EVERYDAY
Slow Cooker
& ONE DISH RECIPES

Taste of Home

TRUSTED MEDIA BRANDS, INC • MILWAUKEE, WI

© 2016 RDA Enthusiast Brands, LLC
1610 N. 2nd St., Suite 102, Milwaukee WI 53212-3906

INTERNATIONAL STANDARD BOOK NUMBER:
978-1-61765-558-6
INTERNATIONAL STANDARD SERIAL NUMBER:
1944-6382
COMPONENT NUMBER:
119400037H

PICTURED ON THE FRONT COVER:
Southwestern Shredded Beef Sandwiches, page 60;
Potluck Bacon Mac & Cheese, page 48;
Salty-Sweet Peanut Treat, page 81;
Upside-Down Frito Pie, page 27.

PICTURED ON THE BACK COVER:
Alfredo Chicken & Biscuits, page 36;
Asian Turkey Lettuce Cups, page 121;
Cajun Beef Casserole, page 163.

CONTENTS

Slow Cooker

Stovetop Suppers

Oven Entrees

Bonus Chapter:

GET SOCIAL WITH US

 **LIKE US**
facebook.com/tasteofhome

 **PIN US**
pinterest.com/taste_of_home

 **FOLLOW US**
@tasteofhome

 **TWEET US**
twitter.com/tasteofhome

To find a recipe tasteofhome.com

To submit a recipe tasteofhome.com/submit

To find out about other *Taste of Home* **products** shoptasteofhome.com

Everyday Dinners have never been easier!

You win with 361 simple, family-pleasing Slow Cooker, Stovetop and Oven recipes in this handy three-in-one cookbook.

There's always time to set a hot homemade meal on the table using this beautiful collection. Keep the comfort food coming all year with 361 amazing make-again specialties from home cooks like you!

Simmer up 125+ slow-cooked dishes, perfect for potlucks, parties and busy workdays. Toss together 105 stovetop suppers, such as tacos, pork chops and sloppy joes. And 100+ oven favorites are guaranteed to warm hearts: potpies, meat loaves and casseroles are just the beginning.

Every dish in this big volume is another home cook's cherished favorite. So grab an apron and make them your own!

HANDY ICONS IN THIS BOOK

EAT SMART Recipes are lower in calories, fat and/or sodium, as determined by a registered dietitian. Consider these when you're cooking for someone following a special diet or you just want to eat lighter.

FREEZE IT Freeze It recipes may be stored in the freezer if you choose. These fix-ahead dishes include directions for freezing and reheating.

ROASTED CHICKEN
WITH LEMON SAUCE
PAGE 194

Slow-Cook with Confidence
Follow these tips for **slow-cooking success every time.**

PLAN AHEAD TO PREP AND GO.
In most cases, you can prepare and load ingredients into the slow cooker insert beforehand and store it in the refrigerator overnight. But an insert can crack if exposed to rapid temperature changes. Let the insert sit out just long enough to reach room temperature before placing in the slow cooker.

USE THAWED INGREDIENTS.
Although throwing frozen chicken breasts into the slow cooker may seem easy, it's not a smart shortcut. Foods thawing inside the slow cooker can create the ideal environment for bacteria to grow, so thaw frozen meat and veggies ahead of time. The exception is if you're using a prepackaged slow-cooker meal kit and follow the instructions as written.

LINE THE CROCK FOR EASE OF USE.
Some recipes in this book call for a **foil collar** or **sling**. Here's why:

▶ A **foil collar** prevents scorching of rich, saucy dishes, such as *Potluck Bacon Mac & Cheese,* near the slow cooker's heating element. To make, fold two 18-in.-long pieces of foil into strips 4 in. wide. Line the crock's perimeter with the strips; spray with cooking spray.

▶ A **sling** helps you lift layered foods, such as *Slow Cooker Cheesy White Lasagna,* out of the crock without much fuss. To make, fold one or more pieces of heavy-duty foil into strips. Place on bottom and up sides of the slow cooker; coat with cooking spray.

TAKE THE TIME TO BROWN.
Give yourself a few extra minutes to brown your meat in a skillet before placing in the slow cooker. Doing so will add rich color and more flavor to the finished dish.

KEEP THE LID CLOSED.
Don't peek! It's tempting to lift the lid and check on your meal's progress, but resist the urge. Every time you open the lid, you'll have to add about 30 minutes to the total cooking time.

ADJUST COOK TIME AS NEEDED.
Live at a high altitude? Slow cooking will take longer. Add about 30 minutes for each hour of cooking the recipe calls for; legumes will take roughly twice as long.

Want your food done sooner? Cooking one hour on high is roughly equal to two hours on low, so adjust the recipe to suit your schedule.

POTLUCK BACON
MAC & CHEESE, PAGE 48

SLOW COOKER CHEESY
WHITE LASAGNA, PAGE 29

Stovetop Suppers Are Super Convenient

Stovetop cooking is quick and easy. Many stovetop meals in this book are **ready in just one pot**, which makes cleanup a breeze. These tips will help you enjoy cooking on the stove.

CHOOSE THE RIGHT PAN FOR THE JOB.

The right cookware can simplify meal preparation when cooking on the stovetop. The basic skillets every kitchen needs include a 10- or 12-in. skillet with lid and an 8- or 9-in. saute/omelet pan.

Good quality cookware conducts heat quickly and cooks food evenly. The type of metal and thickness of the pan affect its performance. There are pros and cons to each of the most common cookware metals:

COPPER

Copper conducts heat the best. However, it is expensive, it tarnishes (and usually requires periodic polishing) and it reacts with acidic ingredients, which is why the interior of a copper pan is usually lined with tin or stainless steel.

Aluminum is a good conductor of heat and is less expensive than copper. However, aluminum reacts with acidic ingredients.

Anodized aluminum has the same positive qualities as aluminum, but the surface is electrochemically treated so it will not react to acidic ingredients. The surface is resistant to scratches and is nonstick.

Cast iron conducts heat very well. It is usually heavy. Cast iron also needs regular seasoning to prevent sticking and rusting.

STAINLESS STEEL

Stainless steel is durable and retains its new look for years. It isn't a good conductor of heat, which is why it often has an aluminum or copper core or bottom.

Nonstick is especially preferred for cooking delicate foods, such as eggs, pancakes or thin fish fillets. It won't scorch foods if you're cooking in batches. It can be scratched easily and has maximum temperature limitations.

PORK CHOPS WITH HONEY-GARLIC SAUCE, PAGE 140

CILANTRO SHRIMP & RICE, PAGE 155

MASTER THESE COMMON STOVETOP COOKING TECHNIQUES.

Sauteeing
Add a small amount of oil to a hot skillet and heat over medium-high heat. For best results, cut the food into uniformly sized pieces before adding. Don't overcrowd. Stir frequently while cooking.

Searing
Heat oil in a large skillet over medium-high heat until it almost begins to smoke. Pat food dry. Cook the food until a deeply colored crust has formed, being careful not to crowd the pan. Reduce heat if food browns too quickly.

Braising
Season meat; coat with flour if recipe directs. In Dutch oven, brown meat in oil in batches. To ensure nice browning, do not crowd. Set meat aside; cook vegetables, adding flour if recipe directs. Add broth gradually, stirring to deglaze pan and to keep lumps from forming. Return meat to pan and stir until mixture comes to a boil.

Steaming
Place a steamer basket or bamboo steamer in a pan with water. Bring water to a boil (boiling water should not touch the steamer) and place food in basket; cover and steam. Add more boiling water to pan as necessary, making sure pan does not run dry.

ITALIAN BURRITOS
PAGE 168

BAKED SPAGHETTI, PAGE 183

Oven Entrees Bake Hands-Free
And they **warm up the kitchen on a chilly day,** too! Follow these tips for success every time.

CHOOSE THE RIGHT BAKEWARE.
Metal baking pans
These great conductors of heat create nice browning on rolls, coffee cakes and other baked goods. Metal is a safe, smart choice for under the broiler. It may react with acidic foods such as tomato sauce or cranberries and create a metallic taste or discoloration.

Glass baking dishes
Glass provides slower, more even baking for egg dishes, custards and casseroles. It takes longer to heat than metal, but once heated, the dish holds the heat longer. This is undesirable for many desserts, because a sugary batter may overbrown in glass. If you wish to bake in a glass dish even though the recipe calls for a metal pan, decrease the oven temperature by 25°.

Other baking dishes
Ceramic or stoneware baking dishes generally perform like glass, but are more attractive. They may also be safe for higher temperatures than glass; refer to the manufacturer's instructions.

CONFIRM THE OVEN'S TEMPERATURE.
Use an oven thermometer to check. Preheat the oven to the desired temperature; place an oven thermometer on the center rack. Close the oven door and leave the oven on at the set temperature. Keep the thermometer in the oven for 15 minutes before reading. Adjust the temperature accordingly to ensure the best baking results.

NEGATE HOT OR COOL SPOTS.
To test your oven for uneven temperatures, try a bread test. Heat the oven to 350° while arranging six to nine slices of white bread on a large cookie sheet. Place in oven for 5-10 minutes; check if slices are starting to brown or burn. If some slices are noticeably darker or lighter than others, the oven may have hot or cool spots. To negate this, rotate your pans while baking.

ELIMINATE SPILLS—THE SMART WAY.
Line a rimmed baking sheet with foil and place it on the bottom oven rack directly below the dish you are using to bake a recipe. Any drips or spills from the recipe will fall onto the foil-lined pan instead of the oven bottom.

TURKEY SAUSAGE-STUFFED
ACORN SQUASH, PAGE 184

We don't recommend lining the bottom of your oven with aluminum foil or other liners, as there's a chance that they could melt and stick to or damage the oven.

Want to clean up a drip while it's still hot? Grab your oven mitt, a pair of tongs and a damp dishcloth. Using the tongs to move the cloth will help prevent burns.

SLOW COOKER CHEESY
WHITE LASAGNA, PAGE 29

Slow Cooker

Come home to a **hot homemade dinne**r that's ready when you are with one of the 126 fabulous recipes in this section. From **cozy** soups and family meals to **crowd-pleasing** sandwiches and dips for **entertaining with ease,** you'll find plenty of **new favorites.**

Beef & Ground Beef

CIDER MUSHROOM BRISKET

Apple juice and gingersnaps give an autumn feel to this tender brisket. It's quick to prep, and the pleasing aroma will linger for hours.

—COLLEEN WESTON DENVER, CO

PREP: 10 MIN. • **COOK:** 6 HOURS
MAKES: 12 SERVINGS

- 1 **fresh beef brisket (6 pounds)**
- 2 **jars (12 ounces each) mushroom gravy**
- 1 **cup apple cider or juice**
- 1 **envelope onion mushroom soup mix**
- ⅓ **cup crushed gingersnap cookies**

1. Cut brisket into thirds; place in a 5- or 6-qt. slow cooker. In a large bowl, combine the gravy, cider, soup mix and cookie crumbs; pour over beef. Cover and cook on low for 6-8 hours or until meat is tender.
2. Thinly slice meat across the grain. Skim fat from cooking juices; thicken if desired.
NOTE *This is a fresh beef brisket, not corned beef.*
PER SERVING *6 ounces cooked meat with ½ cup cooking juices equals 336 cal., 11 g fat (4 g sat. fat), 101 mg chol., 566 mg sodium, 9 g carb., trace fiber, 47 g pro.* **Diabetic Exchanges:** *6 lean meat, ½ starch, ½ fat.*

FARM-STYLE BBQ RIBS

FARM-STYLE BBQ RIBS

I got this recipe from a newspaper, and it was an instant hit with my husband and my friends. I originally prepared this meal in the oven, but I've since discovered how easy it is to make in the slow cooker.
—BETTE JO WELTON EUGENE, OR

PREP: 20 MIN. • **COOK:** 6 HOURS
MAKES: 4 SERVINGS

- 4 **pounds bone-in beef short ribs**
- 1 **can (15 ounces) thick and zesty tomato sauce**
- 1½ **cups water**
- 1 **medium onion, chopped**
- 1 **can (6 ounces) tomato paste**
- ⅓ **cup packed brown sugar**
- 3 **tablespoons cider vinegar**
- 3 **tablespoons Worcestershire sauce**
- 2 **tablespoons chili powder**
- 4 **garlic cloves, minced**
- 2 **teaspoons ground mustard**
- 1½ **teaspoons salt**

Place ribs in a 5- or 6-qt. slow cooker. In a large saucepan, combine the remaining ingredients. Bring to a boil. Reduce the heat; simmer, uncovered, 5 minutes or until slightly thickened. Pour over ribs; cook, covered, on low 6-8 hours or until tender.

FABULOUS FAJITAS

I've enjoyed cooking since I was a girl growing up in the Southwest. When friends call to ask me for new recipes to try, I suggest these flavorful fajitas. It's wonderful to put the beef in the slow cooker before church and come home to a hot, delicious main dish.

—**JANIE REITZ** ROCHESTER, MN

PREP: 20 MIN. • **COOK:** 3 HOURS
MAKES: 6-8 SERVINGS

- 1½ **pounds beef top sirloin steak, cut into thin strips**
- 2 **tablespoons canola oil**
- 2 **tablespoons lemon juice**
- 1 **garlic clove, minced**
- 1½ **teaspoons ground cumin**
- 1 **teaspoon seasoned salt**
- ½ **teaspoon chili powder**
- ¼ **to ½ teaspoon crushed red pepper flakes**
- 1 **large green pepper, julienned**
- 1 **large onion, julienned**
- 6 **to 8 flour tortillas (8 inches)**
  Shredded cheddar cheese, salsa, sour cream, lettuce and tomatoes, optional

1. In a large skillet, brown steak in oil over medium heat. Place steak and drippings in a 3-qt. slow cooker. Stir in the lemon juice, garlic, cumin, salt, chili powder and red pepper flakes.
2. Cover; cook on high for 2-3 hours or until meat is almost tender. Add green pepper and onion; cover and cook for 1 hour or until meat and vegetables are tender.
3. Warm tortillas according to package directions; spoon beef and vegetables down the center of tortillas. Top each with cheese, salsa, sour cream, lettuce and tomatoes if desired.

MEAT LOAF DINNER

What could be more comforting to come home to than juicy and tender homemade meat loaf? Because potatoes and carrots cook along with it, the entire dinner is ready at the same time.

—**MARNA HEITZ** FARLEY, IA

PREP: 10 MIN. • **COOK:** 8 HOURS
MAKES: 4 SERVINGS

- 1 **large egg**
- ¼ **cup milk**
- 2 **slices day-old bread, cubed**
- ¼ **cup finely chopped onion**
- 2 **tablespoons finely chopped green pepper**
- 1 **teaspoon salt**
- ¼ **teaspoon pepper**
- 1½ **pounds lean ground beef (90% lean)**
- ¼ **cup ketchup**
- 8 **medium carrots, cut into 1-inch chunks**
- 8 **small red potatoes**

1. In a bowl, beat egg and milk. Stir in the bread cubes, onion, green pepper, salt and pepper. Add the beef and mix well. Shape into a round loaf. Place in a 5-qt. slow cooker. Spread ketchup on top of loaf. Arrange carrots around loaf. Peel a strip around the center of each potato; place potatoes over the carrots.
2. Cover and cook on high for 1 hour. Reduce heat to low; cook 7-8 hours longer or until no pink remains in the meat and vegetables are tender.

FABULOUS FAJITAS

SLOW COOKER BEEF
VEGETABLE STEW

THAI COCONUT BEEF

PREP: 30 MIN. • **COOK:** 8¾ HOURS
MAKES: 10 SERVINGS

- 1 **boneless beef chuck roast (3 pounds), halved**
- 1 **teaspoon salt**
- 1 **teaspoon pepper**
- 1 **large sweet red pepper, sliced**
- 1 **can (13.66 ounces) coconut milk**
- ¾ **cup beef stock**
- ½ **cup creamy peanut butter**
- ¼ **cup red curry paste**
- 2 **tablespoons soy sauce**
- 2 **tablespoons honey**
- 2 **teaspoons minced fresh gingerroot**
- ½ **pound fresh sugar snap peas, trimmed**
- ¼ **cup minced fresh cilantro**
  Hot cooked brown or white rice
  Optional toppings: thinly sliced green onions, chopped peanuts, hot sauce and lime wedges

1. Sprinkle beef with salt and pepper. Place beef and pepper slices in a 5-qt. slow cooker. In a bowl, whisk coconut milk, beef stock, peanut butter, curry paste, soy sauce, honey and ginger; pour over meat. Cook, covered, on low 7-8 hours or until meat is tender.
2. Remove beef; cool slightly. Skim fat from reserved juices. Shred beef with two forks. Return beef to slow cooker; stir in snap peas. Cook, covered, on low 45-60 minutes longer or until peas are crisp-tender. Stir in cilantro. Serve with rice and, if desired, toppings of your choice.
FREEZE OPTION *Place cooled meat mixture in freezer containers. To use, partially thaw in the refrigerator overnight. Microwave, covered, on high in a microwave-safe dish until heated through, gently stirring and adding a little broth or water if necessary.*

EAT SMART

SLOW COOKER BEEF VEGETABLE STEW

Come home to warm comfort food! This is based on my mom's wonderful recipe, though I adjusted it. Add a sprinkle of Parmesan to each bowl for a nice finishing touch.
—**MARCELLA WEST** WASHBURN, IL

PREP: 20 MIN. • **COOK:** 6½ HOURS
MAKES: 8 SERVINGS (3 QUARTS)

- 1½ **pounds boneless beef chuck roast, cut into 1-inch cubes**
- 3 **medium potatoes, peeled and cubed**
- 3 **cups water**
- 1½ **cups fresh baby carrots**
- 1 **can (10¾ ounces) condensed tomato soup, undiluted**
- 1 **medium onion, chopped**
- 1 **celery rib, chopped**
- 2 **tablespoons Worcestershire sauce**
- 1 **tablespoon browning sauce, optional**
- 2 **teaspoons beef bouillon granules**
- 1 **garlic clove, minced**
- 1 **teaspoon sugar**
- ¾ **teaspoon salt**
- ¼ **teaspoon pepper**
- ¼ **cup cornstarch**
- ¾ **cup cold water**
- 2 **cups frozen peas, thawed**

1. Place beef, potatoes, water, carrots, soup, onion, celery, Worcestershire sauce, browning sauce if desired, bouillon granules, garlic, sugar, salt and pepper in a 5- or 6-qt. slow cooker. Cover and cook on low for 6-8 hours or until meat is tender.
2. Combine cornstarch and cold water in a small bowl until smooth; gradually stir into stew. Stir in peas. Cover and cook on high for 30 minutes or until thickened.
PER SERVING *1½ cups (calculated without browning sauce) equals 287 cal., 9 g fat (3 g sat. fat), 55 mg chol., 705 mg sodium, 31 g carb., 4 g fiber, 20 g pro.* **Diabetic Exchanges:** *2 starch, 2 lean meat.*

"My husband and I love Thai food, but going out on weeknights can be challenging with busy schedules. I wanted to create a Thai-inspired dinner that could double as an easy lunch the following day. The beef is fantastic in this dish, but chicken or pork would be equally delicious!" —**AHLEY LECKER** GREEN BAY, WI

THAI COCONUT
BEEF

PORTOBELLO BEEF BURGUNDY

Use your handy slow cooker to create a meal with all the stick-to-your-ribs goodness your family craves. These tender cubes of beef—loaded with a fantastic mushroom flavor and draped in a rich Burgundy sauce—are sure to have guests asking for seconds.

—MELISSA GALINAT LAKELAND, FL

PREP: 30 MIN. • **COOK:** 7½ HOURS
MAKES: 6 SERVINGS

- ¼ cup all-purpose flour
- ½ teaspoon salt
- ½ teaspoon seasoned salt
- 1½ teaspoons minced fresh thyme or ½ teaspoon dried thyme
- ¾ teaspoon minced fresh marjoram or ¼ teaspoon dried thyme
- ½ teaspoon pepper
- 2 pounds beef sirloin tip steak, cubed
- 2 bacon strips, diced
- 3 tablespoons canola oil
- 1 garlic clove, minced
- 1 cup Burgundy wine or beef broth
- 1 teaspoon beef bouillon granules
- 1 pound sliced baby portobello mushrooms
  Hot cooked noodles, optional

1. In a large resealable plastic bag, combine the first six ingredients. Add beef, a few pieces at a time, and shake to coat.

2. In a large skillet, cook bacon over medium heat until crisp. Remove to paper towels with a slotted spoon; drain. In same skillet, brown beef in oil in batches, adding garlic to last batch; cook 1-2 minutes longer. Drain.

3. Transfer to a 4-qt. slow cooker. Add wine to skillet, stirring to loosen browned bits from pan. Add bouillon; bring to a boil. Stir into slow cooker. Stir in bacon. Cover and cook on low for 7-9 hours or until meat is tender.

4. Stir in mushrooms. Cover and cook on high for 30-45 minutes longer or until mushrooms are tender and sauce is slightly thickened. Serve with noodles if desired.

FRESH SPINACH
TAMALE PIE

FRESH SPINACH TAMALE PIE

I got this recipe from my mother, who loved quick and easy meals for dinner. I made a few variations by adding spinach, bell peppers and fresh corn. The changes were well worth it–my family and friends love this dish.

—NANCY HEISHMAN LAS VEGAS, NV

PREP: 20 MIN. • **COOK:** 3 HOURS
MAKES: 10 SERVINGS

- 8 frozen beef tamales, thawed
- 2 cans (15 ounces each) pinto beans, rinsed and drained
- 2 cups fresh or frozen corn
- 4 green onions, chopped
- 1 can (2¼ ounces) sliced ripe olives, drained
- ½ teaspoon garlic powder
- ¾ cup chopped sweet red pepper
- ¾ cup sour cream
- 1 can (4 ounces) whole green chilies, drained and chopped
- 3 cups chopped fresh spinach
- 12 bacon strips, cooked and crumbled
- 2 cups (8 ounces) shredded cheddar cheese
  Additional green onions, chopped

1. Place tamales in single layer in greased 6-qt. slow cooker. In a large bowl, combine beans, corn, onions, olives and garlic powder; spoon over tamales. In the same bowl, combine pepper, sour cream and chilies; spoon over bean mixture. Top with spinach.

2. Cook, covered, on low 3-4 hours or until heated through. Sprinkle with bacon, cheese and additional onions.

SHORT RIBS WITH SALT-SKIN POTATOES

I love short ribs, and they are best prepared low and slow in a flavorful sauce. I also love salt-skin potatoes, so I thought I would combine the two.
—**DEVON DELANEY** WESTPORT, CT

PREP: 40 MIN. • **COOK:** 6 HOURS
MAKES: 8 SERVINGS

- 6 **thick slices pancetta or thick-sliced bacon, chopped**
- 6 **pounds bone-in beef short ribs**
- 1 **teaspoon plus 1 cup kosher salt, divided**
- 1 **teaspoon pepper**
- 1 **tablespoon olive oil**
- 3 **medium carrots, chopped**
- 1 **medium red onion, chopped**
- 1 **cup beef broth**
- 1 **cup dry red wine**
- ¼ **cup honey**
- ¼ **cup balsamic vinegar**
- 1 **tablespoon minced fresh thyme or 1 teaspoon dried thyme**
- 2 **teaspoons minced fresh oregano or ¾ teaspoon dried oregano**
- 2 **garlic cloves, minced**
- 2 **pounds small red potatoes**
- 4 **teaspoons cornstarch**
- 3 **tablespoons cold water**

1. In a large skillet, cook pancetta over medium heat until crisp, stirring occasionally. Remove with a slotted spoon; drain on paper towels. Refrigerate until serving.

2. Meanwhile, sprinkle ribs with 1 teaspoon salt and pepper. In another large skillet, heat oil over medium-high heat. In batches, brown ribs on all sides; transfer to a 4- or 5-qt. slow cooker. To same skillet, add carrots and onion; cook and stir over medium heat 2-4 minutes or until crisp-tender. Add broth, wine, honey and vinegar, stirring to loosen browned bits from pan. Transfer to slow cooker; add pancetta, herbs and garlic.

3. Cook, covered, on low 6-8 hours or until meat is tender. In the last hour of cooking, place potatoes in a 6-qt. stockpot and cover with water. Add the remaining salt. Cover and bring to a boil over medium-high heat; stir to dissolve salt. Cook 15-30 minutes or until tender. Drain well.

4. Remove ribs to a serving platter; keep warm. Strain cooking juices into a small saucepan; skim fat. Add vegetables and pancetta to platter. Bring juices to a boil. Mix cornstarch and water until smooth; stir into cooking juices. Return to a boil; cook and stir 1-2 minutes or until thickened. Serve with ribs.

MUSHROOM-BEEF SPAGHETTI SAUCE

I learned about this sauce through a recipe exchange and wish I could credit the person who gave it to me. My children love it! I added mushrooms, but if you'd like it even chunkier, add some bell pepper and other veggies, too.
—**MEG FISHER** MARIETTA, GA

PREP: 20 MIN. • **COOK:** 6 HOURS
MAKES: 12 SERVINGS (1½ QUARTS)

- 1 **pound lean ground beef (90% lean)**
- ½ **pound sliced fresh mushrooms**
- 1 **small onion, chopped**
- 2 **cans (14½ ounces each) diced tomatoes, undrained**
- 1 **can (12 ounces) tomato paste**
- 1 **can (8 ounces) tomato sauce**
- 1 **cup reduced-sodium beef broth**
- 2 **tablespoons dried parsley flakes**
- 1 **tablespoon brown sugar**
- 1 **teaspoon dried basil**
- 1 **teaspoon dried oregano**
- 1 **teaspoon salt**
- ¼ **teaspoon pepper**
  Hot cooked spaghetti
  Shredded Parmesan cheese, optional

1. In a large nonstick skillet, cook the beef, mushrooms and onion over medium heat until meat is no longer pink; drain. Transfer the mixture to a 3-qt. slow cooker.

2. Stir in the tomatoes, tomato paste, tomato sauce, broth, parsley, brown sugar, basil, oregano, salt and pepper. Cover and cook on low for 6-8 hours. Serve with spaghetti. Sprinkle with cheese if desired.

PER SERVING *½ cup (calculated without spaghetti and cheese) equals 115 cal., 3 g fat (1 g sat. fat), 19 mg chol., 493 mg sodium, 12 g carb., 3 g fiber, 10 g pro.* **Diabetic Exchanges:** *2 vegetable, 1 lean meat.*

SHORT RIBS WITH SALT-SKIN POTATOES

SLOW-COOKED ROUND STEAK

Quick and easy slow cooker recipes like this are a real plus, especially around the holidays. Serve these saucy steaks over mashed potatoes, rice or noodles.

—DONA MCPHERSON SPRING, TX

PREP: 15 MIN. • **COOK:** 7 HOURS
MAKES: 6-8 SERVINGS

- ¼ cup all-purpose flour
- ½ teaspoon salt
- ⅛ teaspoon pepper
- 2 pounds boneless beef round steak, cut into serving-size pieces
- 6 teaspoons canola oil, divided
- 1 medium onion, thinly sliced
- 1 can (10¾ ounces) condensed cream of mushroom soup, undiluted
- ½ teaspoon dried oregano
- ¼ teaspoon dried thyme

1. In a large resealable plastic bag, combine the flour, salt and pepper. Add beef, a few pieces at a time, and shake to coat. In a large skillet, brown meat on both sides in 4 teaspoons oil. Place in a 5-qt. slow cooker.

2. In the same skillet, saute onion in remaining oil until lightly browned; place over beef. Combine the soup, oregano and thyme; pour over onion. Cover and cook on low for 7-8 hours or until meat is tender.

SLOW-COOKED
ROUND STEAK

SLOW COOKER GROUND BEEF STROGANOFF

My mother gave me this recipe 40 years ago. It's a wonderfully tasty dish to share around the dinner table.

—SUE MIMS MACCLENNY, FL

PREP: 25 MIN. • **COOK:** 4¼ HOURS
MAKES: 8 SERVINGS

- 2 pounds ground beef
- 1½ teaspoons salt
- 1 teaspoon pepper
- 1 tablespoon butter
- ½ pound sliced fresh mushrooms
- 2 medium onions, chopped
- 2 garlic cloves, minced
- 1 can (10½ ounces) condensed beef consomme, undiluted
- ⅓ cup all-purpose flour
- 2 tablespoons tomato paste
- 1½ cups (12 ounces) sour cream
  Hot cooked noodles

1. In a large skillet, cook the beef, salt and pepper over medium heat 6-8 minutes or until no longer pink, breaking into crumbles; drain. Transfer the meat to a 3- or 4-qt. slow cooker.

2. In same skillet, heat butter over medium-high heat. Add mushrooms and onions; cook and stir 6-8 minutes or until the onions are tender and the mushrooms have released their liquid and begin to brown. Add the garlic; cook 1 minute longer. Transfer to slow cooker.

3. In a small bowl, whisk together consomme, flour and tomato paste. Pour over the meat mixture; stir to combine. Cook, covered, on low for 4-6 hours or until thickened. Stir in the sour cream. Cook, covered, for 15-30 minutes longer or until heated through. Serve with noodles.

SLOW COOKER
GROUND BEEF STROGANOFF

BEEF-WRAPPED STUFFED PEPPERS

We love Mexican flavors and spicy foods—and this recipe has it all. Try our peppers wrapped with flank steak along with rice, beans and sour cream.
—JANE WHITTAKER PENSACOLA, FL

PREP: 40 MIN. • **COOK:** 6 HOURS
MAKES: 4 SERVINGS

- 1 beef flank steak (1 pound)
- 1 teaspoon olive oil
- 1 small onion, chopped
- 3 ounces fully cooked chorizo chicken sausage links or flavor of your choice, chopped
- 2 garlic cloves, minced
- 5 ounces fat-free cream cheese
- 3 tablespoons minced fresh cilantro
- 1 tablespoon lime juice
- ½ teaspoon pepper
- 4 poblano peppers
- ¼ cup shredded pepper jack cheese
- 1 cup salsa verde

1. Cut steak into four serving-size pieces; pound with a meat mallet to ¼-in. thickness.
In a large skillet, heat the oil over medium-high heat. Add onion; cook and stir 2-3 minutes or until tender. Add sausage; cook 3-4 minutes or until browned. Add garlic; cook 1 minute longer. Remove from heat. Stir in cream cheese, cilantro, lime juice and pepper.
2. Cut and discard tops from peppers; remove seeds. Fill each pepper with 1 tablespoon pepper jack cheese and ⅓ cup filling. Wrap a piece of steak around each pepper and tie with kitchen string.
3. Transfer to a 4-qt. slow cooker coated with cooking spray. Top with salsa. Cook, covered, on low 6-8 hours or until meat is tender.

MEXICAN BEEF & BEAN STEW

I like that this stew is quick to assemble. The beans, veggies and spices taste great together, and it really warms me up on blustery days.
—TACY FLEURY CLINTON, SC

PREP: 20 MIN. • **COOK:** 8 HOURS
MAKES: 10 SERVINGS (2½ QUARTS)

- 1 cup all-purpose flour
- ¼ teaspoon salt
- ⅛ teaspoon pepper
- 1 pound beef stew meat
- 2 tablespoons canola oil
- 1 can (16 ounces) kidney beans, rinsed and drained
- 1 can (15¼ ounces) whole kernel corn, drained
- 2 medium potatoes, cubed
- 2 small carrots, sliced
- 2 celery ribs, sliced
- 1 small onion, chopped
- 2 cans (15 ounces each) tomato sauce
- 1 cup water
- 1 envelope taco seasoning
- ½ teaspoon ground cumin
  Tortilla chips and shredded cheddar cheese

1. Combine the flour, salt and pepper in a large resealable plastic bag. Add beef, a few pieces at a time, and shake to coat.
2. Brown meat in batches in oil in a large skillet; drain. Place in a 5-qt. slow cooker. Add beans, vegetables.
3. Whisk tomato sauce, water, taco seasoning and cumin; pour over top. Cover and cook on low 8-10 hours or until meat is tender. Serve with chips and cheese.

BEEF-WRAPPED
STUFFED PEPPERS

SWEET AND SAVORY PULLED BEEF DINNER

Flavorful pulled beef is great served over rice or noodles for a more formal meal, or inside hard rolls for casual party sandwiches.

—PATTY MANOCCHI GLENVILLE, NY

PREP: 25 MIN. • **COOK:** 6 HOURS
MAKES: 6 SERVINGS

- 1 **teaspoon salt**
- 1 **teaspoon ground mustard**
- 1 **teaspoon barbecue seasoning**
- 1 **teaspoon paprika**
- 1 **teaspoon chili powder**
- ½ **teaspoon pepper**
- 1 **boneless beef chuck roast (3 pounds)**
- 3 **tablespoons olive oil**
- 1 **large onion, halved and sliced**
- 1 **large sweet red pepper, sliced**

SAUCE
- 1 **can (8 ounces) tomato sauce**
- ⅓ **cup packed brown sugar**
- 3 **tablespoons honey**
- 2 **tablespoons Dijon mustard**
- 2 **tablespoons Worcestershire sauce**
- 2 **tablespoons soy sauce**
- 5 **garlic cloves, minced**
- 4 **teaspoons balsamic vinegar**
- ¾ **teaspoon salt**
  Cooked egg noodles

1. Combine the first six ingredients. Cut the roast in half; rub with the seasonings. In a large skillet, brown the beef in oil on all sides. Transfer to a 4- or 5-qt. slow cooker. Top with onion and red pepper.

2. In a small bowl, combine the tomato sauce, brown sugar, honey, mustard, Worcestershire sauce, soy sauce, garlic, vinegar and salt; pour over vegetables. Cover and cook on low for 6-8 hours or until meat is tender.

3. Remove roast; cool slightly. Strain cooking juices, reserving vegetables and 1¼ cups juices; skim fat from reserved juices. Shred beef with two forks and return to slow cooker. Stir in the reserved vegetables and cooking juices; heat through. Serve with noodles.

MEXICAN
BUBBLE PIZZA

MEXICAN BUBBLE PIZZA

This pizza offers a new way to experience Mexican cuisine. Serve it at your next party and watch it disappear before your eyes.

—JACKIE HANNAHS CEDAR SPRINGS, MI

PREP: 15 MIN. • **COOK:** 3 HOURS
MAKES: 6 SERVINGS

- 1½ **pounds ground beef**
- 1 **can (10¾ ounces) condensed tomato soup, undiluted**
- ¾ **cup water**
- 1 **envelope taco seasoning**
- 1 **tube (16.3 ounces) large refrigerated buttermilk biscuits**
- 2 **cups (8 ounces) shredded cheddar cheese**
  Optional toppings: shredded lettuce, chopped tomatoes, salsa, sliced ripe olives, sour cream and thinly sliced green onions

1. Fold an 18-in. square piece of heavy-duty foil in half to make an 18x9-in. strip. Place strip on the bottom and up sides of a 6-qt. slow cooker. Coat strip with cooking spray.

2. In a large skillet, cook beef over medium heat 6-8 minutes or until no longer pink, breaking into crumbles; drain. Stir in soup, water and taco seasoning. Bring to a boil. Reduce heat; simmer, uncovered, 3-5 minutes or until slightly thickened.

3. Cut each biscuit into four pieces; gently stir into beef mixture. Transfer to slow cooker. Cook, covered, on low 3-4 hours or until dough is cooked through. Sprinkle with cheese. Cook, covered, 5 minutes longer or until cheese is melted. Serve with toppings of your choice.

"This recipe offers a great authentic Mexican taste that can be prepared at home. I love having this as a go-to recipe for a weeknight meal."
—MELISSA PELKEY-HASS WALESKA, GA

CUBAN
ROPA VIEJA

CUBAN ROPA VIEJA

PREP: 25 MIN. • **COOK:** 7 HOURS
MAKES: 8 SERVINGS

- 6 **bacon strips, chopped**
- 2 **beef flank steaks (1 pound each), cut in half**
- 1 **can (28 ounces) crushed tomatoes**
- 2 **cups beef stock**
- 1 **can (6 ounces) tomato paste**
- 5 **garlic cloves, minced**
- 1 **tablespoon ground cumin**
- 2 **teaspoons dried thyme**
- ¾ **teaspoon salt**
- ½ **teaspoon pepper**
- 1 **medium onion, thinly sliced**
- 1 **medium sweet red pepper, sliced**
- 1 **medium green pepper, sliced**
- ¼ **cup minced fresh cilantro**
  Hot cooked rice

1. In a large skillet, cook bacon over medium heat until crisp, stirring occasionally. Remove with a slotted spoon; drain on paper towels.
2. In same skillet, heat drippings over medium-high heat; brown the steak in batches. Transfer meat and bacon to a 5- or 6-qt. slow cooker. In a large bowl, combine tomatoes, beef stock, tomato paste, garlic, seasonings and vegetables; pour over meat.
3. Cook, covered, on low 7-9 hours or until meat is tender. Shred beef with two forks; return to slow cooker. Stir in cilantro. Remove with a slotted spoon; serve with rice.
FREEZE OPTION *Place cooled meat mixture in freezer containers. To use, partially thaw in refrigerator overnight. Microwave, covered, on high in a microwave-safe dish until heated through, gently stirring and adding a little stock or water if necessary.*

CILANTRO KNOW-HOW
If you grow cilantro, you also can harvest its seeds, known as coriander. Let the seeds mature from green to brown, then cut heads with a few inches of stem and hang to dry. Gently loosen the seeds and store in a covered jar.

STUFFED CABBAGE CASSEROLE
I love cabbage rolls but don't always have time to prepare them, so I created this easy recipe. It uses the traditional ingredients and delivers the same great taste.
—**JOANN ALEXANDER** CENTER, TX

PREP: 20 MIN. • **COOK:** 4 HOURS
MAKES: 6 SERVINGS

- 1 **pound ground beef**
- ⅓ **cup chopped onion**
- 4 **cups chopped cabbage**
- 1 **medium green pepper, chopped**
- 1 **cup uncooked instant rice**
- 1 **cup water**
- 1 **can (6 ounces) tomato paste**
- 1 **can (14½ ounces) diced tomatoes, undrained**
- ½ **cup ketchup**
- 2 **tablespoons cider vinegar**
- 1 **to 2 tablespoons sugar, optional**
- 1 **tablespoon Worcestershire sauce**
- 1 **teaspoon salt**
- ½ **teaspoon pepper**
- ¼ **teaspoon garlic powder**

1. In a large skillet, cook beef and onion over medium heat until meat is no longer pink; drain. Transfer to a 5-qt. slow cooker; add cabbage, green pepper and rice.
2. In a large bowl, combine the water and tomato paste. Stir in the remaining ingredients. Pour over beef mixture; mix well. Cover and cook on low for 4-5 hours or until rice and vegetables are tender.

SUPER SHORT RIBS
This came from an old recipe my mom had for baked short ribs. I added a few ingredients to her original to suit my taste, and I prepare it in the slow cooker.
—**COLEEN CARTER** MALONE, NY

PREP: 20 MIN. • **COOK:** 8 HOURS
MAKES: 6 SERVINGS

- 3 **medium onions, cut into wedges**
- 3 **to 3½ pounds bone-in beef short ribs**
- 1 **bay leaf**
- 1 **bottle (12 ounces) beer or nonalcoholic beer**
- 2 **tablespoons brown sugar**
- 2 **tablespoons Dijon mustard**
- 2 **tablespoons tomato paste**
- 2 **teaspoons dried thyme**
- 2 **teaspoons beef bouillon granules**
- 1 **teaspoon salt**
- ¼ **teaspoon pepper**
- 3 **tablespoons all-purpose flour**
- ½ **cup cold water**
  Hot cooked noodles

1. Place onions in a 5-qt. slow cooker; add ribs and bay leaf. Combine the beer, brown sugar, mustard, tomato paste, thyme, bouillon, salt and pepper. Pour over meat.
2. Cover and cook on low for 8-10 hours or until meat is tender.
3. Remove meat and vegetables to a serving platter; keep warm. Discard bay leaf. Skim fat from cooking juices; transfer juices to a small saucepan. Bring to a boil.
4. Combine flour and water until smooth. Gradually stir into the pan. Bring to a boil; cook and stir for 2 minutes or until thickened. Serve with meat and noodles.

BEEF 'N' BEAN TORTA

This zesty dish is a favorite of mine because it has a wonderful Southwestern taste and is easy to prepare. I serve it on nights when we have only a few minutes to eat before running off to meetings or sports events.

—JOAN HALLFORD NORTH RICHLAND HILLS, TX

PREP: 30 MIN. • **COOK:** 4 HOURS
MAKES: 4 SERVINGS

- **1 pound ground beef**
- **1 small onion, chopped**
- **1 can (15 ounces) pinto or black beans, rinsed and drained**
- **1 can (10 ounces) diced tomatoes and green chilies, undrained**
- **1 can (2¼ ounces) sliced ripe olives, drained**
- **1½ teaspoons chili powder**
- **½ teaspoon salt**
- **⅛ teaspoon pepper**
- **3 drops hot pepper sauce**
- **4 flour tortillas (8 inches)**
- **1 cup (4 ounces) shredded cheddar cheese**
  Minced fresh cilantro, optional
  Salsa, sour cream, shredded lettuce and chopped tomatoes, optional

1. Cut four 20x3-in. strips of heavy-duty foil; crisscross strips so they resemble the spokes of a wheel. Place the foil strips on the bottom and up the sides of a 5-qt. slow cooker. Coat the foil strips with cooking spray.

2. In a large skillet, cook beef and onion over medium heat until meat is no longer pink; drain. Stir in the beans, tomatoes, olives, chili powder, salt, pepper and hot pepper sauce. Spoon about 1⅔ cups into prepared slow cooker; top with one tortilla and ¼ cup cheese. Repeat layers three times.

3. Cover and cook on low 4-5 hours or until heated through. Using foil strips as handles, remove the tortilla stack to a platter. Sprinkle with the cilantro. Serve with salsa, sour cream, lettuce and tomatoes if desired.

BEEF 'N' BEAN TORTA

TOP-RATED ITALIAN POT ROAST

I'm always collecting recipes from newspapers and magazines, and this one just sounded too good not to try! You'll love the the blend of wholesome ingredients and aromatic spices.

—**KAREN BURDELL** LAFAYETTE, CO

PREP: 30 MIN. • **COOK:** 6 HOURS
MAKES: 8 SERVINGS

- 1 **cinnamon stick (3 inches)**
- 6 **whole peppercorns**
- 4 **whole cloves**
- 3 **whole allspice berries**
- 2 **teaspoons olive oil**
- 1 **boneless beef chuck roast (2 pounds)**
- 2 **celery ribs, sliced**
- 2 **medium carrots, sliced**
- 1 **large onion, chopped**
- 4 **garlic cloves, minced**
- 1 **cup dry sherry or reduced-sodium beef broth**
- 1 **can (28 ounces) crushed tomatoes**
- ¼ **teaspoon salt**
  Hot cooked egg noodles and minced parsley, optional

TOP-RATED
ITALIAN POT ROAST

1. Place first four ingredients on a double thickness of cheesecloth. Gather corners of cloth to enclose spices; tie securely with string.
2. In a large skillet, heat oil over medium-high heat. Brown roast on all sides; transfer to a 4-qt. slow cooker. Add celery, carrots and spice bag.
3. Add onion to skillet; cook and stir until tender. Add garlic; cook 1 minute longer. Add sherry, stirring to loosen browned bits from pan. Bring to a boil; cook and stir until liquid is reduced to ⅔ cup. Stir in tomatoes and salt; pour over roast and vegetables.
4. Cook, covered, on low 6-7 hours or until meat and vegetables are tender. Remove roast from slow cooker; keep warm. Discard spice bag; skim fat from sauce. Serve roast and sauce with noodles and parsley if desired.
FREEZE OPTION *Place sliced pot roast in freezer containers; top with sauce. Cool and freeze. To use, partially thaw in refrigerator overnight. Heat through in a covered saucepan, stirring gently and adding a little broth if necessary.*
PER SERVING *3 ounces cooked beef with ⅔ cup sauce (calculated without noodles) equals 251 cal., 12 g fat (4 g sat. fat), 74 mg chol., 271 mg sodium, 11 g carb., 3 g fiber, 24 g pro.* **Diabetic Exchanges:** *3 lean meat, 2 vegetable, ½ fat.*

STUFFED FLANK STEAK

Flank steak cuts easily into appetizing spirals for serving, and extra stuffing cooks conveniently in a foil packet on top of the steak.

—**DIANE HIXON** NICEVILLE, FL

PREP: 25 MIN. • **COOK:** 6 HOURS
MAKES: 6 SERVINGS

- 1 **package (8 ounces) crushed corn bread stuffing**
- 1 **cup chopped onion**
- 1 **cup chopped celery**
- ¼ **cup minced fresh parsley**
- 2 **large eggs**
- 1¼ **cups beef broth**
- ⅓ **cup butter, melted**
- ½ **teaspoon seasoned salt**
- ½ **teaspoon pepper**
- 1 **beef flank steak (1½ pounds)**

1. In a large bowl, combine the stuffing, onion, celery and parsley. In a small bowl, beat eggs; stir in broth, butter, seasoned salt and pepper. Pour over stuffing mixture; stir well.
2. Pound steak to ½-in. thickness. Spread 1½ cups stuffing mixture over steak. Roll up, starting with a short side; tie with string. Place in a 5-qt. slow cooker. Remaining stuffing can be wrapped tightly in foil and placed over the rolled steak.
3. Cover and cook on low 6-8 hours or until a thermometer inserted in stuffing reads 160° and the meat is tender. Remove string before slicing.
NOTE *No liquid is added to slow cooker. The moisture comes from the meat.*

COFFEE-BRAISED
ROAST BEEF

SLOW-COOKED
BEEF ENCHILADAS

PREP: 15 MIN. • **COOK:** 7¼ HOURS
MAKES: 6 SERVINGS

- 1　**boneless beef chuck roast
　　(2 pounds)**
- 1　**envelope taco seasoning**
- 1　**medium onion, chopped**
- 1　**cup beef broth**
- 2　**tablespoons all-purpose flour**
- 1　**tablespoon cold water**
- 6　**flour tortillas (8 inches)**
- 1　**can (4 ounces) chopped green
　　chilies**
- 1½　**cups (6 ounces) shredded
　　Mexican cheese blend, divided**
- 1　**can (10 ounces) enchilada sauce
　　Chopped lettuce and chopped
　　tomatoes, optional**

1. Rub roast with taco seasoning. Transfer to a greased 3-qt. slow cooker. Top with onion and broth. Cook, covered, on low 7-8 hours or until meat is tender. Remove roast; cool slightly. Reserve ½ cup cooking juices in a saucepan; discard remaining juices. Skim fat from reserved juices. Shred beef with two forks; return to slow cooker.
2. In a small bowl, mix flour and cold water until smooth; return to saucepan. Cook and stir 2 minutes or until thickened. Stir into the meat mixture.
3. Preheat oven to 425°. Spoon ½ cup meat mixture off center on each tortilla; top with chilies and 2 tablespoons cheese. Roll up and place in a greased 13x9-in. baking dish, seam side down. Top with enchilada sauce and remaining cheese. Bake, uncovered, 15-20 minutes or until cheese is melted. If desired, top with chopped lettuce and tomatoes.

COFFEE-BRAISED
ROAST BEEF

This recipe has been a family tradition since 1974. The meat is quick and flavorful, so it's a nice welcome home after a long day of work. The coffee adds an intriguing flavor to the roast and can be thickened for a delicious gravy.
—**NANCY SCHULER** BELLE FOURCHE, SD

PREP: 10 MIN. + MARINATING
COOK: 6 HOURS • **MAKES:** 10 SERVINGS

- 1　**cup cider vinegar**
- 4　**garlic cloves, crushed, divided**
- 1　**boneless beef chuck roast
　　(4 to 5 pounds), trimmed**
- 2　**teaspoons salt**
- 1　**teaspoon pepper**
- 1　**cup strong brewed coffee**
- 1　**cup beef broth**
- 1　**medium onion, sliced**
- 3　**tablespoons cornstarch**
- ¼　**cup cold water**
　　Mashed potatoes

1. In a large resealable plastic bag, combine vinegar and 2 garlic cloves. Add roast; seal bag and turn to coat. Refrigerate overnight, turning occasionally.
2. Drain and discard marinade. Pat roast dry; sprinkle with salt and pepper. Place roast in a 5- or 6-qt. slow cooker; add coffee, broth, onion and remaining garlic. Cook, covered, on low 6-7 hours or until the meat is tender.
3. Remove roast and keep warm. Strain cooking juices, discarding onion and garlic; skim fat. In a small bowl, mix cornstarch and cold water until smooth; gradually stir into slow cooker. Cook, covered, on high for 30 minutes or until gravy is thickened. Slice roast; serve it with mashed potatoes and gravy.

TOP TIP

ENCHILADA SAUCE
Enchilada sauce is a blend of tomatoes, oil and spices thickened with a little flour or cornstarch.

"Enchiladas get a beefy boost of goodness from slow-cooked roast. When the meat is done, assemble with tortillas and bake. Top with lettuce and tomatoes if desired."
—*TASTE OF HOME* TEST KITCHEN

SLOW-COOKED
BEEF ENCHILADAS

Poultry

LEMON-GARLIC
TURKEY BREAST

LEMON-GARLIC TURKEY BREAST

It's simple to prepare a main dish that easily morphs into tender slices of lunch meat. This turkey breast is hearty, healthy and easy to make!

—**SANDRA HALL** DECATUR, TX

PREP: 15 MIN.
COOK: 5 HOURS + STANDING
MAKES: 12 SERVINGS

- 2 **medium lemons, sliced**
- 1 **bone-in turkey breast (6 to 7 pounds), skin removed**
- ¼ **cup minced fresh parsley**
- 8 **garlic cloves, minced**
- 4 **teaspoons grated lemon peel**
- 2 **teaspoons salt-free lemon-pepper seasoning**
- 1½ **teaspoons salt**

1. Line bottom of a greased 6-qt. slow cooker with three-fourths of the lemon slices. Place turkey over lemons, breast side up. Mix parsley, garlic, lemon peel, pepper seasoning and salt; rub over turkey. Top with remaining lemon slices. Cook, covered, on low 5-6 hours or until turkey is tender.
2. Remove turkey from slow cooker; tent with foil. Let stand 15 minutes before carving. If desired, skim fat and thicken cooking juices for sauce; serve with turkey.

CHICKEN CURRY FOR 2

I love to try new recipes for my husband and me, and I actually have cookbooks and recipes from all over the world. When I find a recipe that's well-received, I make a copy and put it in a protective sleeve in a loose-leaf binder. I now have quite a few huge binders!

—SHARON DELANEY-CHRONIS
SOUTH MILWAUKEE, WI

PREP: 20 MIN. • **COOK:** 3 HOURS
MAKES: 2 SERVINGS

- 1 small onion, sliced
- 1 tablespoon plus ⅓ cup water, divided
- ½ pound boneless skinless chicken breasts, cubed
- 1 small apple, peeled and chopped
- ¼ cup raisins
- 1 garlic clove, minced
- 1 teaspoon curry powder
- ¼ teaspoon ground ginger
- ⅛ teaspoon salt
- 1½ teaspoons all-purpose flour
- 1 teaspoon chicken bouillon granules
- ¾ teaspoon cornstarch
- ½ cup sour cream
- 1 tablespoon thinly sliced green onion
  Hot cooked rice

1. Place onion and 1 tablespoon water in a microwave-safe bowl. Cover and microwave on high for 1-1½ minutes or until crisp-tender.

2. In a 1½-qt. slow cooker, combine the chicken, apple, raisins, garlic, curry, ginger, salt and onion. Combine the flour, bouillon and remaining water; pour over chicken mixture. Cover and cook on low 3 -3½ hours or until chicken juices run clear.

3. Bring sour cream to room temperature. Remove chicken mixture to a bowl; keep warm. Transfer juices to a small saucepan. Combine the cornstarch and sour cream until smooth; add to juices. Cook and stir over medium heat until thickened. Pour over chicken mixture; toss to coat. Sprinkle with green onion and serve with rice.

UPSIDE-DOWN FRITO PIE

Using ground turkey is a great way to lighten up this hearty family-pleaser!

—MARY BERG LAKE ELMO, MN

PREP: 15 MIN. • **COOK:** 2 HOURS
MAKES: 6 SERVINGS

- 2 pounds ground turkey or beef
- 1 medium onion, chopped
- 2 envelopes chili seasoning mix
- 1 can (10 ounces) diced tomatoes and green chilies, undrained
- 1 can (8 ounces) tomato sauce
- 1 can (15 ounces) pinto beans, rinsed and drained
- 1 cup (4 ounces) shredded cheddar cheese
- 3 cups corn chips
  Sour cream and additional chopped onion, optional

1. In a large skillet, cook turkey and onion over medium heat 8-10 minutes or until no longer pink, breaking into crumbles; stir in the chili seasoning. Transfer to a 3- or 4-qt. slow cooker. Pour tomatoes and tomato sauce over the turkey.

2. Cook, covered, on low 2-3 hours or until heated through. Stir turkey mixture to combine. Top with beans. Sprinkle with cheese. Cook, covered, 5-10 minutes or until cheese is melted. Top with chips. If desired, serve with sour cream and additional onion.

UPSIDE-DOWN
FRITO PIE

SLOW COOKER CHEESY WHITE LASAGNA

Here's my best version of my favorite food—lasagna! The recipe is a winner, so it's worth the extra prep. You'll have plenty of time to plan side dishes while the main dish is cooking.

—SUZANNE SMITH BLUFFTON, IN

PREP: 30 MIN.
COOK: 3 HOURS + STANDING
MAKES: 8 SERVINGS

- 1 pound ground chicken or beef
- 2 teaspoons canola oil
- 1¾ cups sliced fresh mushrooms
- 1 medium onion, chopped
- 2 medium carrots, chopped
- 2 garlic cloves, minced
- 2 teaspoons Italian seasoning
- ¾ teaspoon salt
- ½ teaspoon pepper
- ½ cup white wine or chicken broth
- 1 cup half-and-half cream
- ½ cup cream cheese, softened
- 1 cup (4 ounces) shredded white cheddar cheese
- 1 cup (4 ounces) shredded Gouda cheese
- 1 large egg, beaten
- 1½ cups (12 ounces) cottage cheese
- ¼ cup minced fresh basil or 4 teaspoons dried basil
- 9 no-cook lasagna noodles
- 4 cups (16 ounces) shredded part-skim mozzarella cheese
  Additional minced fresh basil, optional

1. Fold two 18-in.-square pieces of heavy-duty foil into thirds. Crisscross strips and place on bottom and up sides of a 6-qt. slow cooker. Coat with cooking spray.
2. In a 6-qt. stockpot, cook chicken over medium heat until no longer pink, 6-8 minutes, breaking into crumbles; drain. Set chicken aside.

3. In same pot, heat oil over medium-high heat. Add mushrooms, onion and carrots; cook and stir just until tender, 6-8 minutes. Add the garlic, Italian seasoning, salt and pepper; cook for 1 minute longer. Stir in wine. Bring to a boil; cook until liquid is reduced by half, 4-5 minutes. Stir in cream, cream cheese, cheddar and Gouda. Return chicken to pot. In a large bowl, combine egg, cottage cheese and basil.
4. Spread 1 cup meat mixture into slow cooker. Layer with 3 noodles (breaking noodles as necessary to fit), 1 cup meat mixture, ½ cup cottage cheese mixture and 1 cup mozzarella cheese. Repeat layers twice. Top with remaining meat mixture and cheese. Cook, covered, on low until noodles are tender, 3-4 hours. Remove the slow cooker insert and let stand for 30 minutes. Sprinkle with additional basil if desired.

TOP TIP

PERFECT LASAGNA ACCOMPANIMENTS
- Arugula Salad with Shaved Parmesan, page 242
- Tomato-Herb Focaccia, page 238

HULI HULI CHICKEN THIGHS

EAT SMART

HULI HULI CHICKEN THIGHS

I'm allergic to bottled barbecue sauces, so when I found a marinade recipe I could use, I tweaked it a little to suit my taste and began serving it with chicken thighs. We love it over Parmesan couscous.

—ERIN ROCKWELL LOWELL, MA

PREP: 10 MIN. • **COOK:** 4 HOURS
MAKES: 8 SERVINGS

- 8 boneless skinless chicken thighs (about 2 pounds)
- 1 cup crushed pineapple, drained
- ¾ cup ketchup
- ⅓ cup reduced-sodium soy sauce
- 3 tablespoons brown sugar
- 3 tablespoons lime juice
- 1 garlic clove, minced
  Hot cooked rice
  Thinly sliced green onions

Place chicken in a 3-qt. slow cooker. In a small bowl, mix pineapple, ketchup, soy sauce, brown sugar, lime juice and garlic; pour over chicken. Cook, covered, on low 4-5 hours or until chicken is tender. Serve with rice and top with green onions.
PER SERVING *1 serving (calculated without rice) equals 239 cal., 8 g fat (2 g sat. fat), 76 mg chol., 733 mg sodium, 19 g carb., trace fiber, 22 g pro.* **Diabetic Exchanges:** *3 lean meat, 1 starch.*

EASY CHICKEN 'N' BISCUITS

Rich gravy makes this a classic comfort food, with chicken slow-cooked to tender perfection and served over hot biscuits. My family can't get enough of this meal.

—**KATHY GARRETT** BROWNS MILLS, NJ

PREP: 5 MIN. • **COOK:** 7 HOURS
MAKES: 5 SERVINGS

- 2 envelopes chicken gravy mix
- 2 cups water
- ¾ cup white wine
- 1 tablespoon minced fresh parsley
- 1 to 2 teaspoons chicken bouillon granules
- 1 teaspoon minced garlic
- ½ teaspoon pepper
- 5 medium carrots, cut into 1-inch chunks
- 1 large onion, cut into eight wedges
- 1 broiler/fryer chicken (3 to 4 pounds), cut up, skin removed
- 3 tablespoons all-purpose flour
- ⅓ cup cold water
- 1 tube (6 ounces) refrigerated buttermilk biscuits

1. In a 5-qt. slow cooker, combine the gravy mix, water, wine, parsley, bouillon, garlic and pepper. Add the carrots, onion and chicken. Cover and cook on low for 6-8 hours.
2. In a small bowl, combine flour and cold water until smooth; gradually stir into slow cooker. Cover and cook on high for 1 hour or until thickened.
3. Meanwhile, bake the biscuits according to package directions. Place biscuits in soup bowls; top with stew.

READER RAVE

"Easy to make! Delicious! I add cream of chicken soup to the mixture as well as diced potatoes (right from the can), just to add a little something extra."

—**EMARCELONIS**
FROM TASTEOFHOME.COM

ITALIAN-STYLE TURKEY WITH POLENTA

This recipe is very easy to prepare, and is made even easier when it simmers in a slow cooker. The turkey comes out tender and the veggies add a mix of color and heartiness.

—**GILDA LESTER** MILLSBORO, DE

PREP: 30 MIN. • **COOK:** 4 HOURS
MAKES: 10 SERVINGS

- 4 turkey thighs (about 3 pounds), skin removed
- 1½ teaspoons salt
- ½ teaspoon pepper
- 4 tablespoons olive oil, divided
- 6 medium carrots, cut into 1-inch pieces
- 1 medium onion, cut into 8 wedges
- 1 small fennel bulb, chopped, fronds reserved
- ½ pound sliced fresh mushrooms
- 3 garlic cloves, minced
- 2 tablespoons tomato paste
- 1 teaspoon Italian seasoning
- ½ cup white wine or chicken broth
- 1 can (28 ounces) diced tomatoes, undrained
- 2 tubes (18 ounces each) polenta, each cut into 5 slices

1. Sprinkle turkey thighs with salt and pepper. In a 6-qt. stockpot, heat 2 tablespoons oil over medium-high heat. Brown thighs on all sides in batches. Remove from pan. In same pan, heat 1 tablespoon oil over medium heat. Add carrots, onion, fennel and mushrooms; cook and stir 3-5 minutes or until softened. Add garlic, tomato paste and Italian seasoning; cook 1 minute longer. Add wine, stirring to loosen browned bits from pan; stir in tomatoes.
2. Transfer turkey and vegetable mixture to a 5- or 6-qt. slow cooker. Cook, covered, on low 4-6 hours or until meat is tender. Remove turkey from slow cooker. When cool enough to handle, remove meat from bones; discard bones. Keep meat warm.
3. Preheat oven to 425°. Brush polenta slices with remaining olive oil. Place slices ½ in. apart on an ungreased baking sheet. Bake for 30-40 minutes or until golden brown, turning halfway though baking. To serve, top polenta with turkey and sauce.

ITALIAN-STYLE
TURKEY WITH POLENTA

CAJUN-STYLE BEANS AND SAUSAGE

Beans and rice make the perfect meal because they're well-balanced, an excellent source of protein, and easy to prepare. The sausage adds full flavor to the recipe, and traditional pork sausage lovers won't even notice that chicken sausage is used in this dish.

—**ROBIN HAAS** CRANSTON, RI

PREP: 25 MIN. • **COOK:** 6 HOURS
MAKES: 8 SERVINGS

- 1 **package (12 ounces) fully cooked spicy chicken sausage links, halved lengthwise and cut into ½-inch slices**
- 2 **cans (16 ounces each) red beans, rinsed and drained**
- 2 **cans (14½ ounces each) diced tomatoes, undrained**
- 3 **medium carrots, chopped**
- 1 **large onion, chopped**
- 1 **large green pepper, chopped**
- ½ **cup chopped roasted sweet red peppers**
- 3 **garlic cloves, minced**
- 1 **teaspoon Cajun seasoning**
- 1 **teaspoon dried oregano**
- ½ **teaspoon dried thyme**
- ½ **teaspoon pepper**
- 5⅓ **cups cooked brown rice**

1. In a large nonstick skillet coated with cooking spray, brown sausage. Transfer to a 5-qt. slow cooker. Stir in beans, tomatoes, vegetables, garlic and seasonings.

2. Cook, covered, on low 6-8 hours or until vegetables are tender. Serve with rice.

PER SERVING *1 cup bean mixture with ⅔ cup rice equals 355 cal., 5 g fat (1 g sat. fat), 33 mg chol., 759 mg sodium, 58 g carb., 11 g fiber, 18 g pro.*

CAJUN-STYLE BEANS
AND SAUSAGE

PINEAPPLE CHICKEN

This quick recipe tastes a little like sweet-and-sour chicken. It's delicious and makes a satisfying family dinner.

—**FRANCISCA MESIANO** NEWPORT NEWS, VA

PREP: 15 MIN. • **COOK:** 4 HOURS
MAKES: 4 SERVINGS

- 4 **bone-in chicken breast halves (12 to 14 ounces each), skin removed**
- 1 **tablespoon canola oil**
- 1 **can (20 ounces) sliced pineapple**
- ⅓ **cup packed brown sugar**
- ¼ **cup cornstarch**
- 2 **tablespoons lemon juice**
- ¾ **teaspoon salt**
- ¼ **teaspoon ground ginger**
  Hot cooked rice

1. In a large skillet, brown chicken in oil. Transfer to a greased 4-qt. slow cooker. Drain pineapple, reserving juice; place pineapple over chicken. Whisk the brown sugar, cornstarch, lemon juice, salt, ginger and reserved juice until smooth; pour over top.

2. Cover and cook on low 4-5 hours or until the chicken is tender. Serve with rice.

CITRUS CHICKEN

For a nutritious meal, I serve this chicken with broccoli and rice. It's a recipe that dates back to 1976, when I got my first slow cooker, which is still in use today.

—**BARBARA EASTON** NORTH VANCOUVER, BC

PREP: 15 MIN. • **COOK:** 4 HOURS
MAKES: 4 SERVINGS

- 2 **medium oranges, cut into wedges**
- 1 **medium green pepper, chopped**
- 1 **broiler/fryer chicken (3 to 4 pounds), cut up, skin removed**
- 1 **cup orange juice**
- ½ **cup chili sauce**
- 2 **tablespoons soy sauce**
- 1 **tablespoon molasses**
- 1 **teaspoon ground mustard**
- 1 **teaspoon minced garlic**
- ¼ **teaspoon pepper**
  Hot cooked rice

Place oranges and green pepper in a 5-qt. slow cooker coated with cooking spray. Top with chicken. Combine the next seven ingredients; pour over chicken. Cover and cook on low for 4-5 hours or until chicken juices run clear. Serve with rice.

CREAMY ITALIAN CHICKEN

Italian salad dressing mix is like a secret weapon for adding flavor to this creamy chicken dish. Served over rice or pasta, it's rich, delicious and special enough for company.

—MAURA MCGEE TALLAHASSEE, FL

PREP: 15 MIN. • **COOK:** 4 HOURS
MAKES: 4 SERVINGS

- **4 boneless skinless chicken breast halves (4 ounces each)**
- **1 envelope Italian salad dressing mix**
- **¼ cup water**
- **1 package (8 ounces) cream cheese, softened**
- **1 can (10¾ ounces) condensed cream of chicken soup, undiluted**
- **1 can (4 ounces) mushroom stems and pieces, drained**
- **Hot cooked pasta or rice**
- **Fresh oregano leaves, optional**

1. Place the chicken in a 3-qt. slow cooker. Combine salad dressing mix and water; pour over chicken. Cover and cook on low for 3 hours.

2. In a small bowl, beat the cream cheese and soup until blended. Stir in mushrooms. Pour over chicken. Cook 1 hour longer or until chicken is tender. Serve with pasta or rice. Garnish with oregano if desired.

SLOW COOKER LUAU CHICKEN

As long as you're cooking bacon for breakfast, save some for the slow cooker. In four short hours, you'll be enjoying a Hawaiian-style lunch.

—CINDY LUND VALLEY CENTER, CA

PREP: 15 MIN. • **COOK:** 4 HOURS
MAKES: 6 SERVINGS

- **6 bacon strips, divided**
- **6 boneless skinless chicken thighs (about 1½ pounds)**
- **¼ teaspoon salt**
- **⅛ teaspoon pepper**
- **½ cup chopped red onion**
- **1 cup crushed pineapple, drained**
- **¾ cup barbecue sauce**

1. Cut three bacon strips in half; cook until partially cooked but not crisp. Drain on paper towels.

2. Season chicken with salt and pepper; place in a 3-qt. slow cooker. Top each thigh with a piece of bacon. Top with the onion, pineapple and barbecue sauce.

3. Cover; cook on low for 4-5 hours or until chicken is tender. Cook the remaining bacon until crisp; drain and crumble. Sprinkle over each serving.

TURKEY TACO MACARONI

PREP: 15 MIN.
COOK: 3 HOURS + STANDING
MAKES: 10 SERVINGS

- **2 tablespoons canola oil, divided**
- **4 cups uncooked elbow macaroni**
- **2 pounds ground turkey**
- **1 medium onion, chopped**
- **4 cans (8 ounces each) tomato sauce**
- **1 cup water**
- **1 cup salsa**
- **1 envelope taco seasoning**
- **2 cups (8 ounces) shredded cheddar cheese**

1. In a large skillet, heat 1 tablespoon oil over medium heat. Add the pasta; cook and stir 2-3 minutes or until pasta is toasted. Transfer to a 5-qt. slow cooker. In same skillet, heat the remaining oil over medium-high heat. Add the turkey and onion; cook for 6-8 minutes or until meat is no longer pink, breaking into crumbles.

2. Transfer to slow cooker. Stir in tomato sauce, water, salsa and taco seasoning. Cook, covered, 3-4 hours or until pasta is tender.

3. Remove insert; top with cheese. Let stand, covered, 15 minutes.

SLOW COOKER LUAU CHICKEN

"This is a nice little twist on a classic dish. If you love cheese, feel free to use more, and green peppers are a great addition if you want some vegetables."
—**BARB KONDOLF** HAMLIN, NY

TURKEY TACO
MACARONI

BROCCOLI-CAULIFLOWER
CHICKEN CASSEROLE

BROCCOLI-CAULIFLOWER CHICKEN CASSEROLE

A chicken, broccoli and rice casserole is one of our favorite comfort foods. I make my easy variation in the slow cooker, with no rice. You can swap in whatever cheese you prefer. Sometimes I use dairy-free cheese to create a more paleo-friendly dinner. The dish is also delicious sprinkled with a simple bread crumb topping.

—COURTNEY STULTZ WEIR, KS

PREP: 20 MIN. • **COOK:** 4 HOURS
MAKES: 8 SERVINGS

- 2 **pounds boneless skinless chicken breasts, cut into 1-inch pieces**
- 1 **small head cauliflower, chopped (about 4 cups)**
- 1 **bunch broccoli, chopped (about 4 cups)**
- ½ **pound medium fresh mushrooms, chopped**
- 1 **large onion, chopped**
- 2 **medium carrots, finely chopped**
- 1 **cup reduced-sodium chicken broth**
- 4 **ounces cream cheese, softened**
- 2 **tablespoons olive oil**
- 2 **teaspoons dried sage leaves**
- 1 **teaspoon salt**
- ½ **teaspoon pepper**
- 1 **cup (4 ounces) shredded cheddar cheese**
  Hot cooked brown rice

In a 6-qt. slow cooker, combine the first six ingredients. In a small bowl, whisk broth, cream cheese, oil, sage, salt and pepper; pour over chicken mixture. Sprinkle with cheese. Cook, covered, on low 4-5 hours or until chicken and vegetables are tender. Serve with rice.

SLOW COOKER CHICKEN CACCIATORE

EAT SMART
SLOW COOKER CHICKEN CACCIATORE

Treat company to this perfect Italian meal. You'll have plenty of time to visit with guests as it cooks hands-free. I like to serve it with couscous, green beans and a dry red wine. *Mangia!*

—MARTHA SCHIRMACHER STERLING HEIGHTS, MI

PREP: 15 MIN. • **COOK:** 8½ HOURS
MAKES: 12 SERVINGS

- 12 **boneless skinless chicken thighs (about 3 pounds)**
- 2 **medium green peppers, chopped**
- 1 **can (14½ ounces) diced tomatoes with basil, oregano and garlic, undrained**
- 1 **can (6 ounces) tomato paste**
- 1 **medium onion, sliced**
- ½ **cup reduced-sodium chicken broth**
- ¼ **cup dry red wine or additional reduced-sodium chicken broth**
- 3 **garlic cloves, minced**
- ¾ **teaspoon salt**
- ⅛ **teaspoon pepper**
- 2 **tablespoons cornstarch**
- 2 **tablespoons cold water**

1. Place chicken in a 4- or 5-qt. slow cooker. In a small bowl, combine green peppers, tomatoes, tomato paste, onion, broth, wine, garlic, salt and pepper; pour over chicken. Cook, covered, on low 8-10 hours or until chicken is tender.

2. In a small bowl, mix cornstarch and water until smooth; gradually stir into slow cooker. Cook, covered, on high 30 minutes or until sauce is thickened.

PER SERVING *1 chicken thigh with scant ½ cup sauce equals 207 cal., 9 g fat (2 g sat. fat), 76 mg chol., 410 mg sodium, 8 g carb., 1 g fiber, 23 g pro.*
Diabetic Exchanges: *3 lean meat, 1 vegetable, ½ fat.*

ALFREDO CHICKEN
& BISCUITS

ALFREDO CHICKEN & BISCUITS

For a cute potpie presentation, dish this creamy chicken up in ramekins and top each with a biscuit. I sometimes serve it over hot linguine , too.

—FAITH CROMWELL SAN FRANCISCO, CA

PREP: 40 MIN. • **COOK:** 3 HOURS
MAKES: 10 SERVINGS

- 2 **jars (16 ounces each) Alfredo sauce**
- 2 **cans (15¼ ounces each) whole kernel corn, drained**
- 2 **cups frozen peas, thawed**
- 2 **jars (4½ ounces each) sliced mushrooms, drained**
- 1 **medium onion, chopped**
- 1 **cup water**
- 1 **teaspoon garlic salt**
- ½ **teaspoon pepper**
- 2 **tablespoons canola oil**
- 8 **boneless skinless chicken breast halves (6 ounces each)**
- 1 **tube (12 ounces) refrigerated buttermilk biscuits**
- 3 **tablespoons grated Parmesan cheese**

1. In a large bowl, combine the first eight ingredients. Pour half into a 6-qt. slow cooker.

2. In a large skillet, heat oil over medium-high heat. Brown chicken in batches on both sides. Transfer to slow cooker.

3. Pour remaining Alfredo mixture over chicken. Cook, covered, on low 3-4 hours or until chicken is tender (a thermometer inserted in chicken should read at least 165°).

4. Arrange biscuits on an ungreased baking sheet; sprinkle with cheese. Bake according to package directions.

5. Remove chicken from slow cooker. Shred with two forks; return to slow cooker. Serve chicken mixture in ramekins or shallow bowls topped with a biscuit.

SLOW COOKER SOUTHWESTERN CHICKEN

Prepared salsa and convenient canned corn and beans add color, texture and flavor to this simple chicken dish. I usually serve it with salad and white rice. Our children love it.

—**KAREN WATERS** LAUREL, MD

PREP: 10 MIN. • **COOK:** 6 HOURS
MAKES: 6 SERVINGS

- 2 **cans (15¼ ounces each) whole kernel corn, drained**
- 1 **can (15 ounces) black beans, rinsed and drained**
- 1 **jar (16 ounces) chunky salsa**
- 6 **boneless skinless chicken breast halves (4 ounces each)**
- 1 **cup (4 ounces) shredded cheddar cheese**

1. In a 5-qt. slow cooker, combine the corn, black beans and ½ cup of salsa. Top with chicken and the remaining salsa.
2. Cover slow cooker; cook on low 6-8 hours or until chicken is tender. Sprinkle with cheese. Cover and cook 5 minutes longer or until cheese is melted.

HOW-TO

SLOW-COOK FOR SUCCESS

1. Choose the correct size slow cooker for your recipe. The slow cooker should be from half to two-thirds full.

2. Be sure the lid is sealed properly—not tilted or askew. The steam creates a seal.

3. Unless otherwise instructed in the recipe, don't lift the lid during cooking. Each peek means heat loss and a longer cooking time.

4. Remove food from slow cooker within one hour after cooking. Promptly refrigerate leftovers.

EAT SMART

LENTIL & CHICKEN SAUSAGE STEW

This hearty and healthy stew will warm up your family members right down to their toes! Serve with corn bread or rolls to soak up every last morsel.

—**JAN VALDEZ** CHICAGO, IL

PREP: 15 MIN. • **COOK:** 8 HOURS
MAKES: 6 SERVINGS

- 1 **carton (32 ounces) reduced-sodium chicken broth**
- 1 **can (28 ounces) diced tomatoes, undrained**
- 3 **fully cooked spicy chicken sausage links (3 ounces each), cut into ½-inch slices**
- 1 **cup dried lentils, rinsed**
- 1 **medium onion, chopped**
- 1 **medium carrot, chopped**
- 1 **celery rib, chopped**
- 2 **garlic cloves, minced**
- ½ **teaspoon dried thyme**

In a 4- or 5-qt. slow cooker, combine all ingredients. Cover and cook on low for 8-10 hours or until lentils are tender.

PER SERVING *1½ cups equals 231 cal., 4 g fat (1 g sat. fat), 33 mg chol., 803 mg sodium, 31 g carb., 13 g fiber, 19 g pro.* **Diabetic Exchanges:** *2 lean meat, 2 vegetable, 1 starch.*

LENTIL & CHICKEN SAUSAGE STEW

CREAMY CHICKEN &
BROCCOLI STEW

Bring to a boil. Reduce heat; cover and simmer for 15-20 minutes or until tender. Drain and return to pan. Mash potatoes with the remaining butter, salt and pepper. Serve with chicken and broccoli mixture.

BUFFALO CHICKEN PASTA

Buffalo chicken is a favorite in our household. Combine it with pasta and you have the ultimate comfort food. If you prefer less spicy food, the addition of sour cream, ranch dressing and mozzarella provides a creamy texture that nicely balances the spice.
—**KATHERINE WHITE** CLEMMONS, NC

PREP: 10 MIN. • **COOK:** 4 HOURS
MAKES: 8 SERVINGS

- **2 pounds boneless skinless chicken breasts, cut into 1-inch cubes**
- **2 cans (10¾ ounces each) condensed cream of chicken soup, undiluted**
- **1 cup Buffalo wing sauce**
- **1 medium onion, finely chopped**
- **1½ teaspoons garlic powder**
- **½ teaspoon salt**
- **½ teaspoon pepper**
- **1 package (16 ounces) penne pasta**
- **2 cups (8 ounces) shredded part-skim mozzarella cheese**
- **2 cups (16 ounces) sour cream**
- **½ cup ranch salad dressing**
  Finely chopped celery, optional

1. In a 5-qt. slow cooker, combine the first seven ingredients. Cook, covered, on low 4-5 hours or until chicken is tender. Cook pasta according to package directions for al dente; drain.
2. Remove insert. Stir in cheese until melted. Add pasta, sour cream and ranch dressing. If desired, top with celery.

CREAMY CHICKEN & BROCCOLI STEW

This recipe is so easy to make, but no one would ever guess. My husband, who doesn't like many chicken dishes, requests it regularly.
—**MARY WATKINS** LITTLE ELM, TX

PREP: 15 MIN. • **COOK:** 5¾ HOURS
MAKES: 8 SERVINGS

- **8 bone-in chicken thighs, skin removed (about 3 pounds)**
- **1 cup Italian salad dressing**
- **½ cup white wine or chicken broth**
- **6 tablespoons butter, melted, divided**
- **1 tablespoon dried minced onion**
- **1 tablespoon garlic powder**
- **1 tablespoon Italian seasoning**
- **¾ teaspoon salt, divided**
- **¾ teaspoon pepper, divided**
- **1 can (10¾ ounces) condensed cream of mushroom soup, undiluted**
- **1 package (8 ounces) cream cheese, softened**
- **2 cups frozen broccoli florets, thawed**
- **2 pounds red potatoes, quartered**

1. Place the chicken in a 4-qt. slow cooker. Combine the salad dressing, wine, 4 tablespoons butter, onion, garlic powder, Italian seasoning, ½ teaspoon salt and ½ teaspoon pepper in a small bowl; pour over the chicken.
2. Cover and cook on low for 5 hours. Skim fat. Combine the soup, cream cheese and 2 cups of liquid from slow cooker in a small bowl until blended; add to slow cooker.
3. Cover and cook 45 minutes longer or until chicken is tender, adding the broccoli during the last 30 minutes of cooking.
4. Meanwhile, place potatoes in a large saucepan and cover with water.

BUFFALO
CHICKEN PASTA

"My youngest son had been out of the country for several years teaching English. When he returned to the United States, I made this home-cooked meal for him that combined Asian and American cuisine. He loved it!"
—**SHEILA SUHAN** SCOTTDALE, PA

CHICKEN IN COCONUT PEANUT SAUCE

CHICKEN IN COCONUT PEANUT SAUCE

PREP: 15 MIN. • **COOK:** 5 HOURS
MAKES: 6 SERVINGS

- ½ cup coconut milk
- ½ cup creamy peanut butter
- 1 can (28 ounces) crushed tomatoes
- 1 medium onion, finely chopped
- 2 to 3 jalapeno peppers, seeded and finely chopped
- 2 tablespoons brown sugar
- 3 garlic cloves, minced
- 2 teaspoons ground cumin
- 1 teaspoon salt
- 1 teaspoon pepper
- 12 boneless skinless chicken thighs (about 3 pounds)
  Hot cooked rice
  Minced fresh cilantro

In a 5-qt. slow cooker, whisk coconut milk and peanut butter until smooth. Stir in tomatoes, onion, peppers, brown sugar, garlic and seasonings. Add chicken; cook, covered, on low 5-6 hours or until chicken is tender. Stir before serving. Serve with rice; sprinkle with cilantro.

NOTE *Wear disposable gloves when cutting hot peppers; the oils can burn skin. Avoid touching your face.*

FREEZE IT

CHEESY TURKEY MEAT LOAF

Nothing says comfort food better than meat loaf! Get this one started in the morning and you'll have a delicious hot meal ready by lunchtime.
—**DEANNA LAUGHINGHOUSE** RALEIGH, NC

PREP: 15 MIN.
COOK: 3 HOURS + STANDING
MAKES: 6 SERVINGS

- 1 large egg, lightly beaten
- 1 cup crushed saltines
- 1 cup ketchup
- 2 garlic cloves, minced
- 1 teaspoon salt
- 1 teaspoon pepper
- 2 pounds ground turkey
- 2½ cups (10 ounces) shredded cheddar cheese, divided
- ½ cup shredded Parmesan cheese

1. Fold an 18-in.-square piece of heavy-duty foil in half to make an 18x9-in. strip. Place strip on bottom and up sides of a 5- or 6-qt. slow cooker. Coat strip with cooking spray.
2. In a large bowl, combine the first six ingredients. Add turkey, 2 cups cheddar cheese and Parmesan cheese; mix lightly but thoroughly (mixture will be moist). Shape into an 8x5-in. loaf; place in center of strip.
3. Cook, covered, on low 3-4 hours or until a thermometer reads 165°. Sprinkle with remaining cheese during the last 20 minutes of cooking.

Using ends of foil strip as handles, remove meat loaf to a platter. Let stand 15 minutes.

FREEZE OPTION *Prepare meat loaf as directed, omitting cheddar cheese over top. Securely wrap cooled meat loaf in plastic wrap and foil, then freeze; freeze cheese in a freezer container. To use, partially thaw in refrigerator overnight. Unwrap meat loaf; reheat on a greased 15x10x1-in. baking pan in a preheated 350° oven until heated through and a thermometer inserted in center reads 165°. Sprinkle with cheese.*

CHEESY TURKEY MEAT LOAF

Other Entrees

CURRIED LAMB AND POTATOES

Loads of rich flavors and spices make this a warming, inviting meal. It's a great way to impress at a family get-together.
—**SUBRINA GOOSCH** MONROE, NC

PREP: 30 MIN. + MARINATING
COOK: 4 HOURS • **MAKES:** 6 SERVINGS

- 6 garlic cloves, minced, divided
- 3 tablespoons curry powder, divided
- 2 tablespoons minced fresh gingerroot, divided
- 2 teaspoons garam masala, divided
- 1 teaspoon chili powder
- 1 teaspoon paprika
- 1 teaspoon dried thyme
- 1 teaspoon ground coriander, divided
- 1½ teaspoons salt, divided
- 1 teaspoon pepper, divided
- ¼ teaspoon ground cumin
- 1 tablespoon olive oil
- 2 pounds lamb shoulder blade chops
- 4 medium red potatoes, cut into ½-inch pieces
- 1 can (15 ounces) diced tomatoes, undrained
- 1 cup chicken broth
- 1 small onion, chopped
  Hot cooked brown rice and minced fresh cilantro, optional

CURRIED LAMB AND POTATOES

1. In a large resealable plastic bag, combine 3 garlic cloves, 1 tablespoon curry powder, 1 tablespoon ginger, 1 teaspoon garam masala, chili powder, paprika and dried thyme, ½ teaspoon coriander, ½ teaspoon salt, ½ teaspoon pepper, cumin and olive oil. Add the lamb chops; seal the bag and turn to coat. Refrigerate for 8 hours or overnight.

2. Place potatoes in a 3- or 4-qt. slow cooker. Transfer lamb to slow cooker.

3. Place the tomatoes, broth, onion, and remaining garlic and seasonings in a blender; cover and process until blended. Pour over lamb and potatoes.

Cook, covered, on low for 4-5 hours or until the meat is tender. When cool enough to handle, remove meat from bones; discard bones. Shred the meat with two forks. Strain cooking juices, reserving potatoes; skim fat. Return the lamb, cooking juices and reserved potatoes to slow cooker; heat through. If desired, serve with rice and cilantro.

BBQ COUNTRY-STYLE RIBS

CHOPS 'N' BEANS

This hearty combination of tender pork chops and two kinds of beans makes a satisfying supper from the slow cooker in summer or winter.

—**DOROTHY PRITCHETT** WILLS POINT, TX

PREP: 15 MIN. • **COOK:** 5 HOURS
MAKES: 4 SERVINGS

- 4 **pork loin chops (½ inch thick)**
- ¼ **teaspoon salt**
- ¼ **teaspoon pepper**
- 1 **tablespoon canola oil**
- 2 **medium onions, chopped**
- 2 **garlic cloves, minced**
- ¼ **cup chili sauce**
- 1½ **teaspoons brown sugar**
- 1 **teaspoon prepared mustard**
- 1 **can (16 ounces) kidney beans, rinsed and drained**
- 1¾ **cups frozen lima beans, thawed**

1. Sprinkle pork chops with salt and pepper. In a large skillet, heat oil over medium-high heat. Brown the pork chops on both sides. Transfer to a 3-qt. slow cooker.

2. Discard the drippings, reserving 1 tablespoon drippings in skillet. Add the onions; cook and stir until tender. Add garlic; cook and stir 1 minute. Stir in the chili sauce, brown sugar and prepared mustard. Pour over chops.

3. Cook, covered, on low for 4 hours or until the meat is almost tender. Stir in the beans. Cook, covered, for 1 to 2 hours longer or until heated through.

PER SERVING *1 serving equals 297 cal., 5 g fat (1 g sat. fat), 14 mg chol., 607 mg sodium, 45 g carb., 11 g fiber, 19 g pro.* ***Diabetic Exchanges:*** *3 starch, 3 lean meat.*

BBQ COUNTRY-STYLE RIBS

Quick to prep for your slow cooker, this dish goes great with a salad and side. My family practically cheers when I make this!

—**CHERYL MANN** WINSIDE, NE

PREP: 10 MIN. • **COOK:** 6 HOURS
MAKES: 6 SERVINGS

- 3 **pounds boneless country-style pork ribs**
- ½ **teaspoon salt**
- ½ **teaspoon pepper**
- 1 **large onion, cut into ½-inch rings**
- 1 **bottle (18 ounces) hickory smoke-flavored barbecue sauce**
- ⅓ **cup maple syrup**
- ¼ **cup spicy brown mustard**
   Thinly sliced green onions, optional

1. Sprinkle ribs with salt and pepper. Place the onion in a 6-qt. slow cooker. Top with ribs. In a large bowl, combine the barbecue sauce, maple syrup and spicy brown mustard; pour over ribs. Cook, covered, on low 6-8 hours or until meat is tender.

2. Transfer meat to a serving platter; keep warm. Pour cooking liquid into a large saucepan; bring to a boil. Reduce heat; simmer, uncovered, 10 minutes or until sauce is thickened. Serve with pork. If desired, sprinkle with onions.

"This is my go-to pepper stew. Whenever my garden yields green peppers, I dice and freeze them for those cold, blustery days to come."

—**DEBBIE JOHNSON** CENTERTOWN, MO

SLOW-COOKED STUFFED PEPPER STEW

SLOW-COOKED STUFFED PEPPER STEW

PREP: 20 MIN. • **COOK:** 4¼ HOURS
MAKES: 8 SERVINGS (3 QUARTS)

- 1½ pounds bulk Italian sausage
- 1 large onion, chopped
- 2 medium green peppers, chopped
- 2 to 4 tablespoons brown sugar
- 2 teaspoons beef base
- ½ teaspoon salt
- ¼ teaspoon pepper
- 2 cans (15 ounces each) tomato sauce
- 1 can (28 ounces) diced tomatoes, undrained
- 2 cups tomato juice
- ¾ cup uncooked instant rice

1. In a large skillet, cook the sausage and onion over medium heat for 8-10 minutes or until sausage is no longer pink, breaking up meat into crumbles; drain.
2. In a 6-qt. slow cooker, combine sausage mixture, green peppers, brown sugar, beef base, salt, pepper, tomato sauce, tomatoes and tomato juice. Cook, covered, on low 4-5 hours or until vegetables are tender.
3. Stir in the instant rice. Cook, covered, for 15-20 minutes longer or until rice is tender.
FREEZE OPTION *Freeze cooled stew in freezer containers. To use, partially thaw in refrigerator overnight. Heat through in a saucepan, stirring occasionally and adding a little water if necessary.*
NOTE *Look for beef base near the broth and bouillon.*

SLOW-COOKED PULLED PORK WITH MOJITO SAUCE

Infused with Cuban flavor, this twist on slow-cooked pulled pork is knock-your-socks-off good, whether you serve it up with rice and beans on the side or press it into a classic Cuban sandwich.

—**KRISTINA WILEY** JUPITER, FL

PREP: 25 MIN. + MARINATING
COOK: 8 HOURS
MAKES: 12 SERVINGS (1½ CUPS SAUCE)

- 2 large onions, quartered
- 12 garlic cloves, peeled
- 1 bottle (18 ounces) Cuban-style mojo sauce and marinade
- ½ cup lime juice
- ½ teaspoon salt
- ¼ teaspoon pepper
- 1 bone-in pork shoulder butt roast (5 to 5¼ pounds)

MOJITO SAUCE
- ¾ cup canola oil
- 1 medium onion, finely chopped
- 6 garlic cloves, finely chopped
- ⅓ cup lime juice
- ½ teaspoon salt
- ¼ teaspoon pepper
  Additional chopped onion and lime wedges, optional

1. Place the onions and garlic in a food processor; process until finely chopped. Add mojo marinade, lime juice, salt and pepper; process until blended. Pour half of the marinade into a large resealable plastic bag. Cut roast into quarters; add to bag. Seal bag and turn to coat. Refrigerate 8 hours or overnight. Transfer the remaining marinade to a small bowl; refrigerate, covered, while marinating the meat.
2. Drain pork, discarding marinade in bag. Place the pork in a 5-qt. slow cooker coated with cooking spray. Top with reserved marinade. Cook, covered, on low for 8-10 hours or until meat is tender.
3. For sauce, in a small saucepan, heat oil over medium heat 2½-3 minutes or until a thermometer reads 200°. Carefully add onion; cook 2 minutes, stirring occasionally. Stir in garlic; remove from heat. Stir in lime juice, salt and pepper.
4. Remove pork from slow cooker; cool slightly. Skim fat from cooking juices. Remove meat from bone; discard bone. Shred pork with two forks. Return cooking juices and pork to slow cooker; heat through.
5. Using tongs, transfer the pork to a platter. Serve with warm mojito sauce, stirring just before serving. If desired, sprinkle the pork with chopped onion and serve with lime wedges.

SHRIMP MARINARA

Flavorful marinara sauce simmers for just a few hours. Right before mealtime, toss in the shrimp to cook quickly. Serve over steamy spaghetti for a delicious weeknight dish that feels dressed up.

—**SUE MACKEY** JACKSON, WI

PREP: 30 MIN. • **COOK:** 3¼ HOURS
MAKES: 6 SERVINGS

- 1 can (14½ ounces) Italian diced tomatoes, undrained
- 1 can (6 ounces) tomato paste
- ½ to 1 cup water
- 2 garlic cloves, minced
- 2 tablespoons minced fresh parsley
- 1 teaspoon salt
- 1 teaspoon dried oregano
- ½ teaspoon dried basil
- ¼ teaspoon pepper
- 1 pound uncooked medium shrimp, peeled and deveined
- ¾ pound spaghetti, cooked and drained
  Shredded Parmesan cheese, optional

1. In a 3-qt. slow cooker, combine the first nine ingredients. Cover and cook on low for 3-4 hours.
2. Stir in the shrimp. Cover and cook for 15-25 minutes or just until shrimp turn pink. Serve with the spaghetti. Sprinkle with cheese if desired.
PER SERVING *1 serving equals 328 cal., 2 g fat (trace sat. fat), 92 mg chol., 768 mg sodium, 54 g carb., 3 g fiber, 22 g pro.*

ONION PORK CHOPS

Wine adds delectable flavor to the chops, and the meat falls from the bone. This easy dish just might initiate every family member into the clean-plate club!

—**KRISTINA WYATT** CATAWBA, VA

PREP: 10 MIN. • **COOK:** 8 HOURS
MAKES: 6 SERVINGS

- 6 **bone-in pork loin chops (8 ounces each)**
- ¼ **teaspoon pepper**
- ⅛ **teaspoon salt**
- 1¼ **cups 2% milk**
- 1 **can (10¾ ounces) condensed cream of onion soup, undiluted**
- 1 **can (10¾ ounces) reduced-fat reduced-sodium condensed cream of mushroom soup, undiluted**
- ⅔ **cup white wine or chicken broth**
- 1 **envelope ranch salad dressing mix**
- 3 **tablespoons cornstarch**
- 2 **tablespoons cold water**
  Minced fresh parsley, optional

1. Sprinkle chops with pepper and salt; transfer to a 4-qt slow cooker. In a large bowl, combine the milk, soups, wine and dressing mix; pour over pork. Cover and cook on low for 8-10 hours or until pork is tender.
2. Remove pork to a serving platter and keep warm. Skim fat from cooking juices; transfer to a large saucepan. Bring liquid to a boil. Combine the cornstarch and water until smooth; gradually stir into the pan. Bring to a boil; cook and stir for 2 minutes or until thickened. Serve with the pork. Sprinkle with parsley if desired.

HOW-TO

MINCE PARSLEY

Here's an easy way to mince parsley without dirtying a cutting board. Place sprigs in a small glass container and snip with kitchen shears.

SLOW COOKER TUNA NOODLE CASSEROLE

SLOW COOKER TUNA NOODLE CASSEROLE

We adapted this family-friendly classic to work in the slow cooker. It's easy, wholesome and totally homemade!

—**TASTE OF HOME** TEST KITCHEN

PREP: 25 MIN. • **COOK:** 4 HOURS + STANDING
MAKES: 10 SERVINGS

- ¼ **cup butter, cubed**
- ½ **pound sliced fresh mushrooms**
- 1 **medium onion, chopped**
- 1 **medium sweet red pepper, chopped**
- 1 **teaspoon salt, divided**
- 1 **teaspoon pepper, divided**
- 2 **garlic cloves, minced**
- ¼ **cup all-purpose flour**
- 2 **cups reduced-sodium chicken broth**
- 2 **cups half-and-half cream**
- 3 **cups uncooked egg noodles (about 6 ounces)**
- 3 **cans (5 ounces each) light tuna in water, drained**
- 2 **tablespoons lemon juice**
- 2 **cups (8 ounces) shredded Monterey Jack cheese**
- 2 **cups frozen peas, thawed**
- 2 **cups crushed potato chips**

1. In a large skillet, melt butter over medium-high heat. Add mushrooms, onion, sweet pepper, ½ teaspoon salt and ½ teaspoon pepper; cook and stir 6-8 minutes or until tender. Add the garlic; cook 1 minute longer. Stir in flour until blended. Gradually whisk in the broth. Bring to a boil, stirring constantly; cook and stir 1-2 minutes or until thickened.
2. Transfer to a 5-qt. slow cooker. Stir in cream and noodles. Cook, covered, on low 4-5 hours or until noodles are tender. Meanwhile, in a small bowl, combine tuna, lemon juice and remaining salt and pepper.
3. Remove insert from slow cooker. Stir cheese, tuna mixture and peas into the noodle mixture. Let stand, uncovered, 20 minutes. Just before serving, sprinkle with potato chips.

CONGA LIME PORK

Dinner guests won't be too shy to get in line when this yummy pork in chipotle and molasses sauce moves to the buffet table.

—**JANICE ELDER** CHARLOTTE, NC

PREP: 20 MIN. • **COOK:** 4 HOURS
MAKES: 6 SERVINGS

- 1 teaspoon salt, divided
- ½ teaspoon pepper, divided
- 1 boneless pork shoulder butt roast (2 to 3 pounds)
- 1 tablespoon canola oil
- 1 large onion, chopped
- 3 garlic cloves, peeled and thinly sliced
- ½ cup water
- 2 chipotle peppers in adobo sauce, seeded and chopped
- 2 tablespoons molasses
- 2 cups broccoli coleslaw mix
- 1 medium mango, peeled and chopped
- 2 tablespoons lime juice
- 1½ teaspoons grated lime peel
- 6 prepared corn muffins, halved

1. Sprinkle ¾ teaspoon salt and ¼ teaspoon pepper over roast. In a large skillet, brown pork in oil on all sides. Transfer meat to a 3- or 4-qt. slow cooker.

2. In the same skillet, saute onion until tender. Add garlic; cook 1 minute longer. Add water, chipotle peppers and molasses, stirring to loosen browned bits from pan. Pour over pork. Cover and cook on high for 4-5 hours or until meat is tender.

3. Remove roast; cool slightly. Skim fat from cooking juices. Shred pork with two forks and return to slow cooker; heat through. In a large bowl, combine the coleslaw mix, mango, lime juice, lime peel and remaining salt and pepper.

4. Place muffin halves cut side down on an ungreased baking sheet. Broil 4 in. from the heat for 2-3 minutes or until lightly toasted. Serve pork with muffins; top with slaw.

FREEZE IT

ITALIAN PORK CHOPS

Not only is it easy to use my slow cooker, the results are fabulous. Meat cooked this way always comes out so tender and juicy. These pork chops are simmered in a thick tomato sauce.

—**BONNIE MARLOW** OTTOVILLE, OH

PREP: 15 MIN. • **COOK:** 5½ HOURS
MAKES: 6 SERVINGS

- 6 boneless pork loin chops (6 ounces each)
- 1 tablespoon canola oil
- 1 medium green pepper, diced
- 1 can (6 ounces) tomato paste
- 1 jar (4½ ounces) sliced mushrooms, drained
- ½ cup water
- 1 envelope spaghetti sauce mix
- ½ to 1 teaspoon hot pepper sauce

1. In a large skillet, brown the pork chops in oil over medium heat for 3-4 minutes on each side; drain. In a 5-qt. slow cooker, combine remaining ingredients. Top with the pork chops.

2. Cover and cook on low 5½-6 hours or until the meat is tender.

FREEZE OPTION *Cool pork chop mixture. Freeze in freezer containers. To use, partially thaw in refrigerator overnight. Heat through slowly in a covered skillet, stirring occasionally, until a thermometer inserted in pork reads 165°.*

CONGA LIME PORK

LIP SMACKIN' RIBS

POTLUCK BACON MAC & CHEESE

PREP: 30 MIN. • **COOK:** 2 HOURS
MAKES: 8 SERVINGS

- 1 pound bacon strips, chopped
- 1 package (16 ounces) elbow macaroni
- ¼ cup all-purpose flour
- 2 teaspoons garlic powder
- 2 teaspoons onion powder
- ½ paprika, optional
- 2 cans (12 ounces each) evaporated milk
- 2 cups reduced-sodium chicken broth
- 8 ounces process cheese (Velveeta), cubed
- 2 cups (8 ounces) shredded cheddar cheese

1. Fold two 18-in.-long pieces of foil into two 18x4-in. strips. Line perimeter of slow cooker with foil strips; spray with cooking spray.
2. In a large skillet, cook the bacon strips over medium heat until crisp, stirring occasionally. Remove with a slotted spoon; drain on paper towels, reserving drippings. In same skillet, heat 2 tablespoons bacon drippings over medium heat; cook macaroni in drippings 2 minutes or until edges turn translucent. Transfer to a 4-qt. slow cooker.
3. In same skillet, heat ¼ cup bacon drippings over medium heat. Add flour, garlic powder, onion powder and, if desired, paprika. Cook and stir 1-2 minutes or until flour begins to turn pale golden brown. Gradually whisk in milk and broth. Bring to a boil, stirring constantly; cook and stir 1-2 minutes or until thickened. Stir in cheeses; transfer to slow cooker. Stir in macaroni. Cook, covered, 2-3 hours or until the macaroni is tender. Top with bacon.

LIP SMACKIN' RIBS

No matter what time of year you eat them, these ribs taste like summer. They never fail to gear me up for grilling season. It's feel-good food!

—**RON BYNAKER** LEBANON, PA

PREP: 20 MIN. • **COOK:** 6 HOURS
MAKES: 8 SERVINGS

- 3 tablespoons butter
- 3 pounds boneless country-style pork ribs
- 1 can (15 ounces) tomato sauce
- 1 cup packed brown sugar
- 1 cup ketchup
- ¼ cup prepared mustard
- 2 tablespoons honey
- 3 teaspoons pepper
- 2 teaspoons dried savory
- 1 teaspoon salt

In a large skillet, heat butter over medium heat. Brown ribs in batches; transfer to a 5-qt. slow cooker. Add the remaining ingredients. Cook, covered, on low 6-8 hours or until meat is tender.

TOP TIP

COUNTRY-STYLE RIBS

Country-style ribs come from the loin, close to the shoulder. Generally considered the meatiest type of rib, they're sold in three ways: as a bone-in rack, as single ribs (similar to pork chops), and boneless.

"This rich mac & cheese is slow-cooker easy. Make it during the week or take it to your next get-together!"
—**KELLY SILVERS** EDMOND, OK

POTLUCK BACON
MAC & CHEESE

SUPREME PIZZA-STYLE PASTA

I guarantee that if this pizza mac is on the menu, everybody will be at the table come dinnertime! Use any of your favorite pizza toppings. I have used Canadian bacon and pinneapple, and my family really loved that. The combinations are only limited by your imagination.

—KELLLY SILVERS EDMOND, OK

PREP: 20 MIN. • **COOK:** 3 HOURS
MAKES: 8 SERVINGS

- 1 **pound bulk Italian sausage**
- 1 **package (16 ounces) elbow macaroni**
- 2 **jars (14 ounces each) pasta sauce**
- ½ **cup water**
- 1 **package (8 ounces) sliced pepperoni**
- 3 **cups (12 ounces) shredded part-skim mozzarella cheese, divided**
- 1 **medium green pepper, chopped**
- 1 **small onion, chopped**
- 1 **can (6½ ounces) sliced ripe olives, drained**
- 1 **can (6 ounces) sliced mushrooms, drained**
- ⅓ **cup grated Parmesan cheese**
  Additional pasta sauce, optional

1. Fold an 18-in.-long piece of foil into an 18x4-in. strip. Line perimeter of a 5-qt. slow cooker with foil strip; spray with cooking spray.

2. In a 6-qt. stockpot, cook sausage over medium heat until no longer pink, breaking into crumbles. Add the pasta; cook and stir 3-4 minutes or until edges become translucent. Stir in pasta sauce, water, pepperoni, and half of each of the following: mozzarella cheese, pepper, onion, olives and mushrooms. Transfer pasta mixture to slow cooker. Top with remaining mozzarella cheese; sprinkle with remaining vegetables.

3. Cook, covered, on low 3-4 hours or until pasta is tender. Just before serving, sprinkle with the grated Parmesan cheese. If desired, serve with additional pasta sauce.

SUPREME
PIZZA-STYLE PASTA

ITALIAN SAUSAGE DINNER

My family loves this dish. It's easy to prepare before I go to work, and it makes the house smell so good by the end of the day.

—**KATHY KASPROWICZ** ARLINGTON HEIGHTS, IL

PREP: 20 MIN. • **COOK:** 6 HOURS
MAKES: 5 SERVINGS

- 1 **pound small red potatoes**
- 2 **large zucchini, cut into 1-inch slices**
- 2 **large green peppers, cut into 1½-inch pieces**
- 1 **large onion, cut into wedges**
- ¼ **teaspoon salt**
- ¼ **teaspoon pepper**
- 1 **pound Italian sausage links, cut into 1½-inch pieces**
- 1 **tablespoon olive oil**
- ½ **cup white wine or chicken broth**
- 1 **tablespoon Italian seasoning**

Place the first six ingredients in a 6-qt. slow cooker. In a large skillet, brown sausages in oil. Reduce heat. Add the wine and Italian seasoning, stirring to loosen browned bits from pan. Transfer to slow cooker. Cover and cook on low 6-8 hours or until potatoes are tender.

CHALUPAS

This is such a refreshing change of pace from traditional chili. It's also fun to serve to guests. Nearly everyone who has sampled it has requested the recipe.

—**GINNY BECKER** TORRINGTON, WY

PREP: 10 MIN. + STANDING
COOK: 8¼ HOURS • **MAKES:** 6-8 SERVINGS

- 1 **cup dried pinto beans**
- 3½ **cups water**
- ¼ **cup chopped onion**
- 1 **can (4 ounces) chopped green chilies**
- 1 **garlic clove, minced**
- 1 **tablespoon chili powder**
- 1½ **teaspoons salt**
- 1½ **teaspoons ground cumin**
- ½ **teaspoon dried oregano**
- 1 **boneless pork shoulder butt roast (1½ pounds)**
- 1 **package (10½ ounces) corn chips**
- ¼ **cup sliced green onions**
  Shredded lettuce, shredded cheddar cheese, chopped fresh tomatoes and salsa

1. Place beans and enough water to cover in a 3-qt. saucepan. Bring to a boil; boil for 2 minutes. Remove from the heat; let stand for 1 hour. Drain beans and discard liquid.

2. In a 3-qt. slow cooker, combine the water, chopped onion, chilies, garlic, chili powder, salt, cumin and oregano. Add roast and beans. Cover and cook on high for 2 hours. Reduce heat to low and cook 6 hours longer or until pork is very tender.

3. Remove roast and shred with a fork. Drain beans, reserving cooking liquid in a saucepan. Combine beans and meat; set aside. Skim and discard fat from cooking liquid; bring to a boil. Boil, uncovered, for 20 minutes or until reduced to 1½ cups. Add meat and bean mixture; heat through.

4. To serve, spoon meat mixture over corn chips; top with green onions, lettuce, cheese, tomatoes and salsa.

CHALUPAS

SPICE TRADE
BEANS & BULGUR

SPICE TRADE BEANS & BULGUR

A rich blend of treasured spices flavors tender, nutritious bulgur and chickpeas in a tangy, nutritious stew that has just the right amount of heat. A hint of sweetness from golden raisins is the perfect accent.

—**FAITH CROMWELL** SAN FRANCISCO, CA

PREP: 30 MIN. • **COOK:** 3½ HOURS
MAKES: 10 SERVINGS

- 3 **tablespoons canola oil, divided**
- 2 **medium onions, chopped**
- 1 **medium sweet red pepper, chopped**
- 5 **garlic cloves, minced**
- 1 **tablespoon ground cumin**
- 1 **tablespoon paprika**
- 2 **teaspoons ground ginger**
- 1 **teaspoon salt**
- 1 **teaspoon pepper**
- ½ **teaspoon ground cinnamon**
- ½ **teaspoon cayenne pepper**
- 1½ **cups bulgur**
- 1 **can (28 ounces) crushed tomatoes**
- 1 **can (14½ ounces) diced tomatoes, undrained**
- 1 **carton (32 ounces) vegetable broth**
- 2 **tablespoons brown sugar**
- 2 **tablespoons soy sauce**
- 1 **can (15 ounces) garbanzo beans or chickpeas, rinsed and drained**
- ½ **cup golden raisins**
  Minced fresh cilantro, optional

1. In a skillet, heat 2 tablespoons oil over medium-high heat. Add onions and pepper; cook and stir 3-4 minutes or until tender. Add the minced garlic and seasonings; cook 1 minute longer. Transfer to a 5-qt. slow cooker.
2. In same skillet, heat the remaining oil over medium-high heat. Add the bulgur; cook and stir 2-3 minutes or until lightly browned.
3. Add the bulgur, tomatoes, broth, brown sugar and soy sauce to slow cooker. Cook, covered, on low for 3-4 hours or until bulgur is tender. Stir in beans and raisins; cook 30 minutes longer. If desired, sprinkle with cilantro.

HAM WITH CHERRY SAUCE

I often make my cherry ham for church breakfasts. It's such a favorite that I've even served it at Easter dinners and at a friend's wedding brunch.

—**CAROL LEE JONES** TAYLORS, SC

PREP: 20 MIN. • **COOK:** 4 HOURS
MAKES: 10-12 SERVINGS

- 1 **boneless fully cooked ham (3 to 4 pounds)**
- ½ **cup apple jelly**
- 2 **teaspoons prepared mustard**
- ⅔ **cup ginger ale, divided**
- 1 **can (21 ounces) cherry pie filling**
- 2 **tablespoons cornstarch**

1. Score the surface of the cooked ham, making diamond shapes ½ in. deep. In a small bowl, combine the jelly, mustard and 1 tablespoon ginger ale; rub over scored surface of ham. Cut ham in half; place in a 5-qt. slow cooker. Cover and cook on low for 4-5 hours or until a thermometer reads 140°, basting with cooking juices near the end of cooking time.
2. For sauce, place pie filling in a saucepan. Combine cornstarch and remaining ginger ale; stir into pie filling until blended. Bring to a boil; cook and stir for 2 minutes or until thickened. Serve over ham.

FAMILY-FAVORITE SPAGHETTI SAUCE

This wonderful recipe has become an annual tradition at our campers' potluck.

—HELEN ROWE SPRING LAKE, MI

PREP: 30 MIN. • **COOK:** 6 HOURS
MAKES: 2¼ QUARTS

- 1 pound bulk Italian sausage
- ½ pound ground beef
- 1 large onion, chopped
- 1 celery rib, chopped
- 3 garlic cloves, minced
- 1 tablespoon olive oil
- 1 can (28 ounces) diced tomatoes
- 1 can (10¾ ounces) condensed tomato soup, undiluted
- 1 can (8 ounces) mushroom stems and pieces, drained
- 1 can (8 ounces) tomato sauce
- 1 can (6 ounces) tomato paste
- 1 tablespoon sugar
- ½ teaspoon pepper
- ½ teaspoon dried basil
- ¼ teaspoon dried oregano
  Hot cooked spaghetti

1. In a large skillet, cook the sausage, beef, onion, celery and garlic in oil over medium heat until meat is no longer pink; drain. In a 4-qt. slow cooker, combine the diced tomatoes, tomato soup, mushrooms, tomato sauce, tomato paste, sugar and seasonings. Stir in sausage mixture.
2. Cook, covered, on low 6-8 hours to blend flavors. Serve with spaghetti.

READER RAVE

"Whole family loves this recipe. We leave out the mushrooms and add 2 or 3 diced carrots. I prepare two batches at once and freeze one before the slow-cooker stage. Then, it's easy-peasy to pop it into the slow cooker another day."

—LISA64801
FROM TASTEOFHOME.COM

MEATY SLOW-COOKED JAMBALAYA

This recipe makes a big batch of delicious, meaty gumbo. Stash some away in the freezer for days you don't feel like cooking.

—DIANE SMITH PINE MOUNTAIN, GA

PREP: 25 MIN. • **COOK:** 7¼ HOURS
MAKES: 12 SERVINGS (3½ QUARTS)

- 1 can (28 ounces) diced tomatoes, undrained
- 1 cup reduced-sodium chicken broth
- 1 large green pepper, chopped
- 1 medium onion, chopped
- 2 celery ribs, sliced
- ½ cup white wine or additional reduced-sodium chicken broth
- 4 garlic cloves, minced
- 2 teaspoons Cajun seasoning
- 2 teaspoons dried parsley flakes
- 1 teaspoon dried basil
- 1 teaspoon dried oregano
- ¾ teaspoon salt
- ½ to 1 teaspoon cayenne pepper
- 2 pounds boneless skinless chicken thighs, cut into 1-inch pieces
- 1 package (12 ounces) fully cooked andouille or other spicy chicken sausage links
- 2 pounds uncooked medium shrimp, peeled and deveined
- 8 cups hot cooked brown rice

1. In a large bowl, combine the first 13 ingredients. Place the chicken and sausage in a 6-qt. slow cooker. Pour the tomato mixture over top. Cook, covered, on low 7-9 hours or until chicken is tender.
2. Stir in the shrimp. Cook, covered, 15-20 minutes longer or until shrimp turn pink. Serve with rice.

PER SERVING *1 cup jambalaya with ⅔ cup cooked rice equals 387 cal., 10 g fat (3 g sat. fat), 164 mg chol., 674 mg sodium, 37 g carb., 4 g fiber, 36 g pro.* **Diabetic Exchanges:** *3 lean meat, 2½ starch.*

MEATY SLOW-COOKED JAMBALAYA

SAUSAGE, ARTICHOKE
& SUN-DRIED TOMATO RAGU

SAUSAGE, ARTICHOKE & SUN-DRIED TOMATO RAGU

It's simple to make this robust ragu. Like all good spaghetti sauces, this version tastes even better the next day. If you prefer a little celery or bell pepper in your sauce, go ahead and throw them in. The results will taste great.
—AYSHA SCHURMAN AMMON, ID

PREP: 20 MIN. • **COOK:** 6 HOURS
MAKES: 2 QUARTS

- 1 pound bulk Italian sausage
- ½ pound lean ground beef (90% lean)
- 1 medium onion, finely chopped
- 3 cans (14½ ounces each) diced tomatoes, undrained
- 1 cup oil-packed sun-dried tomatoes, chopped
- 2 cans (6 ounces each) Italian tomato paste
- 1 jar (7½ ounces) marinated quartered artichoke hearts, drained and chopped
- 3 garlic cloves, minced
- 2 teaspoons minced fresh rosemary
- 1 teaspoon pepper
- ½ teaspoon salt
- 1 bay leaf
- 3 tablespoons minced fresh parsley
  Hot cooked spaghetti
  Grated Parmesan cheese, optional

1. In a large skillet, cook sausage, beef and onion over medium-high heat 4-6 minutes or until meat is no longer pink, breaking into crumbles; drain. Transfer to a 5- or 6-qt. slow cooker. Stir in tomatoes, tomato paste, artichokes, garlic, rosemary, pepper, salt and bay leaf.
2. Cook, covered, on low for 6-8 hours or until heated through. Remove the bay leaf. Stir in minced parsley. Serve with spaghetti. If desired, top with grated Parmesan.
FREEZE OPTION *Freeze cooled sauce in freezer containers. To use, partially thaw in the refrigerator overnight. Heat through in a saucepan, stirring occasionally.*

LOW & SLOW PORK VERDE

PREP: 15 MIN. • **COOK:** 5 HOURS
MAKES: 8 SERVINGS

- 1 boneless pork shoulder butt roast (3½-4 pounds)
- 1 large onion, chopped
- 1 jar (16 ounces) salsa verde
- 2 cans (4 ounces each) chopped green chilies
- 2 teaspoons ground cumin
- 1 teaspoon dried oregano
- 1 teaspoon salt
- 1 teaspoon pepper
- ¼ teaspoon crushed red pepper flakes
- ⅛ teaspoon ground cinnamon
- ¼ cup minced fresh cilantro
  Hot cooked grits
  Sour cream, optional

1. Place pork and onion in a 4-qt. slow cooker. In a small bowl, combine salsa, chilies, cumin, oregano, salt, pepper, pepper flakes and cinnamon; pour over meat. Cook, covered, on low 5-6 hours or until meat is tender.
2. Remove roast; cool slightly. Skim fat from cooking juices. Shred pork with two forks. Return pork to slow cooker; heat through. Stir in cilantro. Serve with cooked grits and, if desired, sour cream.
FREEZE OPTION *Place cooled meat mixture in freezer containers. To use, partially thaw in the refrigerator overnight. Microwave, covered, on high in a microwave-safe dish until heated through, gently stirring and adding a little broth if necessary.*

"My family loves this versatile pork dish. We like to have it over a serving of cheesy grits, but it also goes well with rice or potatoes. Leftovers make an excellent starter for white chili." —**VAL RUBLE** AVA, MO

LOW & SLOW PORK VERDE

LENTIL AND PASTA STEW

Warm up with a big bowl of this stick-to-your-ribs stew. Loaded with chopped smoked sausage, earthy veggies and tender lentils, it's terrific.

—**GERALDINE SAUCIER** ALBUQUERQUE, NM

PREP: 25 MIN. • **COOK:** 8 HOURS
MAKES: 8 SERVINGS

- ½ pound smoked kielbasa, chopped
- 3 tablespoons olive oil
- 3 tablespoons butter
- 1 cup cubed peeled potatoes
- ¾ cup sliced fresh carrots
- 1 celery rib, sliced
- 1 small onion, finely chopped
- 5 cups beef broth
- 1 cup dried lentils, rinsed
- 1 cup canned diced tomatoes
- 1 bay leaf
- 1 teaspoon coarsely ground pepper
- ¼ teaspoon salt
- 1 cup uncooked ditalini or other small pasta
  Shredded Romano cheese

1. Brown kielbasa in oil and butter in a large skillet. Add the potatoes, carrots, celery and onion. Cook and stir for 3 minutes over medium heat. Transfer to a 4- or 5-qt. slow cooker. Stir in the broth, lentils, tomatoes, bay leaf, pepper and salt.

2. Cover and cook on low 8-10 hours or until the lentils are tender. Cook pasta according to package directions; drain. Stir the pasta into slow cooker. Discard bay leaf. Sprinkle servings with cheese.

READER RAVE

"We loved this—it's good and healthy. I used a pound of sausage instead of 1/2 pound so that it would be filling enough even for my husband. So yummy."

—**KIMANDTOMMY**
FROM TASTEOFHOME.COM

SIMPLE SPARERIB & SAUERKRAUT SUPPER

SIMPLE SPARERIB & SAUERKRAUT SUPPER

Try a stout serving of old-fashioned goodness in a bowl. Toss in a little of everything for a simple meal in one.

—**DONNA HARP** CINCINNATI, OH

PREP: 30 MIN. • **COOK:** 6 HOURS
MAKES: 4 SERVINGS

- 1 pound fingerling potatoes
- 1 medium onion, chopped
- 1 medium Granny Smith apple, peeled and chopped
- 3 slices thick-sliced bacon strips, cooked and crumbled
- 1 jar (16 ounces) sauerkraut, undrained
- 2 pounds pork spareribs
- ½ teaspoon salt
- ¼ teaspoon pepper
- 1 tablespoon vegetable oil
- 3 tablespoons brown sugar
- ¼ teaspoon caraway seeds
- ½ pound smoked Polish sausage, cut into 1-inch slices
- 1 cup beer

1. Place the potatoes, onion, apple and bacon in a 6-qt. slow cooker. Drain sauerkraut, reserving ⅓ cup of the liquid; add sauerkraut and reserved liquid to slow cooker.

2. Cut spareribs into serving-size portions; sprinkle with salt and pepper. In a large skillet, heat oil over medium-high heat; brown ribs in batches. Transfer to slow cooker; sprinkle with brown sugar and caraway seeds.

3. Add the sausage; pour in the beer. Cover and cook on low for 6-7 hours or until ribs are tender.

AFRICAN PEANUT SWEET POTATO STEW

When I was in college, my mom made an addicting sweet potato stew. I shared it with friends, and now all of us serve it to our own kids. They all love it, of course.
—**ALEXIS SCATCHELL** NILES, IL

PREP: 20 MIN. • **COOK:** 6 HOURS
MAKES: 8 SERVINGS (2½ QUARTS)

- 1 can (28 ounces) diced tomatoes, undrained
- 1 cup fresh cilantro leaves
- ½ cup chunky peanut butter
- 3 garlic cloves, halved
- 2 teaspoons ground cumin
- 1 teaspoon salt
- ½ teaspoon ground cinnamon
- ¼ teaspoon smoked paprika
- 3 pounds sweet potatoes (about 6 medium), peeled and cut into 1-inch pieces
- 1 can (15 ounces) garbanzo beans or chickpeas, rinsed and drained
- 1 cup water
- 8 cups chopped fresh kale
  Chopped peanuts and additional cilantro leaves, optional

1. Place the first eight ingredients in a food processor; process until pureed. Transfer to a 5-qt. slow cooker; stir in sweet potatoes, beans and water.
2. Cook, covered, on low 6-8 hours or until potatoes are tender, adding kale during the last 30 minutes. If desired, top each serving with chopped peanuts and additional cilantro.
PER SERVING *1¼ cups (calculated without chopped peanuts) equals 349 cal., 9 g fat (1 g sat. fat), 0 chol., 624 mg sodium, 60 g carb., 11 g fiber, 10 g pro.*

AFRICAN PEANUT
SWEET POTATO STEW

SPINACH AND SAUSAGE LASAGNA

Dig into rich layers of home-style lasagna featuring plenty of Italian sausage and gooey cheeses. No-cook noodles, frozen spinach and a jar of sauce simplify the prep. But it tastes far from ordinary!
—**KATHY MORROW** HUBBARD, OH

PREP: 25 MIN. • **COOK:** 3 HOURS
MAKES: 8 SERVINGS

- 1 pound bulk Italian sausage
- 1 jar (24 ounces) garden-style spaghetti sauce
- ½ cup water
- 1 teaspoon Italian seasoning
- ½ teaspoon salt
- 1 carton (15 ounces) ricotta cheese
- 1 package (10 ounces) frozen chopped spinach, thawed and squeezed dry
- 2 cups (8 ounces) shredded part-skim mozzarella cheese, divided
- 9 no-cook lasagna noodles
  Grated Parmesan cheese

1. Cook sausage in a large skillet over medium heat until no longer pink; drain. Stir in the spaghetti sauce, water, Italian seasoning and salt. Combine ricotta, spinach and 1 cup mozzarella cheese in a small bowl.
2. Spread 1 cup sauce mixture in a greased oval 5-qt. slow cooker. Layer with three noodles (breaking the noodles if necessary to fit), 1¼ cups sauce mixture and half of the cheese mixture. Repeat layers. Layer with the remaining noodles and sauce mixture; sprinkle with remaining mozzarella cheese.
3. Cover and cook on low 3-4 hours or until noodles are tender. Sprinkle servings with Parmesan cheese.

PB&J PULLED
PORK

PB&J PULLED PORK

I came up with this recipe for one of my daughters who loves peanut butter and pork! The result has become a family favorite—it's frequently requested for dinner at our house.

—JILL COX LINCOLN, NE

PREP: 15 MIN. • **COOK:** 6 HOURS
MAKES: 6 SERVINGS

- 3 to 4 pounds boneless pork shoulder butt roast
- 1 teaspoon salt
- ½ teaspoon pepper
- 1 can (14½ ounces) reduced-sodium chicken broth
- 1 cup creamy peanut butter
- ¾ cup apricot preserves
- ¼ cup packed brown sugar
- ¼ cup finely chopped onion
- ¼ cup cider vinegar
- 3 tablespoons Dijon mustard
- 1 garlic clove, minced
- 2 tablespoons butter, melted
- 6 ciabatta rolls, split
  Coleslaw, optional

1. Sprinkle the pork roast with salt and pepper; transfer to a 5-qt. slow cooker. In a large bowl, whisk broth, peanut butter, preserves, brown sugar, onion, vinegar, mustard and garlic; pour over meat. Cook, covered, on low 6-8 hours or until meat is tender.

2. Preheat broiler. Remove roast; cool slightly. Shred pork with two forks. Return pork to slow cooker; heat through. Brush butter over cut sides of rolls. Place rolls, buttered side up, on an ungreased baking sheet. Broil 3-4 in. from heat 30-60 seconds or until golden brown. Using a slotted spoon, spoon pork mixture onto roll bottoms; top with coleslaw if desired. Replace tops.

GREEN CHILI CHOPS WITH SWEET POTATOES

It takes only a few minutes to combine the ingredients in a slow cooker, and you'll have a filling, healthy dinner waiting for you at the end of the day. We like to serve it with fresh-baked garlic bread.

—MARINA ASHWORTH DENVER, CO

PREP: 20 MIN. • **COOK:** 6 HOURS
MAKES: 4 SERVINGS

- 3 medium sweet potatoes, peeled and cut into ½-inch slices
- 1 large onion, chopped
- 1 large green pepper, coarsely chopped
- 1½ cups frozen corn
- ½ teaspoon salt
- ¼ teaspoon pepper
- 4 boneless pork loin chops (6 ounces each)
- 1 can (10 ounces) mild green enchilada sauce
- ½ cup sour cream
- 2 tablespoons reduced-sodium teriyaki sauce

1. In a 6-qt. slow cooker, combine sweet potatoes, onion, green pepper, corn, salt and pepper. Top with pork chops. In a small bowl, mix enchilada sauce, sour cream and teriyaki sauce; pour over meat.

2. Cook, covered, on low 6-8 hours or until meat is tender.

GREEN CHILI CHOPS WITH SWEET POTATOES

Soups, Sides & Sandwiches

SOUTHWESTERN SHREDDED
BEEF SANDWICHES

2. Remove roast; cool slightly. Shred meat with two forks. Return meat to slow cooker; heat through. If desired, stir in cilantro. Serve on rolls with cheese and, if desired, coleslaw and pickled jalapeno.

NOTE *Wear disposable gloves when cutting hot peppers; the oils can burn skin. Avoid touching your face.*

HAWAIIAN BARBECUE BEANS

Guests rave and wonder about the unique flavor—fresh ginger is the tasty surprise. It's a hit at every barbecue.

—HELEN REYNOLDS QUINCY, CA

PREP: 10 MIN. • **COOK:** 5 HOURS
MAKES: 9 SERVINGS

- 4 **cans (15 ounces each) black beans, rinsed and drained**
- 1 **can (20 ounces) crushed pineapple, drained**
- 1 **bottle (18 ounces) barbecue sauce**
- 1½ **teaspoons minced fresh gingerroot**
- ½ **pound bacon strips, cooked and crumbled**

In a 4-qt. slow cooker, combine the beans, pineapple, barbecue sauce and ginger. Cover and cook on low for 5-6 hours. Stir in bacon before serving.

SOUTHWESTERN SHREDDED BEEF SANDWICHES

I am the typical busy wife and love a recipe that goes into the slow cooker in the morning and comes out delicious and ready to go when I get home from work.

—ALMA WINDERS SEQUIM, WA

PREP: 20 MIN. • **COOK:** 8 HOURS
MAKES: 8 SERVINGS

- 1 **boneless beef chuck roast (3 to 4 pounds), trimmed**
- 1 **tablespoon ground cumin**
- 1 **tablespoon chili powder**
- 1 **tablespoon smoked paprika**
- 1 **teaspoon salt**
- 1 **teaspoon pepper**
- 1 **medium onion, chopped**
- 1 **can (14½ ounces) stewed tomatoes**
- 1 **can (7 ounces) chopped green chilies**
- 1 **tablespoon chopped seeded jalapeno pepper**
- ¼ **cup minced fresh cilantro, optional**
- 8 **kaiser rolls, split and toasted**
- 2 **cups (8 ounces) shredded Monterey Jack cheese**
  Deli coleslaw and pickled jalapeno slices, optional

1. Place roast in a 5- or 6-qt. slow cooker; sprinkle with seasonings. In a small bowl, mix onion, tomatoes, chilies and jalapeno; pour over roast. Cook, covered, on low 8-10 hours or until meat is tender.

SLOW COOKER LASAGNA SOUP

Every fall and winter, our staff has a soup rotation. I have modified this recipe so I can prep it the night before and put it in the slow cooker in the morning. My colleagues love it!

—SHARON GERST NORTH LIBERTY, IA

PREP: 35 MIN.
COOK: 5 HOURS + STANDING
MAKES: 8 SERVINGS (2½ QUARTS)

- 1½ pounds bulk Italian sausage
- 1 large onion, chopped
- 2 medium carrots, chopped
- 2 cups sliced fresh mushrooms
- 3 garlic cloves, minced
- 1 carton (32 ounces) chicken broth
- 2 cans (14½ ounces each) Italian stewed tomatoes
- 1 can (15 ounces) tomato sauce
- 6 lasagna noodles, broken into 1-inch pieces
- 2 cups coarsely chopped fresh spinach
- 1 cup cubed or shredded part-skim mozzarella cheese
- ½ cup shredded Parmesan cheese Thinly sliced fresh basil, optional

1. In a large skillet, cook the sausage over medium-high heat 8-10 minutes or until no longer pink, breaking into crumbles; drain. Transfer to a 5- or 6-qt. slow cooker.
2. Add onion and carrots to same skillet; cook and stir 2-4 minutes or until softened. Stir in mushrooms and garlic; cook and stir 2-4 minutes or until mushrooms are softened. Transfer to slow cooker. Stir in broth, tomatoes and tomato sauce. Cook, covered, on low 4-6 hours or until vegetables are tender.
3. Add lasagna; cook 1 hour longer or until tender. Stir in spinach. Remove insert; let stand 10 minutes. Divide mozzarella cheese among serving bowls; ladle soup over the cheese. Sprinkle soup with Parmesan cheese and, if desired, basil.

GARLIC & HERB MASHED POTATOES

Cream cheese is my secret ingredient for rich and comforting spuds. Simply mash, mix and then let them heat away in the slow cooker.

—FRIEDA BLIESNER MCALLEN, TX

PREP: 40 MIN. • **COOK:** 2 HOURS
MAKES: 10 SERVINGS

- 4 pounds Yukon Gold potatoes (about 12 medium), peeled and cubed
- 1 package (8 ounces) cream cheese, softened and cubed
- 1 cup (8 ounces) sour cream
- ½ cup butter, cubed
- ⅓ cup heavy whipping cream
- 3 tablespoons minced chives
- 3 garlic cloves, minced
- 1 tablespoon minced fresh parsley
- 1 teaspoon minced fresh thyme
- ½ teaspoon salt
- ¼ teaspoon pepper

1. Place potatoes in a Dutch oven and cover with water. Bring to a boil. Reduce heat; cover and cook for 10-15 minutes or until tender. Drain. Mash potatoes with cream cheese, sour cream, butter and cream. Stir in the remaining ingredients.
2. Transfer to a greased 3- or 4-qt. slow cooker. Cover and cook on low for 2-3 hours to allow flavors to blend.

SLOW COOKER LASAGNA SOUP

"When a hungry crowd's coming over, we make our juicy pork sandwiches. I call the sauce 'mojo' because it's loaded with zingy flavors."
—THERESA YARDAS SHERIDAN, IN

CUBANO PORK
SANDWICHES

CUBANO PORK SANDWICHES

PREP: 1¾ HOURS + MARINATING
COOK: 8 HOURS • **MAKES:** 24 SERVINGS

- ⅓ **cup ground cumin**
- ¼ **cup sugar**
- 2 **tablespoons onion powder**
- 1 **tablespoon kosher salt**
- ½ **teaspoon pepper**
- 1 **boneless pork shoulder roast (6 to 7 pounds)**
- 6 **teaspoons olive oil, divided**
- 1 **large onion, quartered**
- 1 **cup dry red wine or beef broth**
- ⅔ **cup lime juice**
- ⅓ **cup lemon juice**
- ⅓ **cup orange juice**
- 1 **bay leaf**
- 1 **teaspoon dried cilantro flakes**
- 1 **teaspoon dried oregano**
- 1 **teaspoon dried thyme**
- 1 **teaspoon ground allspice**

SANDWICHES
- 2 **loaves unsliced French bread (1 pound each)**
- ¼ **cup sweet pickle relish**
- ¼ **cup Dijon mustard**
- 8 **slices Swiss cheese**

1. In a small bowl, mix the first five ingredients. Cut roast into thirds; rub with 2 teaspoons oil. Rub spice mixture over meat; wrap in plastic wrap. Refrigerate, covered, 24 hours.

2. In a large saucepan, combine onion, wine, juices, bay leaf and seasonings. Bring to a boil. Reduce heat; simmer, uncovered, 45 minutes. Strain sauce, discarding onion and seasonings.

3. In a large skillet, heat the remaining oil over medium heat. Brown roast on all sides; drain. Transfer to a 6-qt. slow cooker. Pour sauce over meat. Cook, covered, on low 8-10 hours or until meat is tender. Remove roast; cool slightly. Skim fat from cooking juices. Shred pork with two forks. Return pork to slow cooker; heat through.

4. Preheat oven to 325°. Split bread horizontally. Hollow out bottoms of loaves, leaving ¾-in. shells. Spread relish and mustard inside shells. Layer with meat and cheese. Replace tops.

5. Wrap sandwiches tightly in heavy-duty foil. Place on baking sheets. Bake 20-25 minutes or until heated through. Cut each crosswise into 12 slices.

PER SERVING *1 slice equals 368 cal., 16 g fat (6 g sat. fat), 76 mg chol., 648 mg sodium, 28 g carb., 2 g fiber, 26 g pro.*

LEMON CHICKEN & RICE SOUP

When buying chicken for this soup, take it to the butcher counter and ask the butcher to cube it for you. It'll save you some prep time.

—**KRISTIN CHERRY** BOTHELL, WA

PREP: 35 MIN. • **COOK:** 4¼ HOURS
MAKES: 12 SERVINGS (4 QUARTS)

- 2 **tablespoons olive oil**
- 2 **pounds boneless skinless chicken breasts, cut into ½-inch pieces**
- 5 **cans (14½ ounces each) reduced-sodium chicken broth**
- 8 **cups coarsely chopped Swiss chard, kale or spinach**
- 2 **large carrots, finely chopped**
- 1 **small onion, chopped**
- 1 **medium lemon, halved and thinly sliced**
- ¼ **cup lemon juice**
- 4 **teaspoons grated lemon peel**
- ½ **teaspoon pepper**
- 4 **cups cooked brown rice**

1. In a large skillet, heat 1 tablespoon oil over medium-high heat. Add half of the chicken; cook and stir until browned. Transfer to a 6-qt. slow cooker. Repeat with remaining oil and chicken.

2. Stir broth, vegetables, lemon slices, lemon juice, peel and pepper into chicken. Cook, covered, on low for 4-5 hours or until chicken is tender. Stir in rice; heat through.

PER SERVING *1⅓ cups equals 203 cal., 5 g fat (1 g sat. fat), 42 mg chol., 612 mg sodium, 20 g carb., 2 g fiber, 20 g pro. Diabetic Exchanges: 2 lean meat, 1 starch, 1 vegetable, ½ fat.*

LEMON CHICKEN & RICE SOUP

HOT PEPPER-BEEF SANDWICHES

If you like your shredded beef with a little kick, then this recipe is for you. For an even zestier version of this recipe, add another jar of jalapenos or use hot peppers instead of the pepperoncini.

—**KRISTEN LANGMEIER** FARIBAULT, MN

PREP: 15 MIN. • **COOK:** 8 HOURS
MAKES: 12 SERVINGS

- 1 boneless beef chuck roast (4 to 5 pounds)
- 2 medium onions, coarsely chopped
- 1 jar (16 ounces) sliced pepperoncini, undrained
- 1 jar (8 ounces) pickled jalapeno slices, drained
- 1 bottle (12 ounces) beer or nonalcoholic beer
- 1 envelope onion soup mix
- 5 garlic cloves, minced
- ½ teaspoon pepper
- 12 kaiser rolls, split
- 12 slices provolone cheese

1. Cut roast in half; place in a 4- or 5-qt. slow cooker. Add the onions, pepperoncini, jalapenos, beer, soup mix, garlic and pepper.

2. Cover roast and cook on low for 8-10 hours or until meat is tender.

3. Remove meat. Skim fat from the cooking liquid. When cool enough to handle, shred meat with two forks and return to slow cooker; heat through. Serve ½ cup meat mixture on each roll with a slice of cheese.

NOTE *Look for pepperoncini (pickled peppers) in the pickle and olive section of your grocery store.*

SLOW COOKER CHICKEN
& SWEET POTATO CHILI

SLOW COOKER CHICKEN & SWEET POTATO CHILI

As a college student, one of the things I miss most is my mom's wonderful cooking...and her well-stocked kitchen! This recipe is perfect because I can make it in my dorm and come back later to a fresh bowl of delicious chili.

—**BAILEY STARKEY** MOUNT VERNON, WA

PREP: 15 MIN. • **COOK:** 5 HOURS
MAKES: 8 SERVINGS (3 QUARTS)

- 1½ pounds sweet potatoes, peeled and cut into ½-inch cubes (about 6 cups)
- 2 cans (15 ounces each) black beans, rinsed and drained
- 1 pound boneless skinless chicken thighs, cubed
- 2 cups chicken broth
- 1 jar (16 ounces) salsa
- 1 can (14½ ounces) diced tomatoes, undrained
- 1 package (10 ounces) frozen corn, thawed
- 1 medium onion, chopped
- 1 tablespoon chili powder
- 3 garlic cloves, minced
- 1 teaspoon ground coriander
- ½ teaspoon ground cinnamon
  Shredded cheddar cheese, sour cream and tortilla chips

In a greased 6-qt. slow cooker, combine the first 12 ingredients. Cook, covered, on low 5-6 hours or until chicken and sweet potatoes are tender. Serve with cheese, sour cream and chips.

SMOKED SAUSAGE GUMBO

Serve up the flavors of the bayou! You'll leave the table satisfied, as this gumbo is brimming with veggies and sausage. For a more authentic Cajun flavor, use andouille instead of Polish sausage.

—SHARON DELANEY-CHRONIS
SOUTH MILWAUKEE, WI

PREP: 20 MIN. • **COOK:** 4 HOURS
MAKES: 5 SERVINGS

- 2 celery ribs, chopped
- 1 medium onion, chopped
- 1 medium green pepper, chopped
- 1 medium carrot, chopped
- 2 tablespoons olive oil
- ¼ cup all-purpose flour
- 1 cup chicken broth
- 1 pound smoked kielbasa or Polish sausage, cut into ½-inch pieces
- 1 can (14½ ounces) diced tomatoes, undrained
- 2 teaspoons dried oregano
- 2 teaspoons dried thyme
- ⅛ teaspoon cayenne pepper
  Hot cooked rice

1. In a large skillet, saute the celery, onion, green pepper and carrot in oil until tender. Stir in flour until blended; gradually add broth. Bring to a boil. Cook and stir for 2 minutes or until thickened.
2. Transfer to a 3-qt. slow cooker. Stir in the sausage, tomatoes, oregano, thyme and cayenne. Cover and cook on low for 4-5 hours or until heated through. Serve with rice.

FREEZE OPTION *Freeze soup in freezer containers. Thaw in the refrigerator overnight. Transfer to a saucepan. Cover and cook over medium heat until heated through, adding a little water if necessary. Serve gumbo with rice.*

PEPPERONI PIZZA SOUP

Once upon a time, my husband and I owned a pizzeria, where this dish was always popular. We've since sold the restaurant, but I still make the soup for potlucks and other gatherings.

—ESTELLA PETERSON MADRAS, OR

PREP: 20 MIN. • **COOK:** 8¼ HOURS
MAKES: 6 SERVINGS (2¼ QUARTS)

- 2 cans (14½ ounces each) Italian stewed tomatoes, undrained
- 2 cans (14½ ounces each) reduced-sodium beef broth
- 1 small onion, chopped
- 1 small green pepper, chopped
- ½ cup sliced fresh mushrooms
- ½ cup sliced pepperoni, halved
- 1½ teaspoons dried oregano
- ⅛ teaspoon pepper
- 1 package (9 ounces) refrigerated cheese ravioli
  Shredded part-skim mozzarella cheese and sliced ripe olives

1. In a 4-qt. slow cooker, combine the first eight ingredients. Cook, covered, on low 8-9 hours.
2. Stir in ravioli; cook, covered, on low 15-30 minutes or until pasta is tender. Top servings with cheese and olives.

PEPPERONI
PIZZA SOUP

SAVORY WINTER SOUP

Even my father, who doesn't particularly like soup, enjoys my full-flavored rendition of vegetable soup. He asked me to share the recipe with Mom, and I gladly obliged!

—DANA SIMMONS LANCASTER, OH

PREP: 20 MIN. • **COOK:** 6 HOURS
MAKES: 14 SERVINGS (3½ QUARTS)

- 2 **pounds ground beef**
- 3 **medium onions, chopped**
- 1 **garlic clove, minced**
- 3 **cans (10½ ounces each) condensed beef broth, undiluted**
- 1 **can (28 ounces) diced tomatoes, undrained**
- 3 **cups water**
- 1 **cup each diced carrots and celery**
- 1 **cup fresh or frozen cut green beans**
- 1 **cup cubed peeled potatoes**
- 2 **tablespoons minced fresh parsley or 2 teaspoons dried parsley flakes**
- 1 **teaspoon dried basil**
- ½ **teaspoon dried thyme**
  Salt and pepper to taste

1. In a large skillet, cook beef and onions over medium heat until the meat is no longer pink. Add garlic; cook 1 minute longer. Drain.

2. Transfer to a 5-qt. slow cooker. Stir in the remaining ingredients. Cover and cook on low for 6-8 hours or until heated through.

SLOW COOKER SPINACH & RICE

I started making this in the slow cooker to save oven space during the holidays. It's so convenient, I no longer reserve it for special occasions!

—ERICA POLLY SUN PRAIRIE, WI

PREP: 20 MIN.
COOK: 3 HOURS + STANDING
MAKES: 8 SERVINGS

- 2 **tablespoons butter**
- 1 **medium onion, finely chopped**
- 2 **garlic cloves, minced**
- ¼ **teaspoon dried thyme**
- 4 **cups reduced-sodium chicken broth**
- 2 **packages (10 ounces each) frozen chopped spinach, thawed and squeezed dry**
- 1 **package (8 ounces) cream cheese, softened**
- 1 **teaspoon salt**
- 1 **teaspoon pepper**
- 2 **cups uncooked converted rice**
- 8 **ounces cheddar cheese, shredded**
- ½ **cup panko (Japanese) bread crumbs**
- ¼ **cup grated Parmesan cheese**

1. In a large saucepan, melt butter over medium heat. Add onion; cook and stir 4-6 minutes or until tender. Add garlic and thyme; cook 1 minute longer. Add broth; bring to a simmer. Remove from heat. Stir in spinach, cream cheese, salt and pepper until blended. Transfer to a 4-qt. slow cooker. Stir in rice.

2. Cook, covered, 3-4 hours or until rice is tender and liquid is absorbed, stirring halfway through cooking. Remove insert; top mixture with cheddar cheese. Let stand, covered, 20 minutes. Top with bread crumbs and Parmesan cheese.

SLOW COOKER
SPINACH & RICE

SHREDDED
CHICKEN GYROS

EAT SMART

SHREDDED CHICKEN GYROS

We go to the annual Greek Festival in Salt Lake City for the awesome food. This chicken with lemon and spices is our salute to Greek food.

—**CAMILLE BECKSTRAND** LAYTON, UT

PREP: 20 MIN. • **COOK:** 3 HOURS
MAKES: 8 SERVINGS

- 2 **medium onions, chopped**
- 6 **garlic cloves, minced**
- 1 **teaspoon lemon-pepper seasoning**
- 1 **teaspoon dried oregano**
- ½ **teaspoon ground allspice**
- ½ **cup water**
- ½ **cup lemon juice**
- ¼ **cup red wine vinegar**
- 2 **tablespoons olive oil**
- 2 **pounds boneless skinless chicken breasts**
- 8 **whole pita breads**
   Toppings: tzatziki sauce, torn romaine and sliced tomato, cucumber and onion

1. In a 3-qt. slow cooker, combine first nine ingredients; add chicken. Cook, covered, on low 3-4 hours or until chicken is tender (thermometer should read at least 165°).

2. Remove chicken from slow cooker. Shred with two forks; return to slow cooker. Using tongs, place chicken mixture on pita breads. Serve with desired toppings.

PER SERVING *1 gyro (calculated without toppings) equals 337 cal., 7 g fat (1 g sat. fat), 63 mg chol., 418 mg sodium, 38 g carb., 2 g fiber, 29 g pro.* **Diabetic Exchanges:** *3 lean meat, 2½ starch, ½ fat.*

VEGGIE MEATBALL SOUP FOR 3

It's a snap to put together this hearty soup before I leave for work. I just add pasta when I get home, and I have a few minutes to relax before supper is ready.
—CHARLA TINNEY TYRONE, OK

PREP: 10 MIN. • **COOK:** 4¼ HOURS
MAKES: 3 CUPS

- 1½ cups reduced-sodium beef broth
- 1 cup frozen mixed vegetables, thawed
- ¾ cup canned stewed tomatoes
- 9 frozen fully cooked homestyle meatballs (½ ounce each), thawed
- 2 bay leaves
- ⅛ teaspoon pepper
- ½ cup uncooked spiral pasta

In a 1½-qt. slow cooker, combine the first six ingredients. Cover and cook on low for 4-5 hours or until heated through. Stir in pasta; cover and cook on high for 15-30 minutes or until pasta is tender. Discard bay leaves.

PER SERVING *1 cup equals 250 cal., 11 g fat (5 g sat. fat), 35 mg chol., 671 mg sodium, 26 g carb., 5 g fiber, 11 g pro. Diabetic Exchanges: 1½ starch, 1½ fat, 1 lean meat, 1 vegetable.*

"What a great, quick meal! Crowd-pleaser. And I loved the low calories. Substituted turkey meatballs and 1.5 quarts of roasted red pepper soup—just what I had on hand."
—GHONES
FROM TASTEOFHOME.COM

VEGGIE MEATBALL SOUP FOR 3

BLACK & WHITE BEAN CHILI

PREP: 30 MIN. • **COOK:** 4 HOURS
MAKES: 8 SERVINGS (2 QUARTS)

- 3 teaspoons olive oil, divided
- 1½ pounds boneless skinless chicken breasts, cut into 1-inch cubes
- 3 medium carrots, chopped
- 3 celery ribs, sliced
- 1 small onion, finely chopped
- 4 teaspoons garlic powder
- 4 teaspoons onion powder
- 4 teaspoons paprika
- 2 teaspoons ground cumin
- ½ cup Marsala wine or reduced-sodium chicken broth
- 1 can (15½ ounces) great northern beans, undrained
- 1 can (15 ounces) black beans, undrained
- 1 can (14½ ounces) diced tomatoes, undrained
- 1 teaspoon salt
- 1 teaspoon pepper
  Hot cooked rice
  Sour cream and shredded cheddar cheese, optional

1. In a large skillet, heat ½ teaspoon oil over medium-high heat. Add half of the chicken; cook and stir until browned. Remove with a slotted spoon to a 4- or 5-qt. slow cooker. Repeat with ½ teaspoon oil and remaining chicken. In same pan, heat remaining oil over medium heat. Add the carrots, celery, onion and spices; cook and stir 6-8 minutes or until tender.

2. Add Marsala wine; increase the heat to medium-high. Cook 1 minute, stirring to loosen browned bits from pan. Transfer to slow cooker. Add beans, tomatoes, salt and pepper. Cook, covered, on low 4-5 hours or until meat is tender.

3. Serve with rice. If desired, top with sour cream and cheese.

"This is one healthy meal that even the kids love! The satisfying chili is great for football games or potluck dinners, too."

—**KATTI SCOTT** MANTEO, NC

BLACK & WHITE
BEAN CHILI

SLOW COOKER DRESSING

SPICY TOUCHDOWN CHILI

Football, cool weather and chili just seem to go together. Whether I'm cheering on the local team on a Friday night or enjoying a Saturday afternoon of Oklahoma Sooner football with some friends, I enjoy serving this chili.

—CHRIS NEAL QUAPAW, OK

PREP: 30 MIN. • **COOK:** 4 HOURS
MAKES: 12 SERVINGS (3 QUARTS)

- 1 **pound ground beef**
- 1 **pound bulk pork sausage**
- 2 **cans (16 ounces each) kidney beans, rinsed and drained**
- 2 **cans (15 ounces each) pinto beans, rinsed and drained**
- 2 **cans (14½ ounces each) diced tomatoes with mild green chilies, undrained**
- 1 **can (14½ ounces) diced tomatoes with onions, undrained**
- 1 **can (12 ounces) beer**
- 6 **bacon strips, cooked and crumbled**
- 1 **small onion, chopped**
- ¼ **cup chili powder**
- ¼ **cup chopped pickled jalapenos**
- 2 **teaspoons ground cumin**
- 2 **garlic cloves, minced**
- 1 **teaspoon dried basil**
- ¾ **teaspoon cayenne pepper**

In a large skillet, cook beef over medium heat until no longer pink, breaking into crumbles; drain. Transfer to a 6-qt. slow cooker. Repeat with sausage. Add remaining ingredients. Cook, covered, on low 4-5 hours or until heated through.

EAT SMART
SLOW COOKER DRESSING

Here's an easy dressing that's perfect for Thanksgiving get-togethers. Once it's in the slow cooker, you're free to turn your attention to the other dishes.

—RITA NODLAND BISMARCK, ND

PREP: 15 MIN. • **COOK:** 3 HOURS
MAKES: 8 SERVINGS

- 2 **tablespoons olive oil**
- 1 **medium celery rib, chopped**
- 1 **small onion, chopped**
- 8 **cups unseasoned stuffing cubes**
- 1 **teaspoon poultry seasoning**
- ¼ **teaspoon salt**
- ¼ **teaspoon pepper**
- 2 **cups reduced-sodium chicken broth**

In a large skillet, heat the oil over medium-high heat. Add celery and onion; cook and stir until tender. In a large bowl, toss bread cubes with poultry seasoning, salt and pepper. Stir in celery mixture. Add broth to the bread mixture and toss to coat. Transfer to a greased 5-qt. slow cooker. Cook, covered, on low for 3-4 hours or until heated through.
PER SERVING ½ cup equals 226 cal., 5 g fat (trace sat. fat), 0 chol., 635 mg sodium, 40 g carb., 3 g fiber, 8 g pro.

READER RAVE

"At first I thought that it was just another chili recipe, pretty much like most others. However, the more I ate the more I decided that it was perfectly seasoned, had just the right amount of heat and was pretty simple to make. I'm giving it 5 stars."
—SCROOGE42 FROM TASTEOFHOME.COM

SPLIT PEA SOUP WITH HAM & JALAPENO

This recipe speaks total comfort food to me. I can't wait for fall and winter so I can make it. I cook it low and slow all day, and it fills the house with a yummy aroma. I curl up next to the fire and enjoy it with a nice crispy baguette. Yum! Jalapeno adds a little jolt of flavor to this classic soup.

—CHELSEA TICHENOR
HUNTINGTON BEACH, CA

PREP: 15 MIN. • **COOK:** 6 HOURS
MAKES: 6 SERVINGS (2¼ QUARTS)

- 2 smoked ham hocks
- 1 package (16 ounces) dried green split peas, rinsed
- 4 medium carrots, cut into ½-inch slices
- 1 medium onion, chopped
- 1 jalapeno pepper, seeded and minced
- 3 garlic cloves, minced
- 8 cups water
- 1 teaspoon salt
- 1 teaspoon pepper

In a 4- or 5-qt. slow cooker, combine all ingredients. Cook, covered, on low 6-8 hours or until meat is tender. Remove meat from bones when cool enough to handle; cut ham into small pieces and return to slow cooker.
NOTE *Wear disposable gloves when cutting hot peppers; the oils can burn skin. Avoid touching your face.*
PER SERVING *1½ cups equals 316 cal., 2 g fat (trace sat. fat), 9 mg chol., 642 mg sodium, 55 g carb., 21 g fiber, 22 g pro.*

SPLIT PEA SOUP WITH
HAM & JALAPENO

VERY BEST BARBECUE BEEF SANDWICHES

These sweet and tangy barbecue beef sandwiches definitely live up to their name. Friends will want the recipe— they're that good.

—TASTE OF HOME TEST KITCHEN

PREP: 20 MIN. • **COOK:** 8 HOURS
MAKES: 12 SERVINGS

- 1 boneless beef chuck roast (3 to 4 pounds)
- 1½ cups ketchup
- 1 small onion, finely chopped
- ¼ cup packed brown sugar
- ¼ cup red wine vinegar
- 1 tablespoon Dijon mustard
- 1 tablespoon Worcestershire sauce
- 2 garlic cloves, minced
- ½ teaspoon salt
- ¼ teaspoon celery seed
- ¼ teaspoon paprika
- ¼ teaspoon pepper
- 2 tablespoons cornstarch
- 2 tablespoons cold water
- 12 kaiser rolls, split
  Dill pickle slices, optional

1. Cut roast in half. Place in a 5-qt. slow cooker. In a small bowl, combine the ketchup, onion, brown sugar, vinegar, mustard, Worcestershire sauce, garlic, salt, celery seed, paprika and pepper; pour over roast. Cover and cook on low for 8-10 hours or until meat is tender.
2. Remove meat. Skim fat from cooking juices; transfer to a large saucepan. Bring to a boil. Combine cornstarch and water until smooth; gradually stir into juices. Return to a boil; cook and stir for 2 minutes or until thickened.
3. When the meat is cool enough to handle, shred with two forks. Return meat to slow cooker and stir in sauce mixture; heat through. Serve on rolls with pickle slices if desired.

BBQ
BRATS

BBQ BRATS

In Wisconsin, brats are a staple food group! We are always looking for new ways to cook them. This recipe is easy and a hit at any tailgate party or cookout, any time of year.

—**JESSICA ABNET** DEPERE, WI

PREP: 20 MIN. • **COOK:** 3 HOURS
MAKES: 10 SERVINGS

- 10 uncooked bratwurst links
- 1 bottle (12 ounces) beer or
  1½ cups chicken broth
- 1 cup ketchup
- 1 cup honey barbecue sauce
- 10 hot dog buns, split
  Spicy brown mustard

1. Grill bratwursts, covered, on an oiled rack over medium heat or broil 4 in. from heat 10 minutes, turning frequently. Transfer to a 5-qt. slow cooker.
2. In a large bowl, mix the beer, ketchup and barbecue sauce; pour over the bratwursts. Cook, covered, on low for 3-4 hours or until cooked through. Place bratwursts on buns. Serve with mustard and, if desired, cooking liquid.

HOW-TO

GREASE A GRILL GRATE

To oil a hot grill grate to prevent foods from sticking, fold a paper towel into a small pad and moisten it with cooking oil. Holding the pad with long-handled tongs, rub it over the grate.

PROVENCAL HAM & BEAN SOUP

PROVENCAL HAM & BEAN SOUP

There is nothing quite like the wonderful feeling of opening the door and smelling this delicious stew bubbling away in the kitchen. To make preparation even easier, I like to start it the night before, and then all I have to do is turn on the slow cooker in the morning.

—**LYNDSAY WELLS** LADYSMITH, BC

PREP: 15 MIN. + SOAKING • **COOK:** 7 HOURS
MAKES: 10 SERVINGS (3½ QUARTS)

- 2 cups assorted dried beans for soup
- 1 can (28 ounces) whole plum tomatoes, undrained
- 2 cups cubed fully cooked ham
- 1 large Yukon Gold potato, peeled and chopped
- 1 medium onion, chopped
- 1 cup chopped carrot
- 1 celery rib, chopped
- 2 garlic cloves, minced
- 2 teaspoons herbes de Provence
- 1½ teaspoons salt
- 1 teaspoon pepper
- 1 carton (32 ounces) unsalted chicken stock
  French bread

1. Rinse and sort beans; soak according to package directions. Drain and rinse beans, discarding the liquid.
2. Transfer beans to a 6-qt. slow cooker. Add tomatoes; crush with a wooden spoon until chunky. Stir in ham, vegetables, garlic, seasonings and stock. Cook, covered, on low 7-9 hours or until beans are tender. Serve with bread.

WHISKEY BARBECUE PORK

The ingredient list may seem long for my saucy pork, but most of these items are common things you'll already have in your kitchen. Plus, once the sauce is mixed up, the slow cooker does the rest and you can focus on other things. I think the liquid smoke is what gives the barbecue its authentic taste!

—REBECCA HORVATH JOHNSON CITY, TN

PREP: 15 MIN. • **COOK:** 6 HOURS
MAKES: 8 SERVINGS

- ½ to ¾ cup packed brown sugar
- 1 can (6 ounces) tomato paste
- ⅓ cup barbecue sauce
- ¼ cup whiskey
- 2 tablespoons liquid smoke
- 2 tablespoons Worcestershire sauce
- 3 garlic cloves, minced
- ½ teaspoon chili powder
- ½ teaspoon salt
- ½ teaspoon pepper
- ½ teaspoon hot pepper sauce
- ¼ teaspoon ground cumin
- 1 boneless pork shoulder butt roast (3 to 4 pounds)
- 1 medium onion, quartered
- 8 hamburger buns, split

1. Mix the first 12 ingredients in a small bowl. Place pork roast and onion in a 5-qt. slow cooker. Add the sauce mixture. Cook, covered, on low for 6-8 hours or until pork is tender.
2. Remove roast and onion. Cool pork slightly; discard onion. Meanwhile, skim fat from sauce. If desired, transfer sauce to a small saucepan; bring to a boil and cook to thicken slightly.
3. Shred pork with two forks. Return pork and sauce to slow cooker; heat through. Serve on buns.

TOP TIP

PORK SHOULDER

Pork shoulder is a flavorful cut with plenty of fatty marbling throughout. Trim any excess fat before cooking. The meat needs a long cook time to become tender.

CREAM OF POTATO & CHEDDAR SOUP

EAT SMART

CREAM OF POTATO & CHEDDAR SOUP

The Yukon Gold potatoes my daughter shares from her garden make this soup incredible. Add some cheddar cheese and crisp croutons, and it's just heavenly. Total comfort with the simplicity of good ingredients!

—CINDI BAUER MARSHFIELD, WI

PREP: 25 MIN. • **COOK:** 7½ HOURS
MAKES: 11 SERVINGS (2¾ QUARTS)

- 8 medium Yukon Gold potatoes, peeled and cubed
- 1 large red onion, chopped
- 1 celery rib, chopped
- 2 cans (14½ ounces each) reduced-sodium chicken broth
- 1 can (10¾ ounces) condensed cream of celery soup, undiluted
- 1 teaspoon garlic powder
- ½ teaspoon white pepper
- 1½ cups (6 ounces) shredded sharp cheddar cheese
- 1 cup half-and-half cream
  Optional toppings: salad croutons, crumbled cooked bacon and additional shredded sharp cheddar cheese

1. Combine the first seven ingredients in a 4- or 5-qt. slow cooker. Cover and cook on low for 7-9 hours or until potatoes are tender.
2. Stir in cheese and cream. Cover and cook 30 minutes longer or until cheese is melted. Garnish servings with toppings of your choice.
PER SERVING *1 cup (calculated without optional ingredients) equals 212 cal., 8 g fat (5 g sat. fat), 28 mg chol., 475 mg sodium, 27 g carb., 3 g fiber, 8 g pro.* **Diabetic Exchanges:** *2 starch, 1½ fat.*

SLOW-COOKED CHICKEN CHILI

Lime juice gives this chili a zesty twist, while canned tomatoes and beans make preparation a breeze. It's fun to serve with toasted tortilla strips.

—**DIANE RANDAZZO** SINKING SPRING, PA

PREP: 25 MIN. • **COOK:** 4 HOURS
MAKES: 6 SERVINGS (2 QUARTS)

- 1 **medium onion, chopped**
- 1 **each medium sweet yellow, red and green peppers, chopped**
- 2 **tablespoons olive oil**
- 3 **garlic cloves, minced**
- 1 **pound ground chicken**
- 2 **cans (14½ ounces each) diced tomatoes, undrained**
- 1 **can (15 ounces) white kidney or cannellini beans, rinsed and drained**
- ¼ **cup lime juice**
- 1 **tablespoon all-purpose flour**
- 1 **tablespoon baking cocoa**
- 1 **tablespoon ground cumin**
- 1 **tablespoon chili powder**
- 2 **teaspoons ground coriander**
- 1 **teaspoon grated lime peel**
- ½ **teaspoon salt**
- ½ **teaspoon garlic pepper blend**
- ¼ **teaspoon pepper**
- 2 **flour tortillas (8 inches), cut into ¼-inch strips**
- 6 **tablespoons reduced-fat sour cream**

1. In a large skillet, saute onion and peppers in oil 7-8 minutes or until crisp-tender. Add the garlic; cook for 1 minute longer. Add chicken; cook and stir over medium heat until meat is no longer pink, 8-9 minutes.
2. Transfer to a 3-qt. slow cooker. Stir in the tomatoes, beans, lime juice, flour, cocoa, cumin, chili powder, coriander, lime peel, salt, garlic pepper and pepper.
3. Cover and cook on low 4-5 hours or until heated through.
4. Place tortilla strips on a baking sheet coated with cooking spray. Bake at 400° for 8-10 minutes or until crisp. Serve chili with sour cream and tortilla strips.

PER SERVING *1¼ cups with 10 tortilla strips and 1 tablespoon sour cream equals 356 cal., 14 g fat (3 g sat. fat), 55 mg chol., 644 mg sodium, 39 g carb., 8 g fiber, 21 g pro.*

TZIMMES

Tzimmes is a sweet Jewish dish consisting of a variety of fruits and vegetables, and may or may not include meat. Traditionally (as it is here), it's tossed with honey and cinnamon and slowly cooked to blend the flavors.

—**LISA RENSHAW** KANSAS CITY, MO

PREP: 20 MIN. • **COOK:** 5 HOURS
MAKES: 12 SERVINGS (⅔ CUP EACH)

- ½ **medium butternut squash, peeled and cubed**
- 2 **medium sweet potatoes, peeled and cubed**
- 6 **medium carrots, sliced**
- 2 **medium tart apples, peeled and sliced**
- 1 **cup chopped sweet onion**
- 1 **cup chopped dried apricots**
- 1 **cup golden raisins**
- ½ **cup orange juice**
- ¼ **cup honey**
- 2 **tablespoons finely chopped crystallized ginger**
- 3 **teaspoons ground cinnamon**
- 3 **teaspoons pumpkin pie spice**
- 2 **teaspoons grated orange peel**
- 1 **teaspoon salt**
  Vanilla yogurt, optional

1. Place the first seven ingredients in a 5- or 6-qt. slow cooker. Combine the orange juice, honey, ginger, cinnamon, pie spice, orange peel and salt; pour over top and mix well.
2. Cover and cook on low for 5-6 hours or until vegetables are tender. Dollop servings with yogurt if desired.

SLOW-COOKED CHICKEN CHILI

SLOW-COOKED LEMONY SPRING VEGGIES

These spuds do a slow simmer with carrots and onion for a comfort side that bucks up any entree. Finish with a sprinkle of chives.

—*TASTE OF HOME* TEST KITCHEN

PREP: 10 MIN. • **COOK:** 4¼ HOURS
MAKES: 8 SERVINGS

- **4   medium carrots, halved lengthwise and cut into 1-inch pieces**
- **1   large sweet onion, coarsely chopped**
- **1½ pounds baby red potatoes, quartered**
- **3   tablespoons butter, melted**
- **¾ teaspoon salt**
- **¼ teaspoon pepper**
- **1   cup frozen peas, thawed**
- **1   teaspoon grated lemon peel**
- **¼ cup minced fresh chives**

1. Place carrots and onion in a 4-qt. slow cooker; top with the potatoes. Drizzle with melted butter; sprinkle with salt and pepper. Cook, covered, on low 4-5 hours or until vegetables are tender.

2. Add peas to slow cooker. Cook, covered, on high 10-15 minutes or until heated through. Stir in lemon peel. Sprinkle with chives.

SLOW-COOKED LEMONY SPRING VEGGIES

EAT SMART

BROWN SUGAR-GLAZED BABY CARROTS

PREP: 10 MIN. • **COOK:** 6 HOURS
MAKES: 6 SERVINGS

- **2   pounds fresh baby carrots**
- **1   celery rib, finely chopped**
- **1   small onion, finely chopped**
- **¼ cup packed brown sugar**
- **3   tablespoons butter, cubed**
- **½ teaspoon salt**
- **½ teaspoon pepper**

In a 3-qt. slow cooker, combine all ingredients. Cover and cook on low for 6-8 hours or until carrots are tender.

PER SERVING *¾ cup equals 144 cal., 6 g fat (4 g sat. fat), 15 mg chol., 364 mg sodium, 23 g carb., 3 g fiber, 1 g pro.*

FRENCH DIP SANDWICHES

I found this recipe in one of our local publications. It's great for an easy winter meal, since the meat cooks all day without any attention.

—**DIANNE JOY RICHARDSON**
COLORADO SPRINGS, CO

PREP: 15 MIN. • **COOK:** 10 HOURS
MAKES: 12 SANDWICHES

- **1   beef sirloin tip roast (3 to 4 pounds)**
- **½ cup reduced-sodium soy sauce**
- **1   teaspoon beef bouillon granules**
- **1   bay leaf**
- **3   to 4 whole peppercorns**
- **1   teaspoon dried rosemary, crushed**
- **1   teaspoon dried thyme**
- **1   teaspoon garlic powder**
      Hard rolls, split

1. Cut roast in half. Place in a 5-qt. slow cooker. Combine the soy sauce, bouillon and seasonings; pour over roast. Add water to almost cover roast. Cover and cook on low for 10-12 hours or until meat is very tender.

2. Remove the roast; cool slightly. Discard bay leaf. Shred meat with two forks and return to slow cooker; heat through. Serve on rolls with broth.

"When things get hectic on a special holiday, these delicious glazed carrots are my 'rescue me' side dish because they cook while I'm preparing other parts of the meal. Also, I'm able to use my oven for other dishes, like the turkey!"

—ANNDREA BAILEY HUNTINGTON BEACH, CA

BROWN SUGAR-GLAZED BABY CARROTS

BARBECUED PORK SANDWICHES

TURKEY & CANNELLINI BEAN SOUP

This hearty dinner soup will stick to your ribs on a cold night. Slow cooking makes it so convenient!

—AMY MARTELL CANTON, PA

PREP: 35 MIN. • **COOK:** 5 HOURS
MAKES: 8 SERVINGS (3 QUARTS)

- 1 pound bulk pork sausage
- 4 cups cubed cooked turkey
- 2 cans (14½ ounces each) beef broth
- 1 can (15 ounces) white kidney or cannellini beans, rinsed and drained
- 1 can (14½ ounces) diced tomatoes, undrained
- 4 medium carrots, chopped
- 1 medium onion, chopped
- 1 medium green pepper, chopped
- 1 celery rib, chopped
- 2 teaspoons Italian seasoning
- ¼ teaspoon cayenne pepper

Crumble sausage into a large skillet; cook and stir until no longer pink. Drain. Transfer to a 5- or 6-qt. slow cooker. Stir in all of the remaining ingredients. Cover and cook on low for 5-6 hours or until the vegetables are tender.

BARBECUED PORK SANDWICHES

PREP: 20 MIN. • **COOK:** 7 HOURS
MAKES: 10 SERVINGS

- 1 medium onion, chopped
- 1 tablespoon butter
- 1 can (15 ounces) tomato puree
- ½ cup packed brown sugar
- ¼ cup steak sauce
- 2 tablespoons lemon juice
- ½ teaspoon salt
- 1 boneless pork shoulder butt roast (3 pounds)
- 10 hard rolls, split
    Coleslaw, optional

1. In a large skillet, saute onion in butter until tender. Stir in the tomato puree, brown sugar, steak sauce, lemon juice and salt. Cook over medium heat until sugar is dissolved.
2. Place roast in a 5-qt. slow cooker; pour sauce over the top. Cover and cook on low for 7-9 hours or until meat is tender. Remove roast; cool slightly. Skim fat from cooking juices. Shred meat with two forks and return to the slow cooker; heat through. Serve on rolls. Top with coleslaw if desired.

VEGETARIAN VEGETABLE SOUP

You just have to try this hearty soup for its unique blend of flavors and beautiful appearance. With all the rich foods served during the holidays, it's nice to have this soup loaded with fiber and vitamins.

—CHRISTINA TILL SOUTH HAVEN, MI

PREP: 20 MIN. • **COOK:** 9 HOURS
MAKES: 12 SERVING (ABOUT 3 QUARTS)

- ¾ cup chopped onion
- ½ cup chopped celery
- ½ cup chopped green pepper
- 2 tablespoons olive oil
- 1 large potato, peeled and diced
- 1 medium sweet potato, peeled and diced
- 1 to 2 garlic cloves, minced
- 3 cups vegetable broth
- 2 medium fresh tomatoes, chopped
- 1 can (16 ounces) kidney beans, rinsed and drained
- 1 can (15 ounces) garbanzo beans or chickpeas, rinsed and drained
- 2 teaspoons soy sauce
- 1 teaspoon paprika
- ½ teaspoon dried basil
- ¼ teaspoon salt
- ¼ teaspoon ground turmeric
- 1 bay leaf
  Dash cayenne pepper

1. In a large skillet, saute the onion, celery and green pepper in oil until crisp-tender. Add potato, sweet potato and garlic; saute 3-5 minutes longer.
2. Transfer to a 5-qt. slow cooker. Stir in the remaining ingredients. Cover and cook on low for 9-10 hours or until vegetables are tender. Discard bay leaf.

SMOKY WHITE BEANS & HAM

I had never made or eaten this dish before meeting my husband here in Kentucky. Now I make it at least once a week. I serve it with some homemade sweet corn bread. Delicious!

—CHRISTINE DUFFY STURGIS, KY

PREP: 15 MIN. + SOAKING • **COOK:** 6 HOURS
MAKES: 10 SERVINGS

- 1 pound dried great northern beans
- 3 smoked ham hocks
- 1 large onion, chopped
- 3 cans (14½ ounces each) reduced-sodium chicken or beef broth
- 2 cups water
- 1 tablespoon onion powder
- 1 tablespoon garlic powder
- 2 teaspoons pepper
  Thinly sliced green onions, optional

1. Rinse and sort beans; soak according to package directions.
2. Drain and rinse beans, discarding liquid. Transfer beans to a 6-qt. slow cooker. Add ham hocks. Stir in onion, broth, water and seasonings. Cook, covered, on low 6-8 hours or until beans are tender.
3. Remove meat from bones when cool enough to handle; cut ham into small pieces and return to slow cooker. Serve with a slotted spoon. Sprinkle with onions if desired.

SMOKY WHITE BEANS & HAM

Snacks & Sweets

SLOW COOKER SWEET AND SOUR MEATBALLS

My family asks for these saucy meatballs all year long. I like to make them with ground beef in the winter and ground turkey in the spring.

—**RACHELLE STRATTON** ROCK SPRINGS, WY

PREP: 30 MIN. • **COOK:** 3 HOURS
MAKES: 3 DOZEN

- 2 large eggs, lightly beaten
- ¼ cup panko (Japanese) bread crumbs
- 2 garlic cloves, minced
- 2 teaspoons salt-free garlic herb seasoning blend
- ½ teaspoon salt
- ¼ teaspoon pepper
- 2 pounds ground beef
- 1 can (15 ounces) tomato sauce
- 1 cup chicken broth
- 1 bottle (8 ounces) chili sauce
- ½ cup packed brown sugar
- ½ cup cider or white vinegar
- 1 green onion, thinly sliced

1. Preheat oven to 375°. In a large bowl, combine the first six ingredients. Add the ground beef; mix lightly but thoroughly. Shape into 1½-in. balls. Place the meatballs on a greased rack in a 15x10x1-in. baking pan. Bake for 15-20 minutes or until meatballs are lightly browned.

2. In large bowl, combine tomato sauce, broth, chili sauce, brown sugar and vinegar. Transfer meatballs to a 5-qt. slow cooker. Pour sauce over top. Cook, covered, on low 3-4 hours or until meatballs are cooked through. To serve, sprinkle with green onion.

SLOW COOKER SWEET AND SOUR MEATBALLS

SALTY-SWEET
PEANUT TREAT

CRAB & ARTICHOKE DIP

Nearly every time my girlfriends and I get together, we dip into this rich and creamy snack and our favorite bottle of wine. It's so convenient to use the slow cooker to make this recipe—it's a perfect fit for our relaxed friends nights.
—**CONNIE McKINNEY** MARSHALL, MO

PREP: 20 MIN. • **COOK:** 2 HOURS
MAKES: 3½ CUPS

- 3 **cups fresh baby spinach**
- 1 **can (14 ounces) water-packed artichoke hearts, rinsed, drained and chopped**
- 1 **package (8 ounces) cream cheese, softened**
- 2 **cups (8 ounces) shredded Havarti cheese**
- 1 **can (6 ounces) lump crabmeat, drained**
- ½ **cup sour cream**
- ⅛ **teaspoon salt**
- ⅛ **teaspoon pepper**
  Assorted crackers

1. In a large saucepan, bring ½ in. of water to a boil. Add spinach; cover and boil 3-5 minutes or until wilted. Drain.
2. In a 1½-qt. slow cooker, combine the artichokes, cheeses, crabmeat, sour cream, salt, pepper and spinach. Cover and cook on low for 2-3 hours or until cheese is melted. Serve with assorted crackers.

SALTY-SWEET PEANUT TREAT

Slow cooking transforms chocolate, peanuts and pretzels—who knew? After it's cooked, we drop the mix into mini muffin papers for a takeaway treat.
—**LIBBY WALP** CHICAGO, IL

PREP: 10 MIN. • **COOK:** 1 HOUR + CHILLING
MAKES: ABOUT 6 DOZEN

- 24 **ounces milk chocolate, coarsely chopped**
- 2 **cups salted peanuts**
- ¼ **cup packed brown sugar**
- 1 **teaspoon vanilla extract**
- 2 **cups crushed pretzels**

In a 3-qt. slow cooker, combine the chocolate, peanuts and brown sugar. Cook, covered, on low 1 hour or until chocolate is melted, stirring halfway through cooking. Stir in vanilla and pretzels. Drop by tablespoonfuls onto waxed paper-lined baking sheets. Refrigerate 10-15 minutes or until set. Store in an airtight container.

MAKE-AHEAD EGGNOG

Sipping homemade eggnog is a holiday tradition for many families. Our slow cooker version of the classic drink couldn't be easier to make.
—*TASTE OF HOME* TEST KITCHEN

PREP: 10 MIN. • **COOK:** 2 HOURS
MAKES: 9 SERVINGS (¾ CUP EACH)

- 6 **cups whole milk**
- 1 **cup egg substitute**
- ⅔ **cup sugar**
- 2 **teaspoons rum extract**
- 1½ **teaspoons pumpkin pie spice**
  French vanilla whipped topping, optional

In a 3-qt. slow cooker, combine the first five ingredients. Cover and cook on low for 2-3 hours or until heated through. Serve in mugs; dollop with whipped topping if desired.

BABY SPINACH

Using baby spinach saves prep time because you don't have to remove the tough stems from mature spinach. Some people prefer baby spinach's tender texture in salads, too.

QUINOA GRANOLA

This is a healthy and tasty snack that I feed to my kids often. They love it!

—**CINDY REAMS** PHILIPSBURG, PA

PREP: 5 MIN. • **COOK:** 2 HOURS + COOLING
MAKES: 6 CUPS

- ¼ cup honey
- 2 tablespoons coconut or canola oil
- 1 teaspoon ground cinnamon
- 3 cups old-fashioned oats
- 1 cup uncooked quinoa
- 1 cup flaked coconut
- 1 cup chopped mixed dried fruit
- 1 cup chopped pecans

1. In a 3- or 4-qt. slow cooker, combine honey, oil and cinnamon. Gradually stir in oats and quinoa until well blended. Cook, covered, on high 2 hours, stirring well every 20 minutes.

2. Stir in coconut, dried fruit and pecans. Spread evenly on waxed paper or baking sheets; cool completely. Store in airtight containers.

QUINOA GRANOLA

BRISKET SLIDERS WITH CARAMELIZED ONIONS

PREP: 25 MIN. + MARINATING
COOK: 7 HOURS • **MAKES:** 2 DOZEN

- 2 tablespoons plus ⅛ teaspoon salt
- 2 tablespoons sugar
- 2 tablespoons whole peppercorns, crushed
- 5 garlic cloves, minced
- 1 fresh beef brisket (about 4 pounds)
- 1 cup mayonnaise
- ½ cup crumbled blue cheese
- 2 teaspoons horseradish
- ⅛ teaspoon cayenne pepper
- 2 medium onions, chopped
- 3 medium carrots, cut into 1-inch pieces
- 2 celery ribs, chopped
- 1 cup dry red wine or beef broth
- ¼ cup stone-ground mustard
- 3 bay leaves
- 1 tablespoon olive oil
- 3 medium onions, sliced
- 24 mini buns
    Arugula and tomato slices, optional

1. Combine 2 tablespoons salt, sugar, peppercorns and garlic; rub onto all sides of brisket. Wrap in plastic; refrigerate for 8 hours or overnight. Combine the mayonnaise, cheese, horseradish and cayenne; refrigerate.

2. Place chopped onions, carrots and celery in a 6- or 7-qt. slow cooker. Unwrap brisket; place on vegetables. Combine the wine, mustard and bay leaves; pour over the brisket. Cook, covered, on low 7-9 hours or until the meat is fork tender. Meanwhile, in a large skillet, heat the oil over medium heat. Add sliced onions and remaining salt; cook and stir until softened. Reduce heat to medium-low; cook 30-35 minutes or until deep golden brown, stirring occasionally.

3. Remove the brisket; cool slightly. Reserve 1 cup cooking juices; discard remaining juices. Skim the fat from reserved juices. Thinly slice brisket across the grain; return to the slow cooker. Pour juices over brisket.

4. Serve the brisket on buns with mayonnaise mixture and onions and, if desired, arugula and tomato slices.

"For a dear friend's going-away party, I made a juicy brisket and turned it into sliders. Cook the brisket ahead, and the slider assembly will be a breeze."
—**MARLIES COVENTRY** NORTH VANCOUVER, BC

BRISKET SLIDERS WITH
CARAMELIZED ONIONS

SLOW COOKER STRAWBERRY-RHUBARB SAUCE

We recently started growing our own rhubarb, and we live in a part of Oregon where strawberries are plentiful. I created this to drizzle over ice cream and filled a crisp with the rest.

—KIM BANICK SALEM, OR

PREP: 15 MIN. • **COOK:** 4½ HOURS
MAKES: 5 CUPS

- 4 cups sliced fresh or frozen rhubarb, thawed (about 10 stalks)
- 4 cups fresh strawberries (about 1¼ pounds), halved
- 1½ cups sugar
- ¼ cup water
- 3 tablespoons butter
- 1 teaspoon vanilla extract
- ¼ cup cornstarch
- 3 tablespoons cold water
  Vanilla ice cream

1. In a 3-qt. slow cooker, combine the first six ingredients. Cook, covered, on low 4-5 hours or until the rhubarb is tender.
2. In a bowl, mix cornstarch and cold water until smooth; gradually stir into the sauce. Cook, covered, on low for 30 minutes longer or until thickened. Serve with ice cream.
NOTE *If using frozen rhubarb, measure rhubarb while still frozen, then thaw completely. Drain in a colander, but do not press liquid out.*

BBQ CHICKEN SLIDERS

Brining the chicken overnight helps make it taste exceptionally good. Plus, it's so tender, it melts in your mouth.

—RACHEL KUNKEL SCHELL CITY, MO

PREP: 25 MIN. + BRINING • **COOK:** 4 HOURS
MAKES: 8 SERVINGS (2 SLIDERS EACH)

BRINE
- 1½ quarts water
- ¼ cup packed brown sugar
- 2 tablespoons salt
- 1 tablespoon liquid smoke
- 2 garlic cloves, minced
- ½ teaspoon dried thyme

CHICKEN
- 2 pounds boneless skinless chicken breast halves
- ⅓ cup liquid smoke
- 1½ cups hickory smoke-flavored barbecue sauce
- 16 slider buns or dinner rolls, split and warmed

1. In a bowl, mix brine ingredients, stirring to dissolve the brown sugar. Reserve 1 cup brine for cooking the chicken; cover and refrigerate.
2. Place chicken in a large resealable bag; add remaining brine. Seal bag, pressing out as much air as possible; turn to coat chicken. Place in a large bowl; refrigerate 18-24 hours, turning occasionally.
3. Remove chicken from brine and transfer to a 3-qt. slow cooker; discard brine in bag. Add reserved 1 cup brine and ⅓ cup liquid smoke to chicken. Cook, covered, on low 4-5 hours or until chicken is tender.
4. Remove chicken; cool slightly. Discard cooking juices. Shred chicken with two forks and return to slow cooker. Stir in barbecue sauce; heat through. Serve on buns.

BBQ CHICKEN SLIDERS

PEPPERONI EXTREME DIP

CHILI BEEF DIP

No last-minute party prep needed! Just put this creamy dip together a couple hours before your shindig, and let your slow cooker do the work.

—**PAT HABIGER** SPEARVILLE, KS

PREP: 25 MIN. • **COOK:** 2 HOURS
MAKES: 8 CUPS

- 2 **pounds lean ground beef (90% lean)**
- 1 **large onion, chopped**
- 1 **jalapeno pepper, seeded and chopped**
- 1 **pound cream cheese, cubed**
- 2 **cans (8 ounces each) tomato sauce**
- 1 **can (4 ounces) chopped green chilies**
- ½ **cup grated Parmesan cheese**
- ½ **cup ketchup**
- 2 **garlic cloves, minced**
- 1½ **teaspoons chili powder**
- 1 **teaspoon dried oregano**
  Tortilla chips

1. In a large skillet, brown the beef, onion and jalapeno until meat is no longer pink; drain. Transfer to a 3- or 4-qt. slow cooker. Stir in the cream cheese, tomato sauce, green chilies, Parmesan cheese, ketchup, garlic, chili powder and oregano.
2. Cook, covered, on low 2-3 hours or until hot. Stir; serve with chips.
NOTE *Wear disposable gloves when cutting hot peppers; the oils can burn skin. Avoid touching your face.*

PEPPERONI EXTREME DIP

Take just 10 minutes to prep, and in a few short hours, your slow cooker will have you serving up a party-worthy appetizer to your hungry bunch, no problem!

—**LAURA MAGEE** HOULTON, WI

PREP: 10 MIN. • **COOK:** 3 HOURS
MAKES: 2¼ QUARTS

- 4 **cups (16 ounces) shredded cheddar cheese**
- 3½ **cups spaghetti sauce**
- 2 **cups mayonnaise**
- 1 **package (8 ounces) sliced pepperoni, chopped**
- 1 **can (6 ounces) pitted ripe olives, chopped**
- 1 **jar (5¾ ounces) sliced green olives with pimientos, drained and chopped**
  Tortilla chips

Combine the first six ingredients in a 4-qt. slow cooker coated with cooking spray. Cover and cook on low 3 hours or until the cheese is melted, stirring halfway through cooking. Serve with tortilla chips.

OLD-FASHIONED TAPIOCA

My family loves old-fashioned tapioca, but I don't always have time to make it. So, I came up with this simple recipe. It lets us enjoy one of our favorites without all the hands-on time.

—**RUTH PETERS** BEL AIR, MD

PREP: 10 MIN. • **COOK:** 4½ HOURS
MAKES: 18 SERVINGS (½ CUP EACH)

- 8 **cups 2% milk**
- 1 **cup pearl tapioca**
- 1 **cup plus 2 tablespoons sugar**
- ⅛ **teaspoon salt**
- 4 **large eggs**
- 1½ **teaspoons vanilla extract**
  Sliced fresh strawberries and whipped cream, optional

1. In a 4- to 5-qt. slow cooker, combine milk, tapioca, sugar and salt. Cover and cook on low for 4-5 hours.
2. In a large bowl, beat eggs; stir in a small amount of hot tapioca mixture. Return all to slow cooker, stirring to combine. Cover and cook 30 minutes longer or until a thermometer reads 160°. Stir in vanilla.
3. Serve with strawberries and whipped cream if desired.

HOW-TO

CHOP AN ONION

Cut onion in half from top to the root, and peel. Leaving the root attached, place flat side down on work surface. Cut vertically through onion, leaving root end uncut. Cut across onion, discarding root end. The closer the cuts, the more finely the onion will be chopped.

"Fresh peaches and tomatoes make my salsa a hands-down winner over store versions. As a treat, I give my co-workers serveral jars throughout the year."
—**PEGGY STAHNKE** CLEVELAND, OH

SLOW-COOKED PEACH SALSA

SLOW-COOKED PEACH SALSA

PREP: 20 MIN. • **COOK:** 3 HOURS
MAKES: 11 CUPS

- 4 **pounds tomatoes (about 12 medium), chopped**
- 1 **medium onion, chopped**
- 4 **jalapeno peppers, seeded and finely chopped**
- ½ to ⅔ **cup packed brown sugar**
- ¼ **cup minced fresh cilantro**
- 4 **garlic cloves, minced**
- 1 **teaspoon salt**
- 4 **cups chopped peeled fresh peaches (about 4 medium), divided**
- 1 **can (6 ounces) tomato paste**

1. In a 5-qt. slow cooker, combine the first seven ingredients; stir in 2 cups peaches. Cook, covered, on low for 3-4 hours or until onion is tender.
2. Stir tomato paste and remaining peaches into slow cooker. Cool.
3. Transfer to covered containers. (If freezing salsa, use freezer-safe containers and fill to within ½ in. of tops.) Refrigerate up to 1 week or freeze up to 12 months. Thaw frozen salsa in refrigerator before serving.
NOTE *Wear disposable gloves when cutting hot peppers; the oils can burn skin. Avoid touching your face.*

BUTTERSCOTCH PEARS

This grand finale simmers during dinner and impresses as soon as you bring it to the table. Serve as is or with vanilla ice cream and a slice of pound cake. Leftover pear nectar is heavenly. Try adding it to sparkling wine or enjoying it over tinkling ice cubes at breakfast.
—**THERESA KREYCHE** TUSTIN, CA

PREP: 20 MIN. • **COOK:** 2 HOURS
MAKES: 8 SERVINGS

- 4 **large firm pears**
- 1 **tablespoon lemon juice**
- ¼ **cup packed brown sugar**
- 3 **tablespoons butter, softened**
- 2 **tablespoons all-purpose flour**
- ½ **teaspoon ground cinnamon**
- ¼ **teaspoon salt**
- ½ **cup chopped pecans**
- ½ **cup pear nectar**
- 2 **tablespoons honey**

1. Cut the pears in half lengthwise; remove cores. Brush pears with lemon juice. In a bowl, combine the brown sugar, butter, flour, cinnamon and salt; stir in pecans. Spoon into pears; place in 4-qt. slow cooker.
2. Combine pear nectar and honey; drizzle over pears. Cover and cook on low 2-3 hours or until pears are tender. Serve warm.

BARBECUED PARTY STARTERS

These sweet and tangy bites will tide just about anyone over until dinner. At the buffet, set out a collection of fun toothpicks to make for easy nibbling.
—**ANASTASIA WEISS** PUNXSUTAWNEY, PA

PREP: 30 MIN. • **COOK:** 2¼ HOURS
MAKES: 16 SERVINGS (⅓ CUP EACH)

- 1 **pound ground beef**
- ¼ **cup finely chopped onion**
- 1 **package (16 ounces) miniature hot dogs, drained**
- 1 **jar (12 ounces) apricot preserves**
- 1 **cup barbecue sauce**
- 1 **can (20 ounces) pineapple chunks, drained**

1. In a large bowl, combine beef and onion, mixing lightly but thoroughly. Shape into 1-in. balls. In a large skillet over medium heat, cook the meatballs in two batches until cooked through, turning occasionally.
2. Using a slotted spoon, transfer the meatballs to a 3-qt. slow cooker. Add hot dogs; stir in the apricot preserves and barbecue sauce. Cook, covered, on high 2-3 hours or until mixture is heated through.
3. Stir in the pineapple chunks and cook, covered, 15-20 minutes longer or until heated through.

BARBECUED PARTY STARTERS

SLOW COOKER SPICED
MIXED NUTS

NACHO RICE DIP

Spanish rice mix adds an interesting twist to this effortless appetizer. Every time I serve this dip at get-togethers, my guests gobble it up.
—AUDRA HUNGATE HOLT, MO

PREP: 20 MIN. • **COOK:** 15 MIN.
MAKES: ABOUT 8 CUPS

- 1 package (6.8 ounces) Spanish rice and pasta mix
- 2 tablespoons butter
- 2 cups water
- 1 can (14½ ounces) diced tomatoes, undrained
- 1 pound ground beef
- 1 pound (16 ounces) process cheese (Velveeta), cubed
- 1 can (14½ ounces) stewed tomatoes
- 1 jar (8 ounces) process cheese sauce
  Tortilla chips

1. In a large saucepan, cook rice mix in butter until golden brown. Stir in water and diced tomatoes; bring to a boil. Reduce heat; cover and simmer 15-20 minutes or until rice is tender.
2. Meanwhile, in a large skillet, cook beef until no longer pink. Drain and add to the rice. Stir in the cheese, stewed tomatoes and cheese sauce; cook and stir until cheese is melted.
3. Transfer to a slow cooker set on low. Serve with chips.

SLOW COOKER SPICED MIXED NUTS

What slow cookers do for soups and stews, they'll do for mixed nuts, too. Just sprinkle, stir and enjoy the sweet, comforting scent of cooking spices.
—STEPHANIE LOAIZA LAYTON, UT

PREP: 15 MIN.
COOK: 1 HOUR 50 MIN. + COOLING
MAKES: 6 CUPS

- 1 large egg white
- 2 teaspoons vanilla extract
- 1 cup unblanched almonds
- 1 cup pecan halves
- 1 cup shelled walnuts
- 1 cup unsalted cashews
- 1 cup sugar
- 1 cup packed brown sugar
- 4 teaspoons ground cinnamon
- 2 teaspoons ground ginger
- 1 teaspoon ground nutmeg
- ½ teaspoon ground cloves
- ⅛ teaspoon salt
- 2 tablespoons water

1. In a large bowl, whisk the egg white and vanilla until blended; stir in nuts. In a small bowl, mix the sugars, spices and salt. Add to the nut mixture and toss to coat.
2. Transfer to a greased 3-qt. slow cooker. Cook, covered, on high for 1½ hours, stirring every 15 minutes. Gradually stir in the water. Cook, covered, on low 20 minutes.
3. Spread onto waxed paper, and cool completely. Store in airtight containers up to 1 week.

SPICE IT UP

Like zesty flavor? Spice up the dip by stirring in one of these.

- A 4-ounce can of chopped green chilies
- Minced seeded jalapeno
- 1½ cans of tomatoes and green chilies instead of the larger can of regular tomatoes
- Chili powder or cayenne
- Minced chipotle peppers in adobo sauce

BBQ SAUCE MEATBALLS

I whipped these up for my son's first birthday so I could serve something savory alongside the cake and ice cream. They're delicious!

—**TARA REEDER** MASON, MI

PREP: 20 MIN. • **COOK:** 7 HOURS
MAKES: 2 DOZEN

- 1 large egg, beaten
- ½ cup shredded Colby-Monterey Jack cheese
- ¼ cup seasoned bread crumbs
- ¼ cup finely chopped onion
- 2 pounds ground beef

SAUCE

- 2 cups ketchup
- 2 tablespoons prepared mustard
- 1 tablespoon brown sugar
- 1 tablespoon cider vinegar
- 1 tablespoon lemon juice
- 1 tablespoon soy sauce

1. In a large bowl, combine the egg, cheese, bread crumbs and onion. Crumble beef over mixture and mix well. Shape into 1½-in. balls. Transfer to a 3-qt. slow cooker.
2. In a small bowl, combine the sauce ingredients; pour over the meatballs. Cover and cook on low for 7-8 hours or until meat is no longer pink.

FIVE-CHEESE SPINACH & ARTICHOKE DIP

This dish has many fans. I've been asked to make it for weddings, Christmas parties and more. Don't have time to make it in the slow cooker? You can bake it in the oven at about 400 degrees for 30 minutes or until it's hot and bubbly.

—**NOELLE MYERS** GRAND FORKS, ND

PREP: 20 MIN. • **COOK:** 2½ HOURS
MAKES: 16 SERVINGS (¼ CUP EACH)

- 1 jar (12 ounces) roasted sweet red peppers
- 1 jar (6½ ounces) marinated quartered artichoke hearts
- 1 package (10 ounces) frozen chopped spinach, thawed and squeezed dry
- 8 ounces fresh mozzarella cheese, cubed
- 1½ cups (6 ounces) shredded Asiago cheese
- 6 ounces cream cheese, softened and cubed
- 1 cup (4 ounces) crumbled feta cheese
- ⅓ cup shredded provolone cheese
- ⅓ cup minced fresh basil
- ¼ cup finely chopped red onion
- 2 tablespoons mayonnaise
- 2 garlic cloves, minced
  Assorted crackers

1. Drain the roasted sweet peppers, reserving 1 tablespoon liquid; chop the peppers. Drain the artichoke hearts, reserving 2 tablespoons liquid; coarsely chop the artichoke hearts.
2. In a 3-qt. slow cooker coated with cooking spray, combine the spinach, cheeses, basil, onion, mayonnaise, garlic, artichoke hearts and peppers. Stir in reserved pepper and artichoke liquids. Cook, covered, on high for 2 hours. Stir the dip; cook, covered, 30-60 minutes longer or until cheese is melted. Stir before serving; serve with crackers.

FIVE-CHEESE SPINACH & ARTICHOKE DIP

WARM APPLE-CRANBERRY DESSERT

Served with ice cream, this heartwarming dessert promises to become a favorite in your house! I love that on nights when we have this, dessert practically makes itself.

—MARY JANE JONES ATHENS, OH

PREP: 20 MIN. • **COOK:** 2 HOURS
MAKES: 10 SERVINGS

- 5 large apples, peeled and sliced
- 1 cup fresh or frozen cranberries, thawed
- ¾ cup packed brown sugar, divided
- 2 tablespoons lemon juice
- ½ cup all-purpose flour
  Dash salt
- ⅓ cup cold butter
  Vanilla ice cream
  Toasted chopped pecans

1. In a greased 5-qt. slow cooker, combine apples, cranberries, ¼ cup brown sugar and lemon juice. In a bowl, mix flour, salt and remaining brown sugar; cut in the butter until crumbly. Sprinkle over fruit mixture.
2. Cook, covered, on high 2-2½ hours or until apples are tender. Serve with ice cream and pecans.

EAT SMART

SLOW COOKER BAKED APPLES

On a cool fall day, coming home to this healthy dessert is just plain wonderful.

—EVANGELINE BRADFORD ERLANGER, KY

PREP: 25 MIN. • **COOK:** 4 HOURS
MAKES: 6 SERVINGS

- 6 medium tart apples
- ½ cup raisins
- ⅓ cup packed brown sugar
- 1 tablespoon grated orange peel
- 1 cup water
- 3 tablespoons thawed orange juice concentrate
- 2 tablespoons butter

1. Core the apples and, if desired, peel the top third of each. Combine raisins, brown sugar and grated orange peel; spoon into the apples. Place in a 5-qt. slow cooker.
2. Pour water around apples. Drizzle with orange juice concentrate. Dot with butter. Cover and cook on low for 4-5 hours or until apples are tender.
PER SERVING *1 stuffed apple equals 203 cal., 4 g fat (2 g sat. fat), 10 mg chol., 35 mg sodium, 44 g carb., 4 g fiber, 1 g pro.*

FREEZE IT

HEARTY PORK AND BLACK BEAN NACHOS

PREP: 15 MIN. • **COOK:** 6 HOURS
MAKES: 10 SERVINGS

- 1 package (4 ounces) beef jerky
- 3 pounds pork spareribs, cut into 2-rib sections
- 4 cans (15 ounces each) black beans, rinsed and drained
- 4 cups beef broth
- 1 medium onion, chopped
- 6 bacon strips, cooked and crumbled
- 3 large garlic cloves, minced
- 1 teaspoon crushed red pepper flakes
  Tortilla chips
  Optional toppings: shredded cheddar cheese, sour cream, thinly sliced green onions, pickled jalapenos and chopped tomatoes

1. Place the beef jerky in a food processor; pulse until finely ground. Place ribs in a 5- or 6-qt. slow cooker; top with jerky, beans, broth, onion, bacon, garlic and pepper flakes. Cook, covered, on low 6-8 hours or until meat is tender.
2. When cool enough to handle, remove meat from bones; discard bones. Shred meat with two forks; return to slow cooker. Strain pork mixture; discard juices. Serve with chips and toppings as desired.
FREEZE OPTION *Freeze cooled shredded meat mixture with juices in freezer containers. To use, partially thaw in refrigerator overnight. Heat through in a saucepan, stirring occasionally. Strain pork mixture; discard juices. Serve with chips and toppings as desired.*

SLOW COOKER
BAKED APPLES

"My husband and I are both graduate students right now, so we don't have a lot of time to cook dinner. Our family loves coming home to this incredible nacho platter, and I love how easy it is to prepare." —**FAITH STOKES** CHICKAMAUGA, GA

HEARTY PORK AND
BLACK BEAN NACHOS

APPLE-TOPPED HAM
STEAKS, PAGE 144

Stovetop Suppers

Quick, **no-fuss dinners** are just a page-flip away with the recipes you'll find here. Discover 105 **savory** pastas, **simmered** stews, **fiery** sautes, **healthy** seafood options and **hearty** main-dish salads. Wondering **what's for dinner tonight?** Let this section be **your new go-to.**

Beef & Ground Beef

GERMAN MEATBALLS

This is one of our favorite main dishes. For variety, the meatballs can be cooked with a sweet cream gravy or tomatoes.

—IONA REDEMER CALUMET, OK

PREP: 20 MIN. • **COOK:** 25 MIN.
MAKES: 6 SERVINGS

- 1 **pound ground beef**
- ½ **pound ground pork**
- ½ **cup finely chopped onion**
- ¾ **cup fine dry bread crumbs**
- 1 **tablespoon snipped fresh parsley**
- 1½ **teaspoons salt**
- ⅛ **teaspoon pepper**
- 1 **teaspoon Worcestershire sauce**
- 1 **large egg, beaten**
- ½ **cup milk**
- 2 **to 3 tablespoons vegetable oil**
- 1 **can (27 ounces) sauerkraut, undrained**
- ⅓ **to ½ cup water, optional**
  Additional snipped parsley

In a bowl, combine the first 10 ingredients; shape into 18 meatballs, 2 in. each. Heat the oil in a skillet; brown the meatballs. Remove the meatballs and drain fat. Spoon the sauerkraut into the skillet; top with meatballs. Cover and simmer for 15-20 minutes or until meatballs are cooked through, adding water if necessary. Sprinkle with parsley.

FREEZE OPTION *Freeze cooled meatball mixture in freezer containers. To use, partially thaw in refrigerator overnight. Microwave, covered, on high in a microwave-safe dish until heated through, stirring gently.*

GERMAN MEATBALLS

SKILLET
LASAGNA

CHICKEN-FRIED STEAKS

These crispy steaks will have people raving about how good they taste.

—DENICE LOUK GARNETT, KS

START TO FINISH: 25 MIN.
MAKES: 4 SERVINGS (2 CUPS GRAVY)

    2   cups all-purpose flour, divided
    2   teaspoons baking powder
    ¾   teaspoon each salt, onion powder,
        garlic powder, chili powder and
        pepper
    1   large egg, lightly beaten
    1¼ cups buttermilk, divided
    4   beef cubed steaks (4 ounces each)
        Oil for frying
    1½ cups 2% milk

1. In a shallow bowl, combine 1¾ cups flour, baking powder and seasonings. In another shallow bowl, combine egg and ¾ cup buttermilk. Dip each cubed steak in buttermilk mixture, then roll in flour mixture.
2. In a large skillet, heat ½ in. of oil on medium-high. Fry steaks for 5-7 minutes. Turn carefully; cook 5 minutes longer or until coating is crisp and meat is no longer pink.
3. Drain oil, reserving ⅓ cup of the drippings; stir in remaining flour until smooth. Cook and stir over medium heat 2 minutes. Gradually whisk in milk and remaining buttermilk. Bring to a boil; cook and stir 2 minutes or until thickened. Serve with steaks.

HOW-TO

PAN-FRY

Heat ½ in. oil in a skillet over medium-high heat. The oil is ready when it shimmers (gives off visible waves of heat). Never leave the pan unattended, and don't overheat the oil or it will smoke. Pat food dry before frying and, if desired, dip in batter or coat with crumbs. Don't overcrowd the pan, as the food will steam rather than fry.

SKILLET LASAGNA

This is hands-down one of the best skillet lasagna recipes for a weekday meal. With classic flavors and cheesy layers, it's definitely kid-friendly.

—TASTE OF HOME TEST KITCHEN

START TO FINISH: 30 MIN.
MAKES: 6 SERVINGS

    ¾   pound ground beef
    2   garlic cloves, minced
    1   can (14½ ounces) diced tomatoes
        with basil, oregano and garlic,
        undrained
    2   jars (14 ounces each) spaghetti
        sauce
    ⅔   cup condensed cream of onion
        soup, undiluted
    2   large eggs, lightly beaten
    1¼ cups 1% cottage cheese
    ¾   teaspoon Italian seasoning
    9   no-cook lasagna noodles
    ½   cup shredded Colby-Monterey
        Jack cheese
    ½   cup shredded part-skim
        mozzarella cheese

1. In a large skillet, cook beef and garlic over medium heat until meat is no longer pink; drain. Stir in tomatoes and spaghetti sauce; heat through. Transfer to a large bowl.
2. In a small bowl, combine the soup, eggs, cottage cheese and the Italian seasoning.
3. Return 1 cup meat sauce to the skillet; spread evenly. Layer with 1 cup cottage cheese mixture, 1½ cups meat sauce and half of the noodles, breaking to fit. Repeat layers of cottage cheese mixture, meat sauce and noodles. Top with remaining meat sauce. Bring to a boil. Reduce heat; cover and simmer for 15-17 minutes or until noodles are tender.
4. Remove from the heat. Sprinkle with shredded cheeses; cover and let stand for 2 minutes or until melted.

BAVARIAN
POT ROAST

BAVARIAN POT ROAST

Since all of my grandparents were German, it's no wonder that so many Bavarian recipes have been handed down to me. Because the Midwest has such a large German population, this recipe represents the area well.

—SUSAN ROBERTSON HAMILTON, OH

PREP: 20 MIN. • **COOK:** 2½ HOURS
MAKES: 8-10 SERVINGS

- 1 boneless beef chuck pot roast (about 3 pounds)
- 2 tablespoons canola oil
- 1¼ cups water
- ¾ cup beer or beef broth
- 1 can (8 ounces) tomato sauce
- ½ cup chopped onion
- 2 tablespoons sugar
- 1 tablespoon vinegar
- 2 teaspoons salt
- 1 teaspoon ground cinnamon
- 1 bay leaf
- ½ teaspoon pepper
- ½ teaspoon ground ginger
  Cornstarch and cold water, optional
  Hot cooked noodles

1. In a Dutch oven, brown roast in hot oil. Combine water, beer or broth, tomato sauce, onion, sugar, vinegar, salt, cinnamon, bay leaf, pepper and ginger. Pour over meat and bring to a boil. Reduce heat; cover and simmer until meat is tender, 2½-3 hours.

2. Remove meat. Discard bay leaf. If desired, thicken juices with cornstarch and water. Serve with cooked noodles.

FREEZE OPTION *Place sliced pot roast in freezer containers; top with cooking juices. If desired, place noodles in separate freezer containers. Cool and freeze. To use, partially thaw in the refrigerator overnight. Microwave, covered, on high in a microwave-safe dish until heated through, gently stirring and adding a little broth to pot roast if necessary.*

"Feta cheese is one of my favorite kinds. It's good in a burger, but it really shines in this Mediterranean-style sloppy joe."

—SONYA LABBE WEST HOLLYWOOD, CA

GREEK SLOPPY JOES

GREEK SLOPPY JOES

START TO FINISH: 25 MIN.
MAKES: 6 SERVINGS

- 1 pound lean ground beef (90% lean)
- 1 small red onion, chopped
- 2 garlic cloves, minced
- 1 can (15 ounces) tomato sauce
- 1 teaspoon dried oregano
- 2 cups chopped romaine
- 6 kaiser rolls, split and toasted
- ½ cup crumbled feta cheese

1. In a large skillet, cook the beef, onion and garlic over medium heat for 6-8 minutes or until beef is no longer pink, breaking up beef into crumbles; drain. Stir in tomato sauce and oregano. Bring to a boil. Reduce heat; simmer, uncovered, for 8-10 minutes or until sauce is slightly thickened, stirring occasionally.

2. Place romaine on roll bottoms; top with meat mixture. Sprinkle with feta cheese; replace tops.

FREEZE OPTION *Freeze cooled meat mixture in freezer containers. To use, partially thaw in the refrigerator overnight. Heat through in a saucepan, stirring occasionally and adding a little water if necessary.*

PER SERVING *1 sandwich equals 335 cal., 10 g fat (4 g sat. fat), 52 mg chol., 767 mg sodium, 36 g carb., 3 g fiber, 23 g pro.* **Diabetic Exchanges:** *3 lean meat, 2 starch, 1 vegetable.*

BEEF FILETS WITH PORTOBELLO SAUCE

These tasty steaks are special and fast enough for everyday dinners. We enjoy the mushroom-topped filets with crusty French bread, mixed salad and a light lemon dessert.

—**CHRISTEL STEIN** TAMPA, FL

START TO FINISH: 30 MIN.
MAKES: 2 SERVINGS

- 2 **beef tenderloin steaks (4 ounces each)**
- ½ **cup dry red wine or reduced-sodium beef broth**
- 1 **teaspoon all-purpose flour**
- ½ **cup reduced-sodium beef broth**
- 1 **teaspoon each steak sauce, Worcestershire sauce and ketchup**
- ½ **teaspoon ground mustard**
- 4 **ounces fresh baby portobello mushrooms, sliced**
- ¼ **teaspoon pepper**
- ⅛ **teaspoon salt**
- 1 **tablespoon minced chives, optional**

1. In a large nonstick skillet coated with cooking spray, brown steaks on both sides over medium-high heat. Remove and keep warm.

2. Reduce heat to medium. Add wine to pan, stirring to loosen browned bits; cook for 2-3 minutes or until liquid is reduced by half. Combine flour and broth until smooth; whisk into the pan juices. Add steak sauce, Worcestershire sauce, ketchup and mustard. Bring to a boil.

3. Return steaks to the skillet; add mushrooms. Cook for 4-5 minutes on each side or until meat reaches desired doneness (for medium-rare, a meat thermometer should read 145°; medium, 160°; well-done, 170°). Sprinkle with pepper, salt and chives if desired.

SIRLOIN STIR-FRY WITH RAMEN NOODLES

SIRLOIN STIR-FRY WITH RAMEN NOODLES

I created this recipe when I was craving good Chinese food. The leftovers taste just as yummy when reheated the next day.

—**ANNETTE HEMSATH** SUTHERLIN, OR

START TO FINISH: 30 MIN.
MAKES: 4 SERVINGS

- 2 **packages (3 ounces each) beef ramen noodles**
- 2 **tablespoons cornstarch**
- 2 **cups beef broth, divided**
- 1 **pound beef top sirloin steak, cut into thin strips**
- 2 **tablespoons canola oil**
- 2 **tablespoons reduced-sodium soy sauce**
- 2 **cans (14 ounces each) whole baby corn, rinsed and drained**
- 2 **cups fresh broccoli florets**
- 1 **cup diced sweet red pepper**
- 1 **cup shredded carrots**
- 4 **green onions, cut into 1-inch pieces**
- ½ **cup unsalted peanuts**

1. Set aside seasoning packets from noodles. Cook noodles according to package directions.

2. Meanwhile, in a small bowl, combine cornstarch and ¼ cup broth until smooth; set aside. In a large skillet or wok, stir-fry beef in oil until no longer pink. Add soy sauce; cook for 3-4 minutes or until liquid has evaporated. Remove the beef and keep warm.

3. Add the corn, broccoli, red pepper, carrots, onions and remaining broth to the pan. Sprinkle with contents of seasoning packets. Stir-fry for 5-7 minutes or until vegetables are crisp-tender.

4. Stir the cornstarch mixture and add to skillet. Bring to a boil; cook and stir for 2 minutes or until thickened. Drain noodles. Add beef and noodles to pan; heat through. Garnish with the peanuts.

CHILI BEEF NOODLE SKILLET

A friend gave me this recipe. My husband likes this entree's hearty blend of beef, onion and tomatoes. I like it because I can get it to the table so quickly.
—**DEBORAH ELLIOTT** RIDGE SPRING, SC

START TO FINISH: 30 MIN.
MAKES: 8 SERVINGS

- 1 package (8 ounces) egg noodles
- 2 pounds ground beef
- 1 medium onion, chopped
- ¼ cup chopped celery
- 2 garlic cloves, minced
- 1 can (28 ounces) diced tomatoes, undrained
- 1 tablespoon chili powder
- ¼ to ½ teaspoon salt
- ⅛ teaspoon pepper
- ½ to 1 cup shredded cheddar cheese

1. Cook noodles according to package directions. Meanwhile, in a large skillet, cook the beef, onion, celery and garlic over medium heat until meat is no longer pink and vegetables are tender; drain. Add the tomatoes, chili powder, salt and pepper. Cook and stir for 2 minutes or until mixture is heated through.

2. Drain the egg noodles; stir into the beef mixture and heat through. Remove from the heat. Sprinkle with the cheddar cheese; cover and let stand for 5 minutes or until the cheese is melted.

CHILI BEEF
NOODLE SKILLET

CLASSIC CABBAGE ROLLS

HUNGARIAN SHORT RIBS

FREEZE IT

PREP: 15 MIN. • **COOK:** 2¼ HOURS
MAKES: 6-8 SERVINGS

- 2 to 3 tablespoons canola oil
- 4 pounds bone-in beef short ribs
- 2 medium onions, sliced
- 1 can (15 ounces) tomato sauce
- 1 cup water
- ¼ cup packed brown sugar
- ¼ cup vinegar
- 1½ teaspoons salt
- 1½ teaspoons ground mustard
- 1½ teaspoons Worcestershire sauce
- ¼ teaspoon paprika
  Cooked wide egg noodles

In a Dutch oven, heat the oil over medium-high heat. Brown ribs on all sides. Add onions; cook until tender. Combine all remaining ingredients except the noodles; pour over ribs. Reduce heat; cover and simmer for 2-2½ hours or until the meat is tender. Thicken gravy if desired. Serve over noodles.

FREEZE OPTION *Freeze cooled rib mixture in freezer containers. To use, partially thaw in the refrigerator overnight. Microwave, covered, on high in a microwave-safe dish until heated through, gently stirring and adding a little water if necessary. Serve with egg noodles.*

CLASSIC CABBAGE ROLLS

I've always enjoyed cabbage rolls but never made them because most recipes seemed too complicated. This one is on the simpler side and is the best I've ever tasted.

—BEVERLY ZEHNER MCMINNVILLE, OR

PREP: 30 MIN. • **COOK:** 1½ HOURS
MAKES: 4 SERVINGS

- 1 medium head cabbage
- 1½ cups chopped onion, divided
- 1 tablespoon butter
- 2 cans (14½ ounces each) Italian stewed tomatoes
- 4 garlic cloves, minced
- 2 tablespoons brown sugar
- 1½ teaspoons salt, divided
- 1 cup cooked rice
- ¼ cup ketchup
- 2 tablespoons Worcestershire sauce
- ¼ teaspoon pepper
- 1 pound lean ground beef (90% lean)
- ¼ pound bulk Italian sausage
- ½ cup V8 juice, optional

1. In a Dutch oven, cook cabbage in boiling water for 10 minutes or until outer leaves are tender; drain. Rinse in cold water; drain. Remove eight large outer leaves (refrigerate the remaining cabbage for another use); set aside.

2. In a large saucepan, saute 1 cup onion in butter until tender. Add tomatoes, garlic, brown sugar and ½ teaspoon salt. Simmer 15 minutes, stirring occasionally.

3. Meanwhile, in a large bowl, combine the cooked rice, ketchup, Worcestershire sauce, pepper and remaining onion and salt. Crumble beef and sausage over mixture and mix well.

4. Remove thick vein from cabbage leaves for easier rolling. Place about ½ cup meat mixture on each leaf; fold in sides. Starting at an unfolded edge, roll up leaf to completely enclose filling. Place seam side down in a skillet. Top with the sauce.

5. Cover and cook over medium-low heat for 1 hour. Add V8 juice if desired. Reduce heat to low; cook 20 minutes longer or until the rolls are heated through and a thermometer inserted in the filling reads 160°.

TOP TIP

WORCESTERSHIRE SAUCE

Worcestershire sauce was originally considered a mistake. In 1835, an English lord commissioned two chemists to duplicate a sauce he had tried in India. The pungent batch was disappointing and wound up in their cellar. When the pair stumbled upon the aged concoction 2 years later, they were pleasantly surprised by its unique taste.

"This is a special meal in our house. As soon as I get ribs, I know which dish my family will ask me to make."
—**JOANNE SHEWCHUK** ST. BENEDICT, SK

HUNGARIAN
SHORT RIBS

BEEF AND BEAN
CHIMICHANGAS

BEEF AND BEAN CHIMICHANGAS

I enjoy trying new recipes, so my family never gets bored at mealtime. My daughter often requests these chimichangas for dinner, and no one ever complains.

—JANICE LYONS EAGLE RIVER, WI

PREP: 25 MIN. • **COOK:** 20 MIN.
MAKES: 16 CHIMICHANGAS

- 1½ pounds ground beef
- 1 medium onion, chopped
- 1 medium green pepper, chopped
- 1 garlic clove, minced
- 2 cans (16 ounces each) refried beans
- ½ cup shredded cheddar cheese
- ½ cup taco sauce
- 16 flour tortillas (10 inches)
  Vegetable oil
  Toppings: shredded lettuce, sour cream, chopped ripe olives, chopped tomatoes, additional cheddar cheese

1. In a large skillet, cook beef, onion, green pepper and garlic over medium heat until the meat is no longer pink; drain. Add the beans, cheese and taco sauce. Cook and stir until cheese is melted, about 5 minutes. Remove from the heat.

2. Spoon about ⅓ cup off-center on each tortilla. Fold up edge nearest filling; fold in both sides and roll up. Secure with a toothpick. In a large skillet, fry tortillas, folded side down, in oil for 2-3 minutes or until lightly browned. Turn; cook 2-3 minutes longer. Drain on paper towels. Discard toothpicks. Serve with toppings of your choice.

SOUTHWESTERN SPAGHETTI

Chili powder and cumin give a mild Mexican flavor to this colorful one-skillet supper. With chunks of fresh zucchini, it's a nice change of pace from typical spaghetti dishes.

—BETH COFFEE HARTFORD CITY, IN

START TO FINISH: 30 MIN.
MAKES: 5 SERVINGS

- ¾ pound lean ground beef (90% lean)
- 2¼ cups water
- 1 can (15 ounces) tomato sauce
- 2 teaspoons chili powder
- ½ teaspoon garlic powder
- ½ teaspoon salt, optional
- ½ teaspoon ground cumin
- 1 package (7 ounces) thin spaghetti, broken into thirds
- 6 small zucchini (about 1 pound), cut into chunks
- ½ cup shredded cheddar cheese

1. In a large skillet, cook beef over medium heat until no longer pink; drain. Remove beef and set aside. In the same skillet, combine the water, tomato sauce, chili powder, garlic powder, salt if desired and cumin; bring to a boil. Stir in spaghetti; return to a boil. Boil for 6 minutes.

2. Add zucchini. Cook 4-5 minutes longer or until spaghetti and zucchini are tender, stirring several times. Stir in beef and heat through. Sprinkle with cheese.

SOUTHWESTERN SPAGHETTI

SPAGHETTI SUPPER

It was such a joy to come home and find my mom making spaghetti and meatballs for dinner. This recipe has always been dear to my heart.

—**DEBBIE HEGGIE** LARAMIE, WY

PREP: 30 MIN. • **COOK:** 1¾ HOURS
MAKES: 10 SERVINGS

- 2 cans (28 ounces each) diced tomatoes, undrained
- 2 teaspoons sugar
- 2 teaspoons dried basil
- 2 garlic cloves, minced
- 1 teaspoon salt
- ½ teaspoon pepper

MEATBALLS

- 3 cups soft bread crumbs
- ½ cup water
- 2 large eggs, lightly beaten
- ½ cup grated Parmesan cheese
- 2 tablespoons minced fresh parsley
- 1 garlic clove, minced
- 1 teaspoon salt
- ¼ teaspoon pepper
- 1 pound ground beef
- 1 pound ground pork
  Hot cooked spaghetti

1. In a 6-qt. stockpot, combine the first six ingredients; bring to a boil. Reduce heat; simmer, covered, 1½ hours, stirring occasionally.

2. For meatballs, preheat oven to 400°. In a large bowl, combine the bread crumbs and water; let stand 5 minutes. Stir in eggs, cheese, parsley, garlic, salt and pepper. Add beef and pork; mix lightly but thoroughly. Shape into 1-in. balls.

3. Place meatballs on a greased rack in a 15x10x1-in. baking pan. Bake 15-20 minutes or until cooked through. Add meatballs to sauce, stirring gently to combine. Serve with spaghetti.

FREEZE OPTION *Freeze cooled meatball mixture in freezer containers. To use, partially thaw in refrigerator overnight. Heat through in a covered saucepan, stirring gently and adding a little water if necessary.*

NOTE *To make soft bread crumbs, tear bread into pieces and place in a food processor or blender. Cover and pulse until crumbs form. One slice of bread yields ½ to ¾ cup crumbs.*

BEEF ROULADEN

Our family was poor when I was growing up in Germany, so we ate garden vegetables for many weekday meals. When my mother made meat for a Sunday dinner, it was a terrific treat. My favorite is this tender beef dish, which gets great flavor from Dijon mustard.

—**KAREN COUSINEAU** BURLINGTON, NC

PREP: 35 MIN. • **COOK:** 1½ HOURS
MAKES: 8 SERVINGS

- ¼ cup Dijon mustard
- 8 slices beef top round steak (¼ inch thick and 4 ounces each)
  Salt and pepper to taste
- 8 bacon strips
- 1 large onion, cut into thin wedges
- 3 tablespoons canola oil
- 3 cups beef broth
- ⅓ cup all-purpose flour
- ½ cup water
  Chopped fresh parsley, optional

1. Lightly spread mustard on each slice of steak; sprinkle with salt and pepper. Place 1 bacon strip and a few onion wedges on each slice; roll up; secure with toothpicks.

2. In a large skillet, brown beef in oil until no longer pink; drain. Add broth; bring to a boil. Reduce heat; cover and simmer for 1½ hours or until the meat is tender.

3. Remove meat and keep warm. Combine the flour and water until smooth; gradually stir into broth. Bring to a boil, stirring constantly until thickened and bubbly. Remove toothpicks and return beef to gravy; heat through. Sprinkle with parsley if desired.

SPAGHETTI SUPPER

MEXI-MAC
SKILLET

2 to 3 bay leaves
16 to 24 small potatoes, peeled
8 to 12 medium carrots, halved
1 large head cabbage, cut into wedges
    Minced fresh parsley, optional

HORSERADISH SAUCE
3 tablespoons butter
2 tablespoons all-purpose flour
1 to 1½ cups cooking liquid (from brisket)
1 tablespoon cider vinegar
1 tablespoon sugar
¼ cup horseradish

SOUR CREAM AND MUSTARD SAUCE
1 cups (8 ounces) sour cream
2 tablespoons Dijon mustard
¼ teaspoon sugar

1. Place brisket in a large Dutch oven; cover with water. Add brown sugar and bay leaves. (If spice packet is enclosed with brisket, add it also.) Bring to a boil. Reduce heat; cover and simmer for 2 hours.

2. Add potatoes and carrots. Return to boiling. Reduce heat; cover and simmer 30-40 minutes or until meat and vegetables are just tender. If your Dutch oven is not large enough for cabbage to fit, remove potatoes and carrots and keep warm (they can be returned to cooking liquid and heated through before serving).

3. Add cabbage; cover and cook about 15 minutes or until tender. Discard bay leaves. Remove cabbage and meat.

4. Strain and remove about 1½ cups cooking liquid. Let meat stand a few minutes. Slice meat across the grain. Serve with Horseradish Sauce or Sour Cream and Mustard Sauce. Garnish with parsley if desired.

HORSERADISH SAUCE *In a small saucepan, melt butter. Blend in flour. Add 1 cup cooking liquid; stir until smooth. Add the vinegar, sugar and horseradish. Cook and stir over medium heat until thickened and bubbly. Adjust seasoning with more vinegar, sugar or horseradish if needed. Thin sauce if necessary with the remaining cooking liquid.*

SOUR CREAM AND MUSTARD SAUCE *Combine all ingredients in a small bowl. Mix until well blended.*

EAT SMART

MEXI-MAC SKILLET

My husband loves this recipe, and I love how simple it is to put together! Because you don't need to precook the macaroni, it's a time-saving dish.

—MAURANE RAMSEY FORT WAYNE, IN

START TO FINISH: 30 MIN.
MAKES: 5 SERVINGS

1 pound lean ground beef (90% lean)
1 large onion, chopped
1 can (14½ ounces) diced tomatoes, undrained
1 can (8 ounces) tomato sauce
1 cup fresh or frozen corn
½ cup water
1¼ teaspoons chili powder
1 teaspoon dried oregano
½ teaspoon salt
⅔ cup uncooked elbow macaroni
⅔ cup shredded reduced-fat cheddar cheese

1. In a large nonstick skillet, cook beef and onion over medium-high heat 5-7 minutes or until beef is no longer pink, breaking up beef into crumbles. Drain.

2. Stir in tomatoes, tomato sauce, corn, water and seasonings; bring to a boil. Stir in macaroni. Reduce heat; simmer, covered, 15-20 minutes or until macaroni is tender. Sprinkle with cheese.

PER SERVING *1 cup equals 283 cal., 11 g fat (5 g sat. fat), 55 mg chol., 716 mg sodium, 23 g carb., 4 g fiber, 25 g pro.* **Diabetic Exchanges:** *3 lean meat, 1 starch, 1 vegetable.*

CORNED BEEF AND CABBAGE

This traditional Irish meal, complete with vegetables, is classic comfort food. We love it as a springtime dinner.

—EVELYN KENNEY TRENTON, NJ

PREP: 10 MIN. • **COOK:** 2¾ HOURS
MAKES: 8-12 SERVINGS

1 corned beef brisket with spice packet (4 to 6 pounds)
2 tablespoons brown sugar

STROGANOFF
SANDWICHES

STROGANOFF SANDWICHES

This recipe is ideal for a game day, either at a tailgate party or at home. I often make the meat mixture ahead of time and add the sour cream just before serving.

—**SUSAN GRAHAM** CHEROKEE, IA

PREP: 10 MIN. • **COOK:** 30 MIN.
MAKES: 8 SERVINGS

- 1½ pounds ground beef
- 1 medium onion, chopped
- 6 to 8 bacon strips, cooked and crumbled
- 2 garlic cloves, minced
- 2 tablespoons all-purpose flour
- ½ teaspoon salt
- ½ teaspoon paprika
- ⅛ teaspoon ground nutmeg
- 1 can (10¾ ounces) condensed cream of mushroom soup, undiluted
- ½ cup sliced fresh mushrooms
- 1 cup (8 ounces) sour cream
- 8 hamburger buns, split

1. In a large skillet, cook beef and onion over medium heat until meat is no longer pink; drain. Add bacon and garlic. Combine the flour, salt, paprika and nutmeg; gradually stir into beef mixture until blended.
2. Stir in soup and mushrooms (mixture will be thick). Bring to a boil. Reduce heat; simmer, uncovered, for 4-5 minutes or until heated through. Stir in sour cream. Cook 3-4 minutes longer or until heated through, stirring occasionally (do not boil). Serve on buns.

FREEZE OPTION *Freeze cooled meat mixture in freezer containers. To use, partially thaw in the refrigerator overnight. Heat through in a saucepan, stirring occasionally and adding a little water if necessary. Serve on buns.*

PEPPERED FILETS WITH TOMATO-MUSHROOM SALSA

The secret to these marvelous filets is in the salsa. It's full of fresh veggies and seasonings that bring a true taste of summer at any time of the year.

—**ANN HILLMEYER** SANDIA PARK, NM

PREP: 30 MIN. • **COOK:** 15 MIN.
MAKES: 6 SERVINGS

- 6 plum tomatoes, seeded and chopped
- 1 cup chopped fresh mushrooms
- ¼ cup minced fresh Italian parsley
- 2 tablespoons finely chopped shallot
- 2 teaspoons minced garlic, divided
- 5 teaspoons olive oil, divided
- 1 tablespoon lime juice
- ½ teaspoon salt
- ¼ teaspoon pepper
- 6 beef tenderloin steaks (4 ounces each)
- 2 teaspoons lemon-pepper seasoning
- ⅓ cup balsamic vinegar
- ¼ cup beef broth
- 4 teaspoons butter
- 6 lime slices

1. For salsa, in a small bowl, combine the tomatoes, mushrooms, parsley, shallot, 1 teaspoon garlic, 3 teaspoons oil, lime juice, salt and pepper; set aside.
2. Sprinkle steaks with lemon-pepper. In a large skillet, cook steaks in remaining oil for 4-5 minutes on each side or until meat reaches desired doneness (for medium-rare, a meat thermometer should read 145°; medium, 160°; well-done, 170°). Remove and keep warm.
3. Combine the vinegar, broth and remaining garlic; add to pan, stirring to loosen browned bits. Cook until the liquid is reduced by half, about 2-3 minutes. Stir in butter.
4. Spoon sauce over steaks. Serve with salsa. Garnish with lime slices.

PER SERVING *1 steak with 1 tablespoon sauce and ⅓ cup of salsa equals 251 cal., 13 g fat (5 g sat. fat), 56 mg chol., 414 mg sodium, 7 g carb., 1 g fiber, 26 g pro.* **Diabetic Exchanges:** *3 lean meat, 1½ fat, ½ starch.*

PEPPERED FILETS WITH TOMATO-MUSHROOM SALSA

VEGGIE SIRLOIN STIR-FRY

Here's a stir-fry that's even faster than Chinese takeout. It's an easy dinnertime winner at my house.

—VICKY PRIESTLEY ALUM CREEK, WV

START TO FINISH: 25 MIN.
MAKES: 6 SERVINGS

- 1½ cups uncooked instant brown rice
- 1 tablespoon cornstarch
- ½ cup cold water
- ¼ cup reduced-sodium soy sauce
- 1 tablespoon brown sugar
- ¾ teaspoon ground ginger
- ½ teaspoon chili powder
- ¼ teaspoon garlic powder
- ¼ teaspoon pepper
- 2 tablespoons canola oil, divided
- 1 pound beef top sirloin steak, cut into ½-inch cubes
- 1 package (16 ounces) frozen stir-fry vegetable blend, thawed

1. Cook rice according to package directions. Meanwhile, in a small bowl, mix cornstarch, water, soy sauce, brown sugar and seasonings until smooth.

2. In a large nonstick skillet coated with cooking spray, heat 1 tablespoon oil over medium-high heat. Add beef; stir-fry until no longer pink. Remove from pan. Stir-fry vegetables in remaining oil until crisp-tender.

3. Stir cornstarch mixture and add to pan. Bring to a boil; cook and stir 1-2 minutes or until the sauce is thickened. Return beef to pan; heat through. Serve with rice.

PER SERVING *¾ cup stir-fry with ½ cup rice equals 304 cal., 8 g fat (2 g sat. fat), 42 mg chol., 470 mg sodium, 37 g carb., 3 g fiber, 19 g pro.* **Diabetic Exchanges:** *2 lean meat, 2 vegetable, 1½ starch, 1 fat.*

BLUE CHEESE-STUFFED STEAKS

For a fast, fancy dinner, try this tender beef with a mild blue cheese stuffing. Grape tomatoes sauteed in garlic make a colorful and flavorful accompaniment.

—TEDDY DEVICO WARREN, NJ

START TO FINISH: 30 MIN.
MAKES: 4 SERVINGS

- 10 garlic cloves, peeled
- 2 tablespoons canola oil
- 4 cups grape tomatoes
- 4 boneless beef top loin steaks (8 ounces each)
- ½ cup crumbled blue cheese
- ½ teaspoon salt
- ¼ teaspoon pepper

1. In a large skillet, saute garlic in oil until tender. Cover and cook over low heat for 5-7 minutes or until golden and softened. Add tomatoes; cook and stir until tomatoes just begin to burst. Remove from the skillet; set aside and keep warm.

2. Cut a pocket in the thickest part of each steak; fill with blue cheese. Sprinkle with salt and pepper.

3. In the same skillet, cook steaks over medium heat for 4-5 minutes on each side or until meat reaches desired doneness (for medium-rare, a thermometer should read 145°; medium, 160°; well-done, 170°). Serve with tomato mixture.

NOTE *Top loin steak may be labeled as strip steak, Kansas City steak, New York strip steak, ambassador steak or boneless club steak in your region.*

VEGGIE SIRLOIN STIR-FRY

BEEF AND PASTA SALAD

My husband and I like zesty pasta salads and have tried many different types. This delightful dish can be eaten warm or cold, so it's a great meal any time of year.

—JO ANN SATSKY BANDERA, TX

START TO FINISH: 30 MIN.
MAKES: 6 SERVINGS

- 3 cups spiral pasta, cooked and drained
- 1 medium green pepper, julienned
- 1 cup halved cherry tomatoes
- ½ cup sliced ripe olives
- 1 pound beef top sirloin steak, cut into strips
- 2 tablespoons canola oil
- 1 bottle (8 ounces) Italian salad dressing
- 1½ cups (6 ounces) shredded provolone or part-skim mozzarella cheese

1. In a large bowl, combine the pasta, green pepper, tomatoes and olives. In a large skillet, stir-fry sirloin in oil until cooked as desired; drain.
2. If serving salad hot, add dressing to skillet and bring to a boil. Pour over pasta mixture; toss to coat. Add cheese; serve immediately.
3. If serving salad cold, let beef cool for 15 minutes. Add the beef, dressing and cheese to pasta mixture; toss to coat. Chill for at least 1 hour.

SALISBURY STEAK WITH ONION GRAVY

SALISBURY STEAK WITH ONION GRAVY

These meat patties simmer in a delicious gravy that starts with French onion soup. Let the noodles cook while you prepare the rest of the recipe, and dinner will be done in a flash.

—KIM KIDD NEW FREEDOM, PA

PREP: 10 MIN. • **COOK:** 25 MIN.
MAKES: 6 SERVINGS

- 1 large egg, lightly beaten
- 1 can (10½ ounces) condensed French onion soup, undiluted, divided
- ½ cup dry bread crumbs
- ¼ teaspoon salt
  Pinch pepper
- 1½ pounds ground beef
- ¼ cup water
- ¼ cup ketchup
- 1 teaspoon Worcestershire sauce
- ½ teaspoon prepared mustard
- 2 tablespoons cold water
- 1 tablespoon all-purpose flour
  6 cups hot cooked egg noodles
  Chopped fresh parsley, optional

1. Combine first five ingredients. Crumble beef over mixture and mix well. Shape into six oval patties.
2. In a large skillet over medium heat, brown patties until a thermometer reads 160° and the juices run clear, 3-4 minutes on each side. Remove and drain; set aside. Add next four ingredients to skillet; bring to a boil.
3. Reduce heat; cover and simmer about 15 minutes. Combine cold water and flour until smooth. Stir into pan. Bring to a boil; cook and stir until thickened, about 2 minutes. Return patties to skillet; heat through. Serve patties and gravy with noodles. If desired, sprinkle with parsley.

"Let me share my busy-day secret weapon: pizza burgers, with the patties made ahead of time so they're ready when you need a meal fast."
—**BARBARA SCHINDLER** NAPOLEON, OH

PRESTO PIZZA
PATTIES

PRESTO PIZZA PATTIES

START TO FINISH: 30 MIN.
MAKES: 6 SERVINGS

- 1 **can (8 ounces) pizza sauce, divided**
- ½ **cup seasoned bread crumbs**
- ½ **cup finely chopped green pepper**
- ¼ **cup finely chopped onion**
- 2 **large egg whites**
- 1 **garlic clove, minced**
- 1 **pound lean ground beef (90% lean)**
- 6 **slices Italian bread (½ inch thick)**
- 2 **teaspoons olive oil**
- 1½ **teaspoons Italian seasoning**
- ½ **cup shredded part-skim mozzarella cheese**

1. In a large bowl, combine ⅓ cup pizza sauce, bread crumbs, pepper, onion, egg whites and garlic. Add the beef; mix lightly but thoroughly. Shape into six oval patties.
2. In a large nonstick skillet, cook the patties over medium heat 4-5 minutes on each side or until a thermometer reads 160°.
3. Meanwhile, place bread on an ungreased baking sheet. Brush tops with oil; sprinkle with the Italian seasoning. Broil 3-4 in. from heat 1-2 minutes or until golden brown.
4. Place remaining pizza sauce in a microwave-safe bowl. Microwave, covered, on high for 10-20 seconds or until heated through. Place patties on toast; top with sauce and cheese.
FREEZE OPTION *Place patties on a plastic wrap-lined baking sheet; wrap and freeze until firm. Remove from pan and transfer to a large resealable plastic bag; return to freezer. Freeze remaining pizza sauce in an airtight container. To use, cook frozen patties and pizza sauce as directed, increasing time as necessary for a thermometer to read 160° for patties and for sauce to be heated through.*
PER SERVING *1 serving equals 299 cal., 11 g fat (4 g sat. fat), 53 mg chol., 527 mg sodium, 26 g carb., 2 g fiber, 23 g pro. Diabetic Exchanges: 3 lean meat, 1½ starch.*

SOUTHWEST STUFFED PEPPERS

Put a quick and zesty twist on a dinnertime staple with this colorful main course. Garlic, chili powder, cumin and more season the ground beef perfectly.
—*TASTE OF HOME* TEST KITCHEN

START TO FINISH: 25 MIN.
MAKES: 4 SERVINGS

- 1 **pound lean ground beef (90% lean)**
- ⅔ **cup chopped sweet red pepper**
- ½ **cup chopped onion**
- 2 **garlic cloves, minced**
- 1¾ **cups chopped seeded tomatoes, divided**
- 4 **teaspoons chili powder**
- 1 **teaspoon cornstarch**
- 1 **teaspoon ground cumin**
- ½ **teaspoon dried oregano**
- ¼ **teaspoon cayenne pepper**
- 1½ **cups water, divided**
- 4 **medium green peppers**
- 2 **tablespoons sour cream**
- 2 **tablespoons shredded cheddar cheese**
- 2 **green onions, chopped**
- 4 **grape tomatoes, halved, optional**

1. In a large skillet, cook the beef, red pepper and onion over medium heat until meat is no longer pink. Add the garlic and cook 1 minute longer. Drain.
2. Stir in ½ cup tomatoes, chili powder, cornstarch, cumin, oregano and cayenne. Gradually stir in ½ cup of water. Bring to a boil. Reduce heat; simmer, uncovered, 15-20 minutes.
3. Meanwhile, cut the green peppers in half lengthwise; remove seeds. Place in an ungreased shallow 3-qt. microwave-safe dish; add remaining water. Cover and microwave on high for 8-10 minutes or until crisp tender. Drain; fill each pepper half with ⅓ cup beef mixture.
4. Top with the remaining tomatoes. Garnish with sour cream, cheese, green onions and grape tomatoes if desired.
PER SERVING *2 stuffed pepper halves equals 278 cal., 12 g fat (5 g sat. fat), 64 mg chol., 138 mg sodium, 18 g carb., 5 g fiber, 26 g pro. Diabetic Exchanges: 3 lean meat, 2 starch, 1 fat.*

SOUTHWEST STUFFED PEPPERS

BEEF TOSTADAS

Chipotle sauce gives these meaty open-faced tacos just the right amount of heat to fire up a fiesta at the dinner table.

—*TASTE OF HOME* TEST KITCHEN

START TO FINISH: 15 MIN.
MAKES: 6 SERVINGS

- 1 **pound lean ground beef (90% lean)**
- 1 **cup chopped sweet red pepper**
- ½ **cup chili sauce**
- 1 **teaspoon taco seasoning**
- ¼ **teaspoon salt**
- ¼ **teaspoon pepper**
- ½ **cup sour cream**
- 3 **teaspoons chipotle sauce**
- 6 **tostada shells**
- 3 **cups shredded lettuce**
- 1½ **cups guacamole**
- 1½ **cups shredded Mexican cheese blend**

1. In a large skillet, cook beef and red pepper over medium heat until meat is no longer pink; drain. Stir in the chili sauce, taco seasoning, salt and pepper; heat through.
2. In a small bowl, combine sour cream and chipotle sauce. Layer each tostada with lettuce, meat mixture, guacamole, cheese and the chipotle sour cream.

CORNED BEEF OMELET

I was raised on a farm, where we had chickens as well as other farm animals, so we ate a lot of egg dishes. We usually serve this simple omelet for breakfast with toast on the side.

—**KITTY JONES** CHICAGO, IL

START TO FINISH: 20 MIN.
MAKES: 4 SERVINGS

- 2 **green onions, sliced**
- 2 **tablespoons butter**
- 6 **large eggs**
- ¼ **cup milk**
- 1 **cup cubed cooked corned beef**
- ½ **cup shredded cheddar cheese Dash pepper**

1. In a large skillet, saute onions in butter until tender. In a large bowl, whisk eggs and milk; pour over onions. Cook over medium heat; as the eggs set, lift edges, letting the uncooked portion flow underneath.
2. When the eggs are nearly set, sprinkle with the corned beef, cheese and pepper. Remove from the heat; cover and let stand for 1-2 minutes or until the cheese is melted. Cut omelet into wedges.

GREEK-STYLE SUPPER

An all-in-one meal like this is great for busy weeknights. I add a pinch of cinnamon to make the dish shine. There's minimal prep work and cleanup is just as easy!

—**ALICE BOWER** ROANOKE, IL

START TO FINISH: 30 MIN.
MAKES: 4 SERVINGS

- ½ **pound lean ground beef (90% lean)**
- ½ **cup chopped onion**
- 1 **can (14½ ounces) reduced-sodium beef broth**
- 1 **can (14½ ounces) diced tomatoes, undrained**
- 1½ **cups uncooked penne pasta**
- 1½ **cups frozen cut green beans, thawed**
- 2 **tablespoons tomato paste**
- 2 **teaspoons dried oregano**
- ½ **teaspoon garlic powder**
- ¼ **teaspoon ground cinnamon**
- ¾ **cup crumbled feta cheese**

1. In a large skillet, cook beef and onion over medium heat until the meat is no longer pink. Meanwhile, in a large saucepan, bring the broth and tomatoes to a boil; add pasta. Reduce the heat; simmer, uncovered, for 15-20 minutes or until the pasta is tender, stirring occasionally.
2. Drain beef mixture; add to pasta. Stir in the green beans, tomato paste, oregano, garlic powder and cinnamon; heat mixture through. Sprinkle with feta cheese.
PER SERVING *1½ cups equals 294 cal., 8 g fat (4 g sat. fat), 41 mg chol., 621 mg sodium, 33 g carb., 6 g fiber, 21 g pro.* **Diabetic Exchanges:** *2 starch, 2 lean meat, 1 vegetable.*

BEEF TOSTADAS

MAPLE POT ROAST

I grew up in my Italian grandmother's home, and whenever I think of her, I remember delicious comfort foods like this amazing pot roast.
—**AMY MIAZGA** BALLSTON SPA, NY

PREP: 15 MIN. • **COOK:** 2 HOURS
MAKES: 2 SERVINGS

- ¾ pound boneless beef chuck roast (¾- to 1-inch thick)
- ¼ cup orange juice
- ¼ cup maple syrup
- 4½ teaspoons red wine vinegar
- 1½ teaspoons Worcestershire sauce
- 1 teaspoon grated orange peel
- ⅛ teaspoon salt
- ⅛ teaspoon pepper
- 1 medium carrot, cut into 2-inch pieces
- 1 celery rib, cut into 2-inch pieces
- 8 fresh pearl onions, peeled
- 1 large potato, peeled and cut into 2-inch pieces

1. In a Dutch oven coated with cooking spray, brown meat on both sides. Combine the orange juice, syrup, vinegar, Worcestershire sauce, orange peel, salt and pepper; pour over roast. Bring to a boil. Reduce heat; cover and simmer for 1 hour.
2. Add the carrot, celery and onions; cover and simmer for 20 minutes. Add potato; cover and simmer for 20 minutes or until tender. Serve roast and vegetables with pan juices.

TOP TIP

MAPLE SYRUP

Maple syrup is made from boiling down maple sap until it is thickened and syrupy. It takes about 40 gallons of sap to make 1 gallon of syrup. Sap is collected beginning in February or early March, when temperatures get above freezing during the day. This natural treat is produced only in Canada and the northern United States—nowhere else in the world.

SAUCY THAI BEEF NOODLES

SAUCY THAI BEEF NOODLES

This stir-fry has been a family favorite for some time. I like to double the recipe and add extra vegetables.
—**JANELLE LEE** APPLETON, WI

START TO FINISH: 30 MIN.
MAKES: 6 SERVINGS

- ½ cup 2% milk
- ½ cup creamy peanut butter
- ¼ cup soy sauce
- 2 tablespoons brown sugar
- 2 tablespoons sherry
- 2 garlic cloves, minced
- ¼ teaspoon crushed red pepper flakes
- 3 drops hot pepper sauce
- 12 ounces uncooked spaghetti
- 1 pound beef top sirloin steak, thinly sliced
- 1½ teaspoons canola oil, divided
- ½ cup thinly sliced fresh carrot
- ½ cup julienned sweet red pepper
- 1 cup fresh snow peas
- 2 green onions, sliced
- ¼ cup chopped salted peanuts
- 2 tablespoons minced fresh cilantro

1. In a small saucepan, bring the first eight ingredients just to a boil, stirring constantly. Remove from the heat; set aside.
2. Cook spaghetti according to the package directions.
3. In a large skillet or wok, stir-fry beef in ½ teaspoon oil until no longer pink. Remove and keep warm.
4. Stir-fry carrot and red pepper in remaining oil for 3-4 minutes. Add snow peas and onions; stir-fry 2-3 minutes longer or until vegetables are crisp-tender. Return beef to skillet.
5. Drain noodles; add to the pan. Add the peanut sauce and toss to coat. Sprinkle with peanuts and cilantro.

Poultry

TURKEY MOLE TACOS

In contrast to traditional tacos, these taste complete as is, without needing further garnishes or sauces. I've also made this using bite-sized pieces of chicken thighs and increasing the cooking time accordingly.

—**HELEN GLAZIER** SEATTLE, WA

PREP: 25 MIN. • **COOK:** 20 MIN.
MAKES: 6 SERVINGS

- 1¼ **pounds lean ground turkey**
- 1 **celery rib, chopped**
- 4 **green onions, chopped**
- 2 **garlic cloves, minced**
- 1 **can (14½ ounces) diced tomatoes, undrained**
- 1 **jar (7 ounces) roasted sweet red peppers, drained and chopped**
- 2 **ounces 53% cacao dark baking chocolate, chopped**
- 4 **teaspoons chili powder**
- 1 **teaspoon ground cumin**
- ½ **teaspoon salt**
- ¼ **teaspoon ground cinnamon**
- ¼ **cup lightly salted mixed nuts, coarsely chopped**
- 12 **corn tortillas (6 inches), warmed**

1. In a large nonstick skillet coated with cooking spray, cook the turkey, celery, green onions and garlic over medium heat until the meat is no longer pink and the vegetables are tender; drain.

2. Stir in the tomatoes, red peppers, chocolate, chili powder, cumin, salt and cinnamon. Bring to a boil. Reduce heat; cover and simmer for 10 minutes, stirring occasionally.

3. Remove from the heat; stir in nuts. Place about ⅓ cup filling on each tortilla.

FREEZE OPTION *Freeze cooled meat mixture in freezer containers. To use, partially thaw in the refrigerator overnight. Heat through in a saucepan,* *stirring occasionally and adding a little water if necessary.*

PER SERVING *2 tacos equals 369 cal., 15 g fat (5 g sat. fat), 75 mg chol., 612 mg sodium, 37 g carb., 6 g fiber, 22 g pro.* ***Diabetic Exchanges:*** *3 lean meat, 2 starch, 1 vegetable, 1 fat.*

TURKEY MOLE TACOS

ROSEMARY CHICKEN WITH SPINACH & BEANS

With two young boys constantly on the go, finding tricks to simplify meals is key. Since this recipe uses just one skillet, it's a cinch to prepare when I only have half an hour to make dinner for my hungry family.

—**SARA RICHARDSON** LITTLETON, CO

START TO FINISH: 30 MIN.
MAKES: 4 SERVINGS

- 1 **can (14½ ounces) stewed tomatoes**
- 4 **boneless skinless chicken breast halves (6 ounces each)**
- 2 **teaspoons dried rosemary, crushed**
- ½ **teaspoon salt**
- ½ **teaspoon pepper**
- 4 **teaspoons olive oil, divided**
- 1 **package (6 ounces) fresh baby spinach**
- 2 **garlic cloves, minced**
- 1 **can (15 ounces) white kidney or cannellini beans, rinsed and drained**

ROSEMARY CHICKEN
WITH SPINACH & BEANS

1. Drain tomatoes, reserving juice; coarsely chop tomatoes. Pound the chicken with a meat mallet to ¼-in. thickness. Rub with rosemary, salt and pepper. In a large skillet, heat 2 teaspoons oil over medium heat. Add chicken; cook 5-6 minutes on each side or until no longer pink. Remove and keep warm.

2. In same pan, heat remaining oil over medium-high heat. Add spinach and garlic; cook and stir 2-3 minutes or until spinach is wilted. Stir in beans, tomatoes and reserved juice; heat through. Serve with chicken.

PER SERVING *1 chicken breast half with ¾ cup sauce equals 348 cal., 9 g fat (2 g sat. fat), 94 mg chol., 729 mg sodium, 25 g carb., 6 g fiber, 41 g pro.*
***Diabetic Exchanges:** 5 lean meat, 2 vegetable, 1 starch, 1 fat.*

CHICKEN NICOISE SALAD

This salad makes it easy to eat what's good for you. It's so versatile, you can use asparagus in place of green beans and salmon instead of tuna. Also feel free to add fresh garden tomatoes.

—**NICHOLAS MONFRE** OAK RIDGE, NJ

START TO FINISH: 30 MIN.
MAKES: 4 SERVINGS

- 1 **cup cut fresh green beans**
- 2 **cups torn mixed salad greens**
- 1 **can (5 ounces) light tuna in water, drained and flaked**
- 2 **tablespoons sliced ripe olives, drained**
- 1 **teaspoon capers, rinsed and drained**
- 1 **small red onion, halved and thinly sliced**
- 1 **medium sweet red pepper, julienned**
- 1 **package (6 ounces) ready-to-use Southwest-style grilled chicken breast strips**
- 2 **hard-cooked eggs, sliced**

DRESSING
- ¼ **cup olive oil**
- 2 **tablespoons lemon juice**
- 2 **teaspoons grated lemon peel**
- 2 **garlic cloves, minced**
- 1 **teaspoon Dijon mustard**
- ⅛ **teaspoon salt**
  Dash pepper

1. In a large saucepan, bring 8 cups water to a boil. Add green beans; cook, uncovered, 2-3 minutes or just until crisp-tender. Remove the beans and immediately drop into ice water. Drain and pat dry.

2. Meanwhile, place salad greens on a platter. In a small bowl, mix tuna, olives and capers; spoon into center of platter. Arrange green beans, onion, red pepper, chicken and eggs around tuna.

3. In a small bowl, whisk dressing ingredients; drizzle over salad.

PER SERVING *1 serving equals 289 cal., 18 g fat (3 g sat. fat), 142 mg chol., 562 mg sodium, 9 g carb., 3 g fiber, 24 g pro.*

CHICKEN IN TOMATO-BASIL CREAM SAUCE

Our fresh garden tomatoes and herbs inspired this recipe. During summer, I grill the chicken with Italian seasonings and a bit of garlic powder, but on rainy days or in winter, I cook it on the stovetop.

—RACHEL KOWASIC VALRICO, FL

PREP: 20 MIN. • **COOK:** 30 MIN.
MAKES: 4 SERVINGS

- 1 pound boneless skinless chicken breasts, cut into ½-inch cubes
- 3 teaspoons butter, divided
- 8 plum tomatoes, seeded and chopped
- 1 small onion, finely chopped
- 1 garlic clove, minced
- ½ cup reduced-sodium chicken broth
- 1 cup uncooked whole wheat orzo pasta
- 1 cup evaporated milk
- ½ cup loosely packed basil leaves, julienned
- ¾ teaspoon salt
- ¼ teaspoon pepper
- ¼ cup crumbled feta cheese

1. In a large nonstick skillet coated with cooking spray, cook chicken in 2 teaspoons butter until no longer pink. Remove and keep warm. In the same skillet, saute tomatoes and onion in remaining butter until onion is softened. Add garlic; cook 1 minute longer.

2. Stir in broth. Bring to a boil; add orzo. Reduce heat. Cover and simmer for 10-12 minutes or until orzo is tender. Stir in the chicken, milk, basil, salt and pepper; heat through (do not boil). Sprinkle with cheese just before serving.

PER SERVING *1½ cups equals 417 cal., 12 g fat (6 g sat. fat), 94 mg chol., 723 mg sodium, 41 g carb., 9 g fiber, 35 g pro.* **Diabetic Exchanges:** *3 lean meat, 2 starch, 1 vegetable, ½ whole milk, ½ fat.*

CHICKEN IN TOMATO-BASIL CREAM SAUCE

CHICKEN SAUSAGE & GNOCCHI SKILLET

START TO FINISH: 30 MIN.
MAKES: 4 SERVINGS

- 1 package (16 ounces) potato gnocchi
- 1 tablespoon butter
- 1 tablespoon olive oil
- 2 fully cooked Italian chicken sausage links (3 ounces each), sliced
- ½ pound sliced baby portobello mushrooms
- 1 medium onion, finely chopped
- 1 pound fresh asparagus, trimmed and cut into ½-inch pieces
- 2 garlic cloves, minced
- 2 tablespoons white wine or chicken broth
- 2 ounces herbed fresh goat cheese
- 2 tablespoons minced fresh basil or 2 teaspoons dried basil
- 1 tablespoon lemon juice
- ¼ teaspoon salt
- ⅛ teaspoon pepper
  Grated Parmesan cheese

1. Cook the gnocchi according to package directions; drain. Meanwhile, in a large skillet, heat butter and oil over medium-high heat. Add sausage, mushrooms and onion; cook and stir until sausage is browned and the vegetables are tender. Add the asparagus and garlic; cook and stir 2-3 minutes longer.

2. Stir in wine. Bring to a boil; cook until liquid is almost evaporated. Add goat cheese, basil, lemon juice, salt and pepper. Stir in the gnocchi; heat through. Sprinkle with the Parmesan cheese.

CHICKEN SAUSAGE & GNOCCHI SKILLET

EAT SMART FREEZE IT

CHICKEN THIGHS WITH SHALLOTS & SPINACH

What could be better than an entree that comes with its own creamy vegetable side? It makes an eye-catching presentation and goes together in no time flat for a healthy supper.
—GENNA JOHANNES WRIGHTSTOWN, WI

START TO FINISH: 30 MIN.
MAKES: 6 SERVINGS

- 6 **boneless skinless chicken thighs (about 1½ pounds)**
- ½ **teaspoon seasoned salt**
- ½ **teaspoon pepper**
- 1½ **teaspoons olive oil**
- 4 **shallots, thinly sliced**
- ⅓ **cup white wine or reduced-sodium chicken broth**
- 1 **package (10 ounces) fresh spinach**
- ¼ **teaspoon salt**
- ¼ **cup fat-free sour cream**

1. Sprinkle chicken with seasoned salt and pepper. In a large nonstick skillet coated with cooking spray, heat oil over medium heat. Add chicken; cook 6 minutes on each side or until a thermometer reads 170°. Remove from pan; keep warm.

2. In same pan, cook and stir shallots until tender. Add wine; bring to a boil. Cook until wine is reduced by half. Add spinach and salt; cook and stir just until spinach is wilted. Stir in sour cream; serve with chicken.

FREEZE OPTION *Before adding sour cream, cool chicken and spinach mixture. Freeze in freezer containers. To use, partially thaw in refrigerator overnight. Heat through slowly in a covered skillet until a thermometer inserted in chicken reads 165°, stirring occasionally. Stir in sour cream.*

PER SERVING *1 chicken thigh with ¼ cup spinach mixture equals 225 cal., 10 g fat (2 g sat. fat), 77 mg chol., 338 mg sodium, 8 g carb., 1 g fiber, 24 g pro.* **Diabetic Exchanges:** *3 lean meat, 1½ fat, 1 vegetable.*

CHICKEN THIGHS WITH SHALLOTS & SPINACH

MEXICAN CHICKEN PENNE

This hearty, satisfying dish gives pasta a Southwestern spin. The whole family will enjoy this easy recipe. It's a nice way to stretch leftover chicken.

—**MARTI GUTWEIN** RENSSELAER, IN

START TO FINISH: 25 MIN.
MAKES: 6 SERVINGS

- 1 package (16 ounces) penne pasta
- 2 cups cubed cooked chicken
- 1¼ cups salsa con queso dip
- ½ cup 2% milk
- ¼ teaspoon salt
- 1 can (15 ounces) black beans, rinsed and drained
- 1 large tomato, chopped
- 3 green onions, sliced
- ¼ cup shredded cheddar cheese

1. Cook pasta according to package directions. Meanwhile, in a large bowl, combine chicken, dip, milk and salt.

2. Drain pasta; return to pan. Stir in chicken mixture and toss to coat. Top with the black beans, tomato, onions and cheese; heat through.

TEXAS TURKEY TACOS

We really enjoy these zesty tacos. In fact, the turkey filling is so good, we've stuffed it into pita bread, mixed it with scrambled eggs and even stood over the stove and eaten it right out of the pan!

—**HEIDI MAHON COOK** DALLAS, TX

START TO FINISH: 20 MIN.
MAKES: 2 SERVINGS

- ½ pound ground turkey
- 1 medium onion, chopped
- 2 garlic cloves, minced
- 1 tablespoon olive oil
- ⅓ cup frozen corn
- 3 tablespoons picante sauce
- 3 tablespoons chicken broth
- ½ teaspoon salt
- ¼ teaspoon ground cumin
- ⅛ teaspoon cayenne pepper
- 4 flour tortillas (7 inches), warmed
  Chopped tomato, shredded lettuce, shredded cheddar cheese and/or sour cream, optional

1. In a saucepan over medium heat, cook and stir the turkey, onion and garlic in oil until meat is no longer pink. Drain if necessary. Add the corn, picante sauce, broth, salt, cumin and cayenne. Cook and stir for 5 minutes or until corn is tender.

2. Spoon over tortillas. Top with the tomato, lettuce, cheese and, if desired, sour cream. Roll up.

CHICKEN ASPARAGUS PASTA

We enjoy this dish often in the spring when asparagus is fresh on the market. It's a favorite with family and friends and a pleasant surprise to those who think they don't like asparagus.

—**TARALYNN PLASTINA** MCHENRY, IL

START TO FINISH: 30 MIN.
MAKES: 2 SERVINGS

- ⅔ cup cut fresh asparagus (1-inch pieces)
- 4 teaspoons canola oil, divided
- ½ teaspoon salt
- ¼ teaspoon pepper
- 4 ounces uncooked fettuccine
- ½ pound boneless skinless chicken breast, cut into ½-inch cubes
- 1 garlic clove, minced
- 2 tablespoons lemon juice
- 1 tablespoon grated lemon peel
- 1 tablespoon butter
- 2 tablespoons grated Parmesan cheese

1. Place asparagus in an ungreased 2-qt. baking dish; drizzle with 2 teaspoons oil and sprinkle with salt and pepper. Bake, uncovered, at 400° for 10-12 minutes or until tender, stirring occasionally.

2. Meanwhile, cook the fettuccine according to package directions. In a large skillet over medium heat, cook chicken and garlic in remaining oil until chicken is no longer pink.

3. Stir in the lemon juice, peel and butter; heat through. Remove from the heat. Drain fettuccine; toss with chicken mixture and asparagus. Sprinkle with cheese.

MEXICAN CHICKEN PENNE

EAT SMART

CHICKEN WITH VEGGIES

Here's a nutritious meal with Italian flair. It's an easy, flavorful way to work in a serving of veggies.

—NIKKI ADAMS CHERRY VALLEY, CA

START TO FINISH: 30 MIN.
MAKES: 2 SERVINGS

- 2 boneless skinless chicken breast halves (6 ounces each)
- ¼ teaspoon salt
- ¼ teaspoon pepper
- 2 tablespoons dry bread crumbs
- 2 teaspoons grated Parmesan cheese
- 2 teaspoons Italian seasoning
- 3 teaspoons olive oil, divided
- 3 cups fresh baby spinach
- 2 plum tomatoes, chopped
- 2 garlic cloves, minced

1. Flatten chicken to ¼-in. thickness; sprinkle with salt and pepper. In a shallow bowl, combine the bread crumbs, cheese and Italian seasoning. Coat chicken in bread crumb mixture.
2. In a large nonstick skillet coated with cooking spray, cook chicken in 2 teaspoons oil over medium heat for 3-4 minutes on each side or until no longer pink. Remove and keep warm.
3. Saute spinach in remaining oil just until wilted. Stir in tomatoes and garlic; cook 3 minutes longer. Serve with chicken.

PER SERVING *1 chicken breast half with 1 cup vegetables equals 302 cal., 12 g fat (2 g sat. fat), 95 mg chol., 484 mg sodium, 10 g carb., 2 g fiber, 38 g pro.* **Diabetic Exchanges:** *5 lean meat, 2 fat, 1 vegetable.*

RAMEN CHICKEN STIR-FRY

Ramen noodles are a great way to stretch this easy stir-fry. You can use whatever vegetables you happen to have on hand. The dish is different every time I make it.

—DARLENE BRENDEN SALEM, OR

START TO FINISH: 25 MIN.
MAKES: 4 SERVINGS

- 1 package (3 ounces) chicken ramen noodles
- 1 pound boneless skinless chicken breasts, cut into strips
- 1 tablespoon canola oil
- 1 cup fresh broccoli florets
- 1 cup fresh cauliflowerets
- 1 cup sliced celery
- 1 cup coarsely chopped cabbage
- 2 medium carrots, thinly sliced
- 1 medium onion, thinly sliced
- ½ cup canned bean sprouts
- ½ cup teriyaki or soy sauce

1. Set aside seasoning packet from noodles. Cook noodles according to package directions. Meanwhile, in a large skillet or wok, stir-fry chicken in oil until no longer pink. Add the vegetables; stir-fry for 3-4 minutes or until crisp-tender.
2. Drain noodles. Stir the noodles, contents of seasoning packet and teriyaki sauce into chicken mixture.

RAMEN CHICKEN STIR-FRY

ISLAND CHICKEN WITH MANGO SLAW AND CURRY SAUCE

The fresh mango slaw on the side is what makes this dish pop. But it wouldn't be complete without my three-ingredient sauce using yogurt, orange marmalade and curry powder.

—EVELYN CLEARE MIAMI, FL

PREP: 30 MIN. + MARINATING
COOK: 10 MIN. • **MAKES:** 4 SERVINGS

- ¼ **cup orange juice**
- 3 **tablespoons canola oil, divided**
- 2 **teaspoons Caribbean jerk seasoning**
- 1 **teaspoon garlic powder**
- 4 **boneless skinless chicken breast halves (5 ounces each)**

SAUCE
- ⅓ **cup plain yogurt**
- 2 **tablespoons plus 2 teaspoons orange marmalade**
- ¾ **teaspoon curry powder**

SLAW
- 1 **medium mango, peeled, cut into thin strips**
- 2 **cups fresh baby spinach, cut into strips**
- 1 **large sweet red pepper, cut into thin strips**
- 1 **tablespoon honey**
- 1 **tablespoon lime juice**
- 1 **tablespoon minced fresh gingerroot**
- ¼ **teaspoon crushed red pepper flakes**

1. In a large resealable plastic bag, combine the orange juice, 2 tablespoons oil, jerk seasoning and garlic powder. Flatten chicken breasts to ½-in. thickness; add to marinade. Seal bag and turn to coat; refrigerate for 2 hours.
2. In a small bowl, whisk the sauce ingredients until blended. Cover and refrigerate until serving.
3. Drain chicken and discard the marinade. In a large skillet, cook chicken in remaining oil 5-6 minutes on each side or until no longer pink.
4. Meanwhile, in a large bowl, combine the mango, spinach and red pepper. In a small bowl, whisk the remaining slaw ingredients until

ASIAN TURKEY LETTUCE CUPS

blended. Drizzle over mango mixture and toss to coat. Serve with chicken and sauce.

PER SERVING *1 chicken breast half with ¾ cup slaw and 2 tablespoons sauce equals 293 cal., 7 g fat (2 g sat. fat), 81 mg chol., 205 mg sodium, 28 g carb., 2 g fiber, 31 g pro.* **Diabetic Exchanges:** *4 lean meat, 1½ starch.*

ASIAN TURKEY LETTUCE CUPS

Here's a cool, crisp idea for a light lunch or even an appetizer for a summer party. When I want to make this easier for my kids to eat, I mix it all up with shredded lettuce and serve as a salad.

—DIANA RIOS LYTLE, TX

START TO FINISH: 30 MIN.
MAKES: 4 SERVINGS

- 3 **tablespoons reduced-sodium soy sauce**
- 2 **teaspoons sugar**
- 2 **teaspoons sesame oil**
- 1 **teaspoon Thai chili sauce, optional**
- 1 **pound lean ground turkey**
- 1 **celery rib, chopped**
- 1 **tablespoon minced fresh gingerroot**
- 1 **garlic clove, minced**
- 1 **can (8 ounces) water chestnuts, drained and chopped**
- 1 **medium carrot, shredded**
- 2 **cups cooked brown rice**
- 8 **Bibb or Boston lettuce leaves**

1. In a small bowl, whisk the soy sauce, sugar, sesame oil and, if desired, chili sauce until blended. In a large skillet, cook turkey and celery for 6-9 minutes or until turkey is no longer pink, breaking up meat into crumbles; drain.
2. Add ginger and garlic to turkey; cook 2 minutes. Stir in soy sauce mixture, water chestnuts and carrot; cook 2 minutes longer. Stir in rice; heat through. Serve in lettuce leaves.

PER SERVING *2 filled lettuce cups equals 353 cal., 13 g fat (3 g sat. fat), 90 mg chol., 589 mg sodium, 35 g carb., 4 g fiber, 24 g pro.* **Diabetic Exchanges:** *3 lean meat, 2 starch, 1 vegetable, ½ fat.*

CHICKEN & VEGETABLE
FETTUCCINE

CHICKEN & VEGETABLE FETTUCCINE

PREP: 10 MIN. • **COOK:** 30 MIN.
MAKES: 6 SERVINGS

- 1 **package (12 ounces) fettuccine**
- 5 **tablespoons butter, divided**
- 1 **small onion, chopped**
- 3 **tablespoons all-purpose flour**
- 1 **can (14½ ounces) chicken broth**
- 1 **cup heavy whipping cream**
- 1¼ **teaspoons salt**
- ¼ **teaspoon pepper**
- 1 **package (12 ounces) frozen mixed vegetables**
- 2 **cups cubed cooked chicken**

1. Cook fettuccine according to the package directions. Drain fettuccine; toss with 3 tablespoons butter.

2. Meanwhile, in a large saucepan, heat remaining butter over medium heat. Add onion; cook and stir for 2-3 minutes or until tender.

3. Stir in the flour until blended; gradually whisk in broth, cream, salt and pepper. Bring to a boil, stirring constantly; cook for 8-10 minutes or until thickened, stirring occasionally.

4. Stir in vegetables; return just to a boil. Stir in chicken; heat through. Serve with fettucine.

FREEZE OPTION *Do not cook the fettuccine. Freeze cooled chicken mixture in freezer containers. Partially thaw in refrigerator overnight. Prepare fettuccine as directed. Place chicken mixture in a saucepan or skillet; cook over medium-low heat until heated through, stirring occasionally. (Sauce may appear curdled initially, but will become smooth upon heating.) Serve with buttered fettuccine.*

TOP TIP

ITALIAN SPIN

Give this fettuccine dish an easy Italian flair by substituting frozen Italian vegetables for the regular. Shake a nice amount of grated Parmesan cheese into the sauce before adding the vegetables.

TURKEY TACO SALAD

I discovered this simple taco salad while I was on a health kick. My husband and I love it now. When I served it at a family birthday party, everyone eagerly asked for the recipe.

—**ANGELA MATSON** KENNEWICK, WA

START TO FINISH: 30 MIN.
MAKES: 4 SERVINGS

- 12 **ounces ground turkey**
- 1 **medium sweet red pepper, chopped**
- 1 **small sweet yellow pepper, chopped**
- ⅓ **cup chopped onion**
- 3 **garlic cloves, minced**
- 1½ **cups salsa**
- ½ **cup canned kidney beans, rinsed and drained**
- 2 **teaspoons chili powder**
- 1 **teaspoon ground cumin**
- 8 **cups torn romaine**
- 2 **tablespoons fresh cilantro leaves**
  Optional toppings: chopped tomatoes, shredded cheddar cheese and crushed tortilla chips

1. In a large skillet, cook turkey, peppers, onion and garlic over medium heat 6-8 minutes or until turkey is no longer pink and the vegetables are tender, breaking up turkey into crumbles; drain.

2. Stir in salsa, beans, chili powder and cumin; heat through. Divide romaine among four plates and top with turkey mixture. Sprinkle with cilantro and the toppings of your choice. Serve immediately.

PER SERVING *1 cup turkey mixture with 2 cups romaine (calculated without optional toppings) equals 275 cal., 13 g fat (4 g sat. fat), 58 mg chol., 525 mg sodium, 21 g carb., 6 g fiber, 18 g pro.* **Diabetic Exchanges:** *2 medium-fat meat, 1½ starch.*

TURKEY TACO SALAD

THAI RED
CURRY CHICKEN

THAI RED
CURRY CHICKEN

I re-created a favorite dish from a restaurant, and now I cook it almost weekly for my family. On a busy night, frozen stir-fry veggies really speed things up.

—MARY SHENK DEKALB, IL

START TO FINISH: 25 MIN.
MAKES: 4 SERVINGS

- 1 **can (13.66 ounces) coconut milk**
- ⅓ **cup chicken broth**
- 2 **tablespoons brown sugar**
- 2 **tablespoons fish sauce**
- 1 **tablespoon red curry paste**
- 2 **cups frozen stir-fry vegetable blend**
- 3 **cups cubed cooked chicken breast**
  Cooked jasmine rice
  Minced fresh cilantro, optional

1. Combine coconut milk, broth, brown sugar, fish sauce and curry paste in a large skillet. Bring to a boil; reduce heat and simmer 5 minutes.
2. Stir in vegetables; return to a boil. Reduce heat and simmer, uncovered, for 9-11 minutes or until vegetables are tender and sauce thickens slightly.
3. Add chicken; heat through. Serve with rice. Sprinkle with fresh cilantro if desired.

GYRO-STYLE
TURKEY PITAS

These are so good! Everyone will love these flavorful hand-held sammies stuffed with turkey, sauerkraut and a zesty cream sauce.

—WANDA ALLENDE ORLANDO, FL

START TO FINISH: 30 MIN.
MAKES: 4 SERVINGS

- 1 **pound ground turkey**
- 1 **small onion, chopped**
- ½ **cup sauerkraut, rinsed and well drained**
- 2 **tablespoons brown sugar**
- ½ **teaspoon salt**
- ⅔ **cup sour cream**
- 3 **tablespoons mayonnaise**
- 2 **tablespoons prepared ranch salad dressing**
- 1 **small tomato, chopped**
- ⅓ **cup chopped cucumber**
- 4 **pita breads (6 inches), halved and warmed**
  Shredded lettuce

1. In a large skillet, cook the turkey, onion, sauerkraut, brown sugar and salt over medium heat until meat is no longer pink; drain.
2. In a small bowl, combine sour cream, mayonnaise and salad dressing. Stir in the tomato and cucumber. Fill pita halves with turkey mixture, lettuce and sauce.

ONE-PAN PAELLA

Packed with chicken, shrimp, rice, veggies and green olives, this vibrant meal is quick and satisfying. It will take the chill off any cool evening.

—**LIBBY WALP** CHICAGO, IL

PREP: 15 MIN. • **COOK:** 25 MIN.
MAKES: 6 SERVINGS

- 1¼ pounds boneless skinless chicken breasts, thinly sliced
- 2 tablespoons olive oil
- 1 medium onion, chopped
- 2 garlic cloves, minced
- 2¼ cups chicken broth
- 1 cup uncooked long grain rice
- 1 teaspoon dried oregano
- ½ teaspoon ground turmeric
- ½ teaspoon paprika
- ¼ teaspoon salt
- ¼ to ½ teaspoon pepper
- 1 pound cooked medium shrimp, peeled and deveined
- 1 can (14½ ounces) diced tomatoes, undrained
- ¾ cup frozen peas, thawed
- ½ cup sliced pimiento-stuffed olives

1. In a large skillet, saute chicken in oil until no longer pink. Remove and keep warm. In the same skillet, saute onion until tender. Add garlic; cook 1 minute longer. Stir in the broth, rice and seasonings. Bring to a boil. Reduce heat; cover and simmer for 15-18 minutes or until rice is tender.
2. Stir in the shrimp, tomatoes, peas, olives and chicken; cover and cook for 3-4 minutes or until heated through.

LEMON CHICKEN TORTELLINI

If you don't have fresh chicken on hand for this recipe, use 3 cups of cubed leftover chicken. Stir it into the dish and heat through before adding the spinach. I like to keep frozen cooked chicken on hand for meals like this. Discard the bones, chop chicken and place in a zippered freezer bag. The chicken takes only minutes to thaw.

—**LORRAINE CALAND** SHUNIAH, ON

PREP: 15 MIN. • **COOK:** 25 MIN.
MAKES: 6 SERVINGS

- 1 package (19 ounces) frozen cheese tortellini
- 1 pound boneless skinless chicken breasts, cut into 1-inch pieces
- 2 tablespoons butter
- ½ small sweet red pepper, julienned
- 2 garlic cloves, minced
- 3 cups reduced-sodium chicken broth, divided
- ⅓ cup all-purpose flour
- ½ teaspoon salt
- ¼ teaspoon pepper
- 2 teaspoons grated lemon peel
- ½ teaspoon hot pepper sauce, optional
- 1 package (6 ounces) fresh baby spinach
- 6 tablespoons shredded Parmesan cheese

1. Cook the tortellini according to package directions. Meanwhile, in a large skillet, saute chicken in butter until no longer pink. Remove and keep warm. In the same pan, cook red pepper until crisp-tender. Add garlic; cook 1 minute longer. Add 2 cups broth; bring to a boil.
2. Combine the flour, salt, pepper and remaining broth until smooth; gradually stir into the pan. Bring to a boil; cook and stir for 2 minutes or until thickened. Stir in the chicken, lemon peel and pepper sauce if desired. Add spinach; cook just until wilted. Drain pasta; toss with sauce. Sprinkle with cheese.

LEMON CHICKEN TORTELLINI

SAUSAGE
ORECCHIETTE PASTA

SAUSAGE ORECCHIETTE PASTA

I adapted this pasta to be like my favorite Italian restaurant version, only lighter—and tastier. I often use spicy sausage and broccoli rabe.

—MELANIE TRITTEN CHARLOTTE, NC

START TO FINISH: 25 MIN.
MAKES: 6 SERVINGS

- 4 **cups uncooked orecchiette or small tube pasta**
- 1 **package (19½ ounces) Italian turkey sausage links, casings removed**
- 3 **garlic cloves, minced**
- 1 **cup white wine or chicken broth**
- 4 **cups small fresh broccoli florets**
- 1 **can (14½ ounces) diced tomatoes, drained**
- ⅓ **cup grated or shredded Parmesan cheese**

1. Cook pasta according to package directions. Meanwhile, in a large skillet, cook sausage over medium heat 6-8 minutes or until no longer pink, breaking into crumbles. Add garlic; cook 1 minute longer. Add wine, stirring to loosen browned bits from pan. Bring to a boil; cook 1-2 minutes or until liquid is reduced by half.
2. Stir in the broccoli and tomatoes. Reduce heat; simmer, covered, for 4-6 minutes or until the broccoli is crisp-tender. Drain pasta; add to skillet and toss to coat. Serve with cheese.

PER SERVING *1⅔ cups equals 363 cal., 8 g fat (2 g sat. fat), 38 mg chol., 571 mg sodium, 48 g carb., 5 g fiber, 20 g pro.* ***Diabetic Exchanges:*** *3 lean meat, 2½ starch, 1 vegetable.*

TURKEY SAUSAGE WITH PASTA

Love Italian food? You'll be craving what's good for you when this turkey dish is on the menu. It balances meat, pasta and the best of the garden's bounty.

—**MARY TALLMAN** ARBOR VITAE, WI

START TO FINISH: 30 MIN.
MAKES: 6 SERVINGS

- 1 **pound Italian turkey sausage links, casings removed**
- 1 **large onion, chopped**
- 1 **large green pepper, chopped**
- 1¼ **cups sliced fresh mushrooms**
- 2 **garlic cloves, minced**
- 2 **cans (14½ ounces each) diced tomatoes, undrained**
- 1 **teaspoon Italian seasoning**
- 1 **teaspoon chili powder**
- 6 **cups uncooked spiral pasta**
- ½ **cup shredded part-skim mozzarella cheese**

1. Crumble sausage into a large nonstick skillet. Add the onion, green pepper and mushrooms. Cook over medium heat until meat is no longer pink. Add the garlic; cook 1 minute longer. Drain.
2. Stir in tomatoes, Italian seasoning and chili powder. Bring to a boil. Reduce heat; simmer, uncovered, for 10 minutes.
3. Meanwhile, cook pasta according to package directions; drain. Serve sausage mixture over pasta; sprinkle with cheese.

PER SERVING *1 cup sausage mixture with 1 cup pasta equals 396 cal., 10 g fat (3 g sat. fat), 51 mg chol., 679 mg sodium, 54 g carb., 5 g fiber, 24 g pro.*

FIESTA SMOTHERED CHICKEN

Topped with ooey-gooey shredded cheese, this tender skillet chicken looks great and tastes even better. You'll get a kick out of its jalapeno zip.

—**TERESA JONES** ASHDOWN, AR

START TO FINISH: 30 MIN.
MAKES: 2 SERVINGS

- 3 **tablespoons reduced-sodium soy sauce**
- 1 **tablespoon Worcestershire sauce**
- ¼ **teaspoon garlic powder**
- 2 **boneless skinless chicken breast halves (5 ounces each)**
- ½ **cup sliced fresh mushrooms**
- ¼ **cup chopped onion**
- 4 **teaspoons chopped seeded jalapeno pepper**
- 6 **teaspoons butter, divided**
- ¼ **cup shredded pepper jack cheese**
- ¼ **cup shredded cheddar cheese**

1. In a large resealable plastic bag, combine first three ingredients. Add chicken; seal bag and turn to coat.
2. In a large nonstick skillet coated with cooking spray, saute the mushrooms, onion and jalapeno in 2 teaspoons butter until tender. Remove and keep warm.
3. Drain chicken and discard the marinade. In same skillet, cook the chicken in remaining butter over medium heat for 4-5 minutes on each side or until a thermometer reads 170°. Spoon vegetable mixture over chicken; sprinkle with cheeses. Cover and cook for 1-2 minutes or until cheese is melted.

NOTE *Wear disposable gloves when cutting hot peppers; the oils can burn skin. Avoid touching your face.*

TURKEY SAUSAGE WITH PASTA

SOBA NOODLE CHICKEN TOSS

This is one of my favorite meals for busy weeknights. You can prepare all the ingredients the day before and then put this healthy dish together just before dinner.

—ELIZABETH BROWN LOWELL, MA

START TO FINISH: 30 MIN.
MAKES: 4 SERVINGS

- 2 teaspoons cornstarch
- ½ cup reduced-sodium chicken broth
- 2 tablespoons brown sugar
- 3 garlic cloves, minced
- 1 tablespoon butter, melted
- 1 tablespoon reduced-sodium soy sauce
- 1 tablespoon hoisin sauce
- 2 teaspoons minced fresh gingerroot
- 2 teaspoons rice vinegar
- ¼ teaspoon pepper
- 6 ounces uncooked Japanese soba noodles
- ¾ pound chicken tenderloins, cubed
- 4 teaspoons canola oil, divided
- 3 cups fresh broccoli stir-fry blend
- ¼ cup chopped unsalted cashews

1. In a small bowl, combine the first 10 ingredients; set aside.
2. Cook noodles according to package directions. Meanwhile, in a large skillet or wok, stir-fry the chicken in 2 teaspoons oil until no longer pink. Remove and keep warm.
3. Stir-fry the broccoli blend in the remaining oil for 4-6 minutes or until vegetables are crisp-tender.
4. Stir cornstarch mixture and add to the pan. Bring to a boil; cook and stir for 2 minutes or until thickened. Drain noodles; add to pan. Add the chicken; heat through. Sprinkle with chopped cashews.
PER SERVING *1½ cups equals 417 cal., 12 g fat (3 g sat. fat), 58 mg chol., 715 mg sodium, 52 g carb., 2 g fiber, 30 g pro.*

CHICKEN AND DUMPLINGS

This is my most treasured comforting main-dish classic. The recipe's a real keeper, so we pared it down to make it perfect for a pair. Enjoy!

—WILLA GOVORO NEVADA, MO

PREP: 35 MIN. • **COOK:** 40 MIN.
MAKES: 2 SERVINGS

- 2 bone-in chicken breast halves (8 ounces each)
- ⅓ cup all-purpose flour
- 2 teaspoons canola oil
- 1 celery rib, cut into 1-inch pieces
- 1 medium carrot, cut into 1-inch pieces
- 1 tablespoon minced fresh parsley or 1 teaspoon dried parsley flakes
- ¼ teaspoon salt
- ¼ teaspoon garlic powder
- ¼ teaspoon dried thyme
- ⅛ teaspoon pepper
- 6 to 8 cups water

DUMPLINGS
- ½ cup all-purpose flour
- ½ teaspoon baking powder
- ¼ teaspoon salt
- 2 tablespoons beaten egg

GRAVY
- 4½ teaspoons all-purpose flour
- ¼ teaspoon salt
- 3 tablespoons water

1. Coat chicken with flour. In a large saucepan, brown chicken in oil. Add the celery, carrot, parsley, salt, garlic powder, thyme and pepper. Add enough water to cover. Bring to a boil. Reduce heat; cover and simmer for 25-30 minutes or until chicken is tender. Remove the chicken and vegetables to a serving dish and keep warm.
2. Set aside ¼ cup broth; cool. Bring remaining broth to a simmer. For dumplings, combine the flour, baking powder and salt; stir in the egg and reserved broth just until moistened. Drop batter in four mounds onto simmering broth. Cover and simmer for 5-7 minutes or until a toothpick inserted into a dumpling comes out clean (do not lift the cover while simmering). Remove dumplings and keep warm.
3. For gravy, transfer 1⅓ cups broth to a small saucepan (save remaining broth for another use). Bring to a boil. Combine the flour, salt and water until smooth; stir into broth. Bring to a boil; cook and stir for 2 minutes or until thickened. Pour over chicken, vegetables and dumplings. Serve immediately.

CHEESEBURGER SKILLET DINNER

START TO FINISH: 25 MIN.
MAKES: 4-6 SERVINGS

- 1 package (7¼ ounces) macaroni and cheese
- 1 pound ground turkey or beef
- ½ cup chopped onion
- 1 package (16 ounces) frozen mixed vegetables
- ⅓ cup ketchup
- ¼ cup water
- ½ teaspoon prepared mustard
- ¼ teaspoon garlic powder
- ¾ cup shredded cheddar cheese
  Salt and pepper to taste

1. Prepare macaroni and cheese according to package directions.
2. Meanwhile, in a large skillet, brown the turkey with the onion; drain. Stir in vegetables, ketchup, water, mustard and garlic powder. Cook until the vegetables are crisp-tender, about 10 minutes. Add cheddar cheese and stir until melted. Mix in macaroni and cheese. Season with salt and pepper.

"This skillet dinner is doubly quick. The leftovers—if there are any—can be reheated to make a second meal as tasty as the first."

—**KAREN GRIMES** STEPHENS CITY, VA

CHEESEBURGER
SKILLET DINNER

DESERT OASIS CHICKEN

Boneless skinless chicken breasts pair nicely with sweet and spicy ingredients, like the ones in this recipe.

—**ROXANNE CHAN** ALBANY, CA

START TO FINISH: 20 MIN.
MAKES: 4 SERVINGS

- 4 **boneless skinless chicken breast halves (5 ounces each)**
- 1 **tablespoon olive oil**
- ¼ **teaspoon salt**
- ¼ **teaspoon crushed red pepper flakes**
- ¼ **teaspoon ground cumin**
- ¼ **teaspoon ground cinnamon**
- 1 **cup canned apricot halves, sliced**
- ⅓ **cup dried tropical fruit**
- ¼ **cup water**
- 1 **tablespoon honey**
  Minced fresh parsley

1. Flatten chicken slightly; rub with oil. Combine the salt, pepper flakes, cumin and cinnamon. Sprinkle over chicken.

2. In a large skillet, brown chicken on both sides. Add the apricots, tropical fruit, water and honey; bring to a boil. Reduce the heat; cover and simmer for 5-6 minutes or until a thermometer reads 170°. Garnish with parsley.

PER SERVING *1 chicken breast with ¼ cup apricot mixture equals 288 cal., 7 g fat (2 g sat. fat), 78 mg chol., 230 mg sodium, 27 g carb., 2 g fiber, 29 g pro.*

TOP TIP

MAKE IT A MEAL

Round out this Middle Eastern-inspired meal with one or more of these accompaniments:

- Minted Orzo, page 231
- Tangy Cucumber Salad, page 245
- A double batch of the couscous on the facing page

DESERT OASIS CHICKEN

SAUSAGE, SPINACH
AND GNOCCHI

2 minutes or until thickened. Stir in the cilantro.

4. For couscous, in a small saucepan, bring the water, broth, salt and cumin to a boil. Stir in couscous. Cover and remove from the heat; let stand for 5-10 minutes or until the water is absorbed. Fluff with a fork, then stir in almonds. Serve with chicken and sauce.

FREEZE IT

SAUSAGE, SPINACH AND GNOCCHI

I get creative in the kitchen with dishes like this when we're too busy to go to the grocery store. My daughter loves this dinner, and it's easy for little fingers to pick up while still learning to use utensils.

—**CARLA ANDREWS** LORTON, VA

START TO FINISH: 30 MIN.
MAKES: 4 SERVINGS

- 1 package (16 ounces) potato gnocchi
- 1 tablespoon olive oil
- 3 Italian turkey sausage links (4 ounces each), casings removed
- 1 garlic clove, minced
- 1 package (6 ounces) fresh baby spinach
- 2 medium tomatoes, coarsely chopped
- 1½ cups spaghetti sauce

1. Cook gnocchi according to package directions; drain.

2. Meanwhile, in a large skillet, heat oil over medium heat; cook sausage 5-7 minutes or until no longer pink, breaking up sausage into crumbles. Add garlic; cook 1 minute longer. Drain. Add spinach and tomatoes; cook and stir just until the spinach is wilted.

3. Stir in the gnocchi and spaghetti sauce; heat through.

FREEZE OPTION *Freeze cooled gnocchi mixture in freezer containers. To use, partially thaw in refrigerator overnight. Heat through in a skillet, stirring occasionally and adding a little water if necessary.*

NOTE *Look for potato gnocchi in the pasta or frozen foods section.*

MOROCCAN CHICKEN THIGHS

My husband and I love Mediterranean and Middle Eastern food. This recipe has quickly become one of our favorites.

—**SUSAN MILLS** THREE RIVERS, CA

PREP: 25 MIN. • **COOK:** 40 MIN.
MAKES: 2 SERVINGS

- ½ teaspoon brown sugar
- ½ teaspoon ground coriander
- ½ teaspoon ground cumin
- ½ teaspoon paprika
- ¼ teaspoon ground cinnamon
- ⅛ teaspoon garlic powder
- ⅛ teaspoon salt
- ⅛ teaspoon pepper
- 2 teaspoons all-purpose flour
- 4 bone-in chicken thighs (about 1½ pounds), skin removed if desired
- 1½ teaspoons olive oil

SAUCE

- 3 shallots, chopped
- ½ cup plus 2 tablespoons reduced-sodium chicken broth, divided
- 4 pitted dates, chopped
- 1 teaspoon all-purpose flour
- 1½ teaspoons minced fresh cilantro

COUSCOUS

- ¼ cup water
- 3 tablespoons reduced-sodium chicken broth
- ⅛ teaspoon salt
  Dash ground cumin
- ⅓ cup uncooked couscous
- 1½ teaspoons slivered almonds, toasted

1. In a small bowl, combine the first eight ingredients. Set aside 1 teaspoon spice mixture; add flour to remaining mixture and sprinkle over chicken.

2. In a large nonstick skillet coated with cooking spray, brown chicken in oil on both sides. Remove and keep warm. Add shallots to pan; cook and stir over medium heat 3 minutes. Stir in ½ cup broth and dates. Bring to a boil. Reduce heat; return chicken to the pan.

3. Cover and simmer 20-25 minutes or until chicken juices run clear. Remove chicken and keep warm. Combine flour with reserved spice mixture and remaining broth until smooth; gradually stir into the pan. Bring to a boil; cook and stir for

"When I have leftover veggies, I dress up the salsa a little bit with some finely chopped green onions and sweet red peppers. If you like a more spicy salsa, toss in a little cayenne pepper."
—**AYSHA SCHURMAN** AMMON, ID

CHICKEN WITH
MANDARIN SALSA

CHICKEN WITH MANDARIN SALSA

START TO FINISH: 20 MIN.
MAKES: 4 SERVINGS

- 1 **can (11 ounces) mandarin oranges**
- ½ **cup chopped pecans**
- ¼ **cup finely chopped red onion**
- 2 **tablespoons minced fresh cilantro**
- 1 **pound boneless skinless chicken breasts, cut into 1-inch cubes**
- ½ **teaspoon salt**
- ½ **teaspoon pepper**
- 1 **tablespoon olive oil**
- 2 **garlic cloves, minced**
- 2⅔ **cups hot cooked brown rice**

1. Drain oranges, reserving ¼ cup juice. For salsa, in a large bowl, combine oranges, pecans, onion and cilantro.
2. Sprinkle chicken with salt and pepper. In a large skillet, heat oil over medium-high heat. Add chicken; cook and stir 4 minutes. Add garlic; cook 1 minute longer. Stir in reserved juice. Bring to a boil. Reduce heat; simmer, uncovered, 4-6 minutes or until the chicken is no longer pink. Top with salsa; serve with rice.
PER SERVING ⅔ *cup chicken mixture with ⅔ cup rice equals 453 cal., 18 g fat (2 g sat. fat), 63 mg chol., 362 mg sodium, 46 g carb., 5 g fiber, 28 g pro.*

HOW-TO

PEEL GARLIC
To quickly peel fresh garlic, gently crush the clove with the flat side of a large knife blade. If you don't have a large knife, you can crush the garlic with a small can.

TURKEY CUTLETS WITH COOL PEPPER SAUCE

A lively jalapeno sauce is the perfect pairing for crispy breaded turkey cutlets. I love to serve the meat with rice noodles, or even on whole wheat sandwich buns with fresh veggies.

—**JEANNIE KLUGH** LANCASTER, PA

START TO FINISH: 25 MIN.
MAKES: 4 SERVINGS (½ CUP SAUCE)

- 3 **tablespoons reduced-fat sour cream**
- 2 **tablespoons reduced-fat mayonnaise**
- 2 **tablespoons minced seeded jalapeno pepper**
- 2 **teaspoons lemon juice**
- ¼ **teaspoon grated lemon peel**
- ⅛ **teaspoon plus ¼ teaspoon pepper, divided**
- ½ **cup seasoned bread crumbs**
- 2 **tablespoons grated Parmesan cheese**
- 1 **tablespoon minced fresh parsley**
- 1 **garlic clove, minced**
- 1 **package (17.6 ounces) turkey breast cutlets**
- 1 **tablespoon olive oil**
  Lemon wedges and sliced jalapeno peppers, optional

1. For sauce, in a small bowl, combine the sour cream, mayonnaise, jalapeno, lemon juice and peel and ⅛ teaspoon pepper; set aside.
2. In a large resealable plastic bag, combine the bread crumbs, Parmesan cheese, parsley, garlic and remaining pepper. Add turkey, a few pieces at a time, and shake to coat.
3. In a large nonstick skillet, cook turkey in oil in batches over medium heat for 1-2 minutes on each side or until no longer pink. Serve with sauce. Garnish with lemon wedges and jalapenos if desired.
NOTE *Wear disposable gloves when cutting hot peppers; the oils can burn skin. Avoid touching your face.*
PER SERVING *4 ounces cooked turkey with 2 tablespoons sauce equals 242 cal., 9 g fat (2 g sat. fat), 78 mg chol., 296 mg sodium, 9 g carb., 1 g fiber, 31 g pro.* **Diabetic Exchanges:** *4 lean meat, 1½ fat, ½ starch.*

PESTO CHICKEN WRAPS

This makes a really quick meal for us. It's so easy, and cleanup is simple if you assemble the wraps on a cookie sheet lined with foil. My wife likes to add a little dollop of sour cream.

—**GARY PHILE** RAVENNA, OH

START TO FINISH: 20 MIN.
MAKES: 4 SERVINGS

- ½ **pound ground chicken**
- 1 **tablespoon canola oil**
- ¼ **cup sun-dried tomato pesto**
- 4 **flour tortillas (8 inches), warmed**
- ½ **cup shredded part-skim mozzarella cheese**
- 8 **grape tomatoes, cut in half**
- 4 **slices red onion, separated into rings**
- 1 **cup shredded lettuce**

1. In a large skillet, cook chicken in oil over medium heat for 5-6 minutes or until no longer pink; drain.
2. Spread pesto over each tortilla; spoon the chicken down the center. Layer with cheese, tomatoes, onion and lettuce; roll up.

Pork

MEXICALI
PORK CHOPS

MEXICALI PORK CHOPS

Grab just a couple pantry staples—taco seasoning and your favorite salsa—to cook up a super-quick dinner of tender pork chops smothered in fun flavors.

—**LAURA COHEN** EAU CLAIRE, WI

START TO FINISH: 10 MIN.
MAKES: 4 SERVINGS

- 1 **envelope taco seasoning**
- 4 **boneless pork loin chops (½ inch thick)**
- 1 **tablespoon canola oil**
  Salsa

1. Rub the taco seasoning over pork chops.
2. In a large skillet, cook chops over medium-high heat in oil until juices run clear, about 4-5 minutes on each side. Serve with salsa.

READER RAVE

"It's a great and simple recipe. For a juicier pork chop, I turned the heat down after searing and then cooked the chops in the salsa."
—**DIHIGGINS**
FROM *TASTEOFHOME.COM*

LIGHT LINGUINE
CARBONARA

WILD RICE HAM SALAD

Wild rice is native to the Midwest, so this dish is popular in our area. We eat it cold or warm it up just enough to soften the cheese and blend the flavors a little more. Serve it as the main event or even as a side for chicken or turkey.

—**KATHI SAARI** AMES, IA

PREP: 30 MIN. • **COOK:** 1 HOUR + CHILLING
MAKES: 6-8 SERVINGS

  1 **cup uncooked wild rice**
  3 **cups water**
  1 **tablespoon chicken bouillon granules**
  1 **cup julienned fully cooked ham**
  1 **cup julienned Monterey Jack cheese**
  1 **cup julienned sweet red pepper**
  1 **cup fresh broccoli florets**
  ½ **cup thinly sliced carrots**
  ½ **cup thinly sliced green onions with tops**

DRESSING
  2 **tablespoons lemon juice**
  2 **tablespoons white vinegar**
  ½ **teaspoon ground mustard**
  ½ to 1 **teaspoon curry powder**
      Salt and pepper to taste
  ½ **cup vegetable oil**

1. In a large saucepan, bring the wild rice, water and chicken bouillon to a boil. Reduce heat; cover and simmer for 1 hour or until the rice is tender. Drain if necessary; cool.

2. In a large bowl, toss the rice with ham, cheese, red pepper, broccoli, carrots and green onions. For the dressing, combine the lemon juice, white vinegar, mustard, curry powder, salt and pepper in a blender or food processor. With the machine on high, slowly add vegetable oil through the feeder cap until well mixed; dressing will thicken slightly.

3. Pour over salad and toss to coat. Cover and chill several hours or overnight.

PER SERVING *1 cup equals 292 cal., 20 g fat (5 g sat. fat), 25 mg chol., 636 mg sodium, 18 g carb., 2 g fiber, 11 g pro.*

LIGHT LINGUINE CARBONARA

When we have to rush off at night, I make this speedy pasta with veggies and bacon. Pass it around the table with breadsticks or garlic toast, and dinner's done.
—**MARY JO MILLER** MANSFIELD, OH

START TO FINISH: 25 MIN.
MAKES: 4 SERVINGS

  8 **ounces uncooked linguine**
  ½ **cup frozen peas**
  1 **large egg**
  1 **cup fat-free evaporated milk**
  ¼ **cup finely chopped sweet red pepper**
  ⅛ **teaspoon crushed red pepper flakes**
  ⅛ **teaspoon pepper**
  ½ **cup grated Parmesan cheese, divided**
  2 **bacon strips, cooked and crumbled**

1. In a 6-qt. stockpot, cook linguine according to the package directions, adding peas during the last 2 minutes of cooking. Meanwhile, in a saucepan, whisk egg, milk, red pepper, pepper flakes and pepper until blended; cook and stir over medium-low heat until mixture is just thick enough to coat a spoon and a thermometer reads at least 160°. Stir in ¼ cup cheese and bacon; remove from heat.

2. Drain linguine; return to pot. Add sauce and toss to coat. Serve with remaining cheese.

PER SERVING *1 cup equals 352 cal., 7 g fat (3 g sat. fat), 66 mg chol., 349 mg sodium, 52 g carb., 3 g fiber, 20 g pro.*

"I made a big pot of this soup when visiting my sister and her family. Now I bring it along when I stop by, or I pack up a few containers for my nephew, who appreciates a home-cooked meal while he's away at college."

—**TIFFANY IHLE** BRONX, NY

SAUSAGE, KALE & LENTIL STEW

SAUSAGE, KALE & LENTIL STEW

PREP: 20 MIN. • **COOK:** 45 MIN.
MAKES: 6 SERVINGS (2 QUARTS)

- 1 pound bulk pork sausage
- 10 baby carrots, chopped (about ¾ cup)
- 1 small onion, finely chopped
- 4 garlic cloves, minced
- 4 plum tomatoes, halved
- ¾ cup roasted sweet red peppers
- 1 cup dried lentils, rinsed
- 2 cans (14½ ounces each) vegetable broth
- 1 bay leaf
- ½ teaspoon ground cumin
- ¼ teaspoon pepper
- 2 cups coarsely chopped fresh kale

1. In a Dutch oven, cook the sausage, carrots and onion over medium-high heat 8-10 minutes or until sausage is no longer pink, breaking up sausage into crumbles. Stir in garlic; cook 2 minutes longer. Drain.

2. Place tomatoes and red peppers in a food processor; process until finely chopped. Add to the sausage mixture; stir in the lentils, broth and seasonings. Bring to a boil. Reduce the heat; simmer, covered, 20 minutes, stirring occasionally.

3. Stir in kale; cook 10-15 minutes longer or until lentils and kale are tender. Remove bay leaf.

FREEZE OPTION *Freeze cooled stew in freezer containers. To use, partially thaw in the refrigerator overnight. Heat through in a small saucepan, stirring occasionally.*

TOP TIP

FRESH BAY LEAVES

Available in the herb section of large supermarkets, fresh bay leaves are more aromatic than dried leaves, and you can mince them to season kabobs and Mediterranean dishes. Freeze unused fresh bay leaves to use for soups.

HAM & BRIE MELTS

TORTELLINI ALFREDO

I jazz up refrigerated tortellini with ham, mushrooms, peas and my homemade Alfredo sauce for a fast supper. When we're having company over, I prepare the dinner shortly before guests arrive, transfer it to a casserole dish and keep it toasty in the oven.
—**CHRIS SNYDER** BOULDER, CO

START TO FINISH: 30 MIN.
MAKES: 4-6 SERVINGS

- 2 packages (9 ounces each) refrigerated cheese tortellini
- ½ cup chopped onion
- ⅓ cup butter, cubed
- 1½ cups frozen peas, thawed
- 1 cup thinly sliced fresh mushrooms
- 1 cup cubed fully cooked ham
- 1¾ cups heavy whipping cream
- ¼ teaspoon coarsely ground pepper
- ¾ cup grated Parmesan cheese
  Shredded Parmesan cheese, optional

1. Cook the tortellini according to package directions. Meanwhile, in a large skillet, saute chopped onion in butter until tender. Add the peas, mushrooms and ham; cook until the mushrooms are tender. Stir in the cream and pepper; heat through. Stir in the grated Parmesan cheese until it's melted.

2. Drain the tortellini and place in a serving dish; add the sauce and toss to coat. Sprinkle with the shredded Parmesan cheese if desired.

HAM & BRIE MELTS

Deli ham and apricot preserves pair up with melty special-occasion cheese in these crispy sandwiches that remind me of baked Brie.
—**BONNIE BAHLER** ELLINGTON, CT

START TO FINISH: 20 MIN.
MAKES: 4 SERVINGS

- 8 slices multigrain bread
- ¼ cup apricot preserves, divided
- ½ pound sliced deli ham
- 1 round (8 ounces) Brie cheese, rind removed, sliced
- 3 tablespoons butter, softened

1. Spread four bread slices with half of the preserves. Layer with ham and cheese. Spread remaining bread with the remaining preserves; place over cheese. Butter outsides of sandwiches.

2. In a large skillet, toast sandwiches over medium heat 2-3 minutes on each side or until golden brown and cheese is melted.

BLACKBERRY-SAUCED PORK CHOPS

My family loved these pork chops from the very first time I made them. They're as tasty in a skillet as they are grilled, so you can eat them all year long. The sauce is also fantastic with chicken.

—PRISCILLA GILBERT
INDIAN HARBOUR BEACH, FL

START TO FINISH: 30 MIN.
MAKES: 4 SERVINGS

- ½ cup seedless blackberry spreadable fruit
- 1 tablespoon lemon juice
- 1 tablespoon reduced-sodium soy sauce
  Dash ground cinnamon
- 4 boneless pork loin chops (5 ounces each)
- 2 teaspoons steak seasoning
- 2 teaspoons olive oil
- 1 cup fresh blackberries

1. In a small saucepan, combine the spreadable fruit, lemon juice, soy sauce and cinnamon. Cook and stir over low heat until spreadable fruit is melted. Remove from heat.

2. Sprinkle pork chops with steak seasoning. In a large nonstick skillet coated with cooking spray, heat the oil over medium heat. Add the pork chops; cook 5-7 minutes on each side or until a thermometer reads 145°. Let stand 5 minutes. Serve with sauce and blackberries.

PER SERVING *1 pork chop with 2 tablespoons sauce and ¼ cup berries equals 311 cal., 10 g fat (3 g sat. fat), 68 mg chol., 531 mg sodium, 25 g carb., 2 g fiber, 28 g pro.* **Diabetic Exchanges:** *4 lean meat, 1½ starch, ½ fat.*

BLACKBERRY-SAUCED
PORK CHOPS

PEPPERED PORK PITAS

Believe it: Cracked black pepper is all it takes to give my pork pitas some pop. Then I fill them up with caramelized onions and garlic mayo. With these, any weeknight meal is awesome.

—**KATHERINE WHITE** CLEMMONS, NC

START TO FINISH: 20 MIN.
MAKES: 4 SERVINGS

- 1 **pound boneless pork loin chops, cut into thin strips**
- 1 **tablespoon olive oil**
- 2 **teaspoons coarsely ground pepper**
- 2 **garlic cloves, minced**
- 1 **jar (12 ounces) roasted sweet red peppers, drained and julienned**
- 4 **whole pita breads, warmed Garlic mayonnaise and torn leaf lettuce, optional**

In a small bowl, combine pork, oil, pepper and garlic; toss to coat. Place a large skillet over medium-high heat. Add pork mixture; cook and stir until no longer pink. Stir in red peppers; heat through. Serve on pita breads. Top with garlic mayonnaise and lettuce if desired.

PER SERVING *¾ cup pork mixture with 1 pita bread equals 380 cal., 11 g fat (3 g sat. fat), 55 mg chol., 665 mg sodium, 37 g carb., 2 g fiber, 27 g pro.* **Diabetic Exchanges:** *3 lean meat, 2 starch, 1 fat.*

PEPPERED
PORK PITAS

THREE-MEAT SAUCE

This authentic Italian spaghetti sauce is a longtime family favorite—and there's enough to feed a table full! Beef roast, pork roast and Italian sausage simmer in a hefty sauce that's big on flavor.

—**LILLIAN DI SENSO** LAKE HAVASU CITY, AZ

PREP: 10 MIN. • **COOK:** 2½ HOURS
MAKES: 18 CUPS

- 1 **boneless beef chuck roast (2½ to 3 pounds), trimmed and cut into 1-inch cubes**
- 1 **boneless pork shoulder butt roast (2 to 2½ pounds), trimmed and cut into 1-inch cubes**
- 1 **pound Italian sausage links, cut into 1-inch slices**
- 3 **tablespoons olive oil**
- 3 **large onions, chopped**
- 5 **cans (15 ounces each) tomato sauce**
- 3 **cans (6 ounces each) tomato paste**
- 1 **cup water**
- ½ **cup minced fresh parsley or 3 tablespoons dried parsley flakes**
- ½ **cup minced fresh oregano or 3 tablespoons dried oregano**
- 5 **teaspoons salt**
- 2 **teaspoons pepper**

1. In a Dutch oven, brown beef, pork and sausage in oil; drain. Add onions; cook until tender. Add tomato sauce, tomato paste, water and seasonings. Bring to a boil.

2. Reduce heat; cover and simmer for 2½-3 hours or until beef and pork are tender. Serve with spaghetti.

FREEZE OPTION *Cool remaining sauce; place in freezer containers. Cover and freeze for up to 3 months. To use, partially thaw in refrigerator overnight. Place in a saucepan and reheat, stirring occasionally. Serve with spaghetti.*

SAUSAGE & PENNE MARINARA

It's hard to beat the classic Italian flavors of this comforting dish. It has a slight kick, so leave out the pepper flakes if you don't want the heat.

—**TAMMY ROWE** BELLEVUE, OH

START TO FINISH: 30 MIN.
MAKES: 6 SERVINGS

- 2½ cups uncooked penne pasta
- 1 pound Italian sausage links, cut into 1-inch pieces
- 1 large onion, halved and sliced
- 1 medium green pepper, sliced
- 1 tablespoon canola oil
- 1 can (14½ ounces) stewed tomatoes, cut up
- 1 can (8 ounces) tomato sauce
- 1 teaspoon garlic powder
- 1 teaspoon dried basil
- 1 teaspoon dried oregano
- ½ teaspoon salt
- ½ teaspoon pepper
- ¼ teaspoon crushed red pepper flakes
  Grated Parmesan cheese, optional

1. Cook the penne pasta according to package directions. Meanwhile, in a large skillet, cook the sausage, onion and green pepper in oil over medium heat until the sausage is no longer pink and the vegetables are tender. Add the tomatoes, tomato sauce and seasonings; heat through.
2. Drain the pasta; toss with tomato mixture. Sprinkle with the Parmesan cheese if desired.

TOASTED SAUSAGE CACCIATORE SAMMIES

To add a little extra texture to these crisp sandwiches, use chunky spaghetti sauce. The result is a delicious Italian dish!

—**TASTE OF HOME** TEST KITCHEN

START TO FINISH: 30 MIN.
MAKES: 8 SERVINGS

- 1 package (11¼ ounces) frozen garlic Texas toast
- 3 Italian sausage links, chopped
- 1 medium eggplant, cubed
- ½ pound sliced fresh mushrooms
- 1 medium onion, halved and thinly sliced
- 1 jar (14 ounces) spaghetti sauce
- ½ teaspoon Italian seasoning
- 8 slices provolone cheese

1. Bake the garlic toast according to the package directions. Meanwhile, cook sausage, eggplant, mushrooms and sliced onion in a large skillet over medium heat until the meat is no longer pink.
2. Stir in spaghetti sauce and Italian seasoning; heat through. Spoon over garlic bread and top with cheese. Let stand until melted.

PORK CHOPS WITH HONEY-GARLIC SAUCE

START TO FINISH: 25 MIN.
MAKES: 4 SERVINGS

- 4 bone-in pork loin chops (6 ounces each)
- ¼ cup lemon juice
- ¼ cup honey
- 2 tablespoons reduced-sodium soy sauce
- 1 garlic clove, minced

1. Place a large nonstick skillet coated with cooking spray over medium heat. Add pork chops; cook 5-6 minutes on each side or until a thermometer reads 145°. Remove and keep warm.
2. In a small bowl, combine lemon juice, honey, soy sauce and garlic; add to pan. Cook over medium heat 3-4 minutes, stirring occasionally. Serve with chops.
PER SERVING *1 pork chop with 2 tablespoons sauce equals 220 cal., 5 g fat (2 g sat. fat), 71 mg chol., 361 mg sodium, 20 g carb., trace fiber, 25 g pro.* **Diabetic Exchanges:** *3 lean meat, 1 starch.*

TOASTED SAUSAGE CACCIATORE SAMMIES

The honey and garlic sauce is so good, I sometimes double it so there's extra for dipping.
—**MICHELLE SMITH** ELDERSBURG, MD

PORK CHOPS WITH HONEY-GARLIC SAUCE

CRANBERRY
SWEET-AND-SOUR PORK

EAT SMART

RANCH HAM 'N' CHEESE PASTA

Our delicious penne has about a third fewer calories than traditional ham and cheese pasta, and it has less than half the fat, saturated fat, cholesterol and sodium.

—*TASTE OF HOME* TEST KITCHEN

START TO FINISH: 25 MIN.
MAKES: 10 SERVINGS

- 1 package (16 ounces) penne pasta
- 1 tablespoon butter
- 1 tablespoon all-purpose flour
- 1 cup fat-free milk
- 2 teaspoons dried parsley flakes
- 1 teaspoon garlic salt
- 1 teaspoon salt-free lemon-pepper seasoning
- ½ teaspoon garlic powder
- ½ teaspoon dried minced onion
- ½ teaspoon dill weed
- ¼ teaspoon onion powder
- ⅛ teaspoon pepper
- 1 cup (8 ounces) reduced-fat sour cream
- 2 cups cubed fully cooked ham
- 1½ cups (6 ounces) shredded reduced-fat Mexican cheese blend
- ¼ cup shredded Parmesan cheese

1. Cook pasta according to package directions; drain. In a Dutch oven, melt butter; whisk in flour until smooth. Gradually add milk and seasonings. Bring to a boil; cook and stir for 2 minutes or until thickened.
2. Reduce heat; fold in sour cream until blended. Add ham and pasta; cook and stir until heated through. Remove from the heat; stir in Mexican cheese blend until melted. Sprinkle with Parmesan cheese.
PER SERVING *1 cup equals 306 cal., 9 g fat (5 g sat. fat), 27 mg chol., 612 mg sodium, 38 g carb., 2 g fiber, 20 g pro.* **Diabetic Exchanges:** *2½ starch, 2 lean meat.*

EAT SMART **FREEZE IT**

CRANBERRY SWEET-AND-SOUR PORK

This fresh take on the beloved Asian-style dish will cause a stir at the dinner table. Get the chopsticks ready!

—**GERT SNYDER** WEST MONTROSE, ON

START TO FINISH: 20 MIN.
MAKES: 6 SERVINGS

- 1 tablespoon cornstarch
- ½ cup unsweetened pineapple juice
- 1 cup whole-berry cranberry sauce
- ½ cup barbecue sauce
- 1½ pounds pork tenderloin, cut into ½-inch cubes
- 1 tablespoon canola oil
- ½ teaspoon salt
- ¼ teaspoon pepper
- 1 medium green pepper, cut into strips
- ¾ cup pineapple tidbits
  Hot cooked rice, chow mein noodles or crispy wonton strips

1. In a bowl, combine the cornstarch and pineapple juice until smooth. Stir in the cranberry and barbecue sauces; set aside.
2. In a large skillet, stir-fry the pork in oil for 3 minutes or until the meat is no longer pink. Sprinkle with salt and pepper. Remove from the pan and keep warm.
3. Add green pepper and pineapple to pan; stir-fry for 2 minutes. Stir cornstarch mixture and add to skillet. Bring to a boil. Cook and stir for 2 minutes or until thickened. Add pork; heat through. Serve with rice, noodles or wonton strips.
FREEZE OPTION *Place cooled meat mixture in freezer containers. To use, partially thaw in the refrigerator overnight. Heat through slowly in a covered skillet, stirring occasionally and adding a little water if necessary.*
PER SERVING *1¼ cups (calculated without rice) equals 268 cal., 7 g fat (2 g sat. fat), 63 mg chol., 444 mg sodium, 28 g carb., 1 g fiber, 23 g pro.*

PUMPKIN & SAUSAGE PENNE

I once made this for my Italian father-in-law, who swears he'll eat pasta only with red sauce. He loved it!

—**KAREN CAMBIOTTI** STROUDSBURG, PA

START TO FINISH: 30 MIN.
MAKES: 2 SERVINGS

- ¾ **cup uncooked penne pasta**
- 2 **Italian sausage links, casings removed**
- ½ **cup chopped sweet onion**
- 1 **garlic clove, minced**
- 1 **teaspoon olive oil**
- ⅓ **cup white wine or chicken broth**
- 1 **bay leaf**
- ¾ **cup chicken broth**
- ⅓ **cup canned pumpkin**
- 3 **teaspoons minced fresh sage, divided**
- ⅛ **teaspoon each salt, pepper and ground cinnamon**
  Dash ground nutmeg
- 3 **tablespoons half-and-half cream**
- 2 **tablespoons shredded Romano cheese**

1. Cook pasta according to package directions. Meanwhile, in a large skillet, cook sausage over medium heat until no longer pink, breaking into crumbles. Remove with a slotted spoon; drain on paper towels. Discard drippings, reserving 1 teaspoon.

2. Cook and stir the onion and garlic in oil and the reserved drippings over medium-high heat until tender. Add wine and bay leaf. Bring to a boil; cook until liquid is reduced by half. Stir in the broth, pumpkin, 1½ teaspoons sage and remaining seasonings; cook 1 minute longer. Add the cream and sausage; heat through. Remove the bay leaf.

3. Drain pasta; transfer to a large bowl. Add sausage mixture; toss to coat. Sprinkle with cheese and the remaining sage.

**PUMPKIN &
SAUSAGE PENNE**

CONEY DOGS

My mom and I always make these top dogs for get-togethers. Leftovers are no problem—there never are any!

—DONNA STERNTHAL SHARPSVILLE, PA

PREP: 15 MIN. • **COOK:** 45 MIN.
MAKES: 24 SERVINGS

- 2 pounds ground beef
- 3 small onions, chopped
- 3 cups water
- 1 can (12 ounces) tomato paste
- 5 teaspoons chili powder
- 2 teaspoons rubbed sage
- 2 teaspoons salt
- 1 teaspoon pepper
- ½ teaspoon garlic salt
- ½ teaspoon dried oregano
- ¼ teaspoon cayenne pepper
- 24 hot dogs, cooked
- 24 hot dog buns
  Shredded cheddar cheese, optional

1. In a Dutch oven, cook beef and onions over medium heat until meat is no longer pink; drain. Stir in the water, tomato paste and seasonings.

2. Cover; simmer 30 minutes, stirring occasionally. Serve on hot dogs in hot dog buns; top with cheese if desired.

ITALIAN SAUSAGE STEW

Here's your answer to what's for dinner on those cold winter nights. We created a quick and flavorful stew that will warm you from head to toe!

—TASTE OF HOME TEST KITCHEN

PREP: 15 MIN. • **COOK:** 30 MIN.
MAKES: 4 SERVINGS

- ½ pound bulk Italian sausage
- 2 garlic cloves, minced
- 1 can (14½ ounces) Italian diced tomatoes, undrained
- 4 small red potatoes, quartered
- ¼ cup sliced fresh carrots
- 1 tablespoon minced fresh basil
- ½ cup sliced zucchini
- 1 can (14½ ounces) reduced-sodium beef broth
- 1 tablespoon cornstarch
- ¼ cup shredded Parmesan cheese, optional

1. In a large saucepan, cook sausage over medium heat until no longer pink. Add the garlic; cook 1 minute longer. Drain.

2. Add tomatoes, potatoes, carrots and basil to sausage mixture. Bring to a boil. Reduce heat; add zucchini. Cover and simmer 10 minutes.

3. Combine the broth and cornstarch until smooth; stir into stew. Simmer until vegetables are tender and stew is thickened, about 5-10 minutes more. Sprinkle with cheese if desired.

APPLE-TOPPED HAM STEAKS

START TO FINISH: 30 MIN.
MAKES: 8 SERVINGS

- 4 fully cooked boneless ham steaks (8 ounces each)
- 1 cup chopped onion
- 3 cups apple juice
- 2 teaspoons Dijon mustard
- 2 medium green apples, thinly sliced
- 2 medium red apples, thinly sliced
- 2 tablespoons cornstarch
- ¼ cup cold water
- 1 tablespoon minced fresh sage or 1 teaspoon rubbed sage
- ¼ teaspoon pepper

1. In a skillet coated with cooking spray, brown steaks in batches over medium heat; remove and keep warm.

2. In same skillet, saute onion until tender. Stir in the apple juice and mustard; bring to a boil. Add apples. Reduce heat; cover and simmer for 4 minutes or until apples are tender.

3. Combine cornstarch and water until smooth; stir into apple juice mixture. Bring to a boil; cook and stir for 2 minutes. Stir in sage and pepper. Return steaks to skillet; heat through.

CONEY DOGS

TOP TIP

IMPROMPTU OVEN RACK

My husband, Brett, and I bought a ham to bake for our family, but we didn't have a rack to cook it on. We decided to use cut apples to prop up the ham. Not only did they keep it upright in the pan, but they added a wonderful flavor to the ham and a tempting aroma to the house.

—ELIZABETH M. PITTSBURGH, PA

When it's time to sit down to dinner with friends, we serve ham with a tangy sauce of sweet and tart apples, zingy mustard and a dash of sage.
—**ELEANOR CHORE** ATHENA, OR

APPLE-TOPPED
HAM STEAKS

**SAVORY
PORK SALAD**

1. Drain peaches, reserving ½ cup syrup; set aside. In a large skillet, brown ham on both sides in butter over medium heat. Remove ham to a platter and keep warm, reserving drippings in skillet.

2. In a bowl, mix the sugar, cornstarch and nutmeg. Add orange juice, lemon juice and reserved peach syrup; stir until smooth. Add to the drippings in skillet. Cook and stir until thickened.

3. Stir in peaches and heat through. Add ham slice and heat 2-3 minutes. Cut into serving-size pieces. Serve over rice.

PORK CHOPS AND SAUERKRAUT

My mother learned to make this dish when she was a young girl in Germany. Typically, we'd eat it with plain boiled potatoes, but for a treat, she'd serve it with steamed dumplings. Whenever I cook this, the wonderful aroma brings back many warm memories.

—ERIKA TAYLOR HOPEDALE, MA

PREP: 10 MIN. • **COOK:** 45 MIN.
MAKES: 4 SERVINGS

- 4 bone-in pork loin chops (¾ inch thick)
- 1 tablespoon canola oil
- 1 cup chopped onion
- 1 can (14½ ounces) chicken broth
- ½ teaspoon caraway seeds
- ¼ teaspoon pepper
- ¼ teaspoon celery seed
- 1 can (14 ounces) sauerkraut, rinsed and well drained
- 1 red apple, chopped
- 4 bacon strips, cooked and crumbled, optional

1. In a skillet, brown the pork chops in oil. Stir in onion, broth, caraway seeds, pepper and celery seed. Cover and cook over medium heat for 30 minutes or until tender. Add the sauerkraut and apple.

2. Cover and cook 10-15 minutes or until heated through. Before serving, sprinkle with bacon if desired.

EAT SMART

SAVORY PORK SALAD

Make a healthy meal in a bowl by tossing veggies, pork tenderloin and herbs with a warm soy dressing.

—*TASTE OF HOME* TEST KITCHEN

START TO FINISH: 25 MIN.
MAKES: 2 SERVINGS

- 1 garlic clove, minced
- ½ teaspoon minced fresh gingerroot
- 2 teaspoons olive oil
- ½ pound pork tenderloin, thinly sliced
- 2 teaspoons brown sugar
- 2 teaspoons minced fresh basil
- 2 teaspoons reduced-sodium soy sauce
- 1½ teaspoons lime juice
- 1½ teaspoons water
- 1 teaspoon minced fresh oregano
- 3 cups torn mixed salad greens
- ½ cup grape tomatoes
- ½ small red onion, sliced and separated into rings
- ½ small sweet yellow pepper, cut into strips

1. In a small skillet, cook the garlic and ginger in oil over medium heat for 30 seconds. Add pork; cook and stir until the meat is no longer pink. Remove and keep warm.

2. In the same skillet, combine the brown sugar, basil, soy sauce, lime juice, water and oregano. Bring to a boil. Remove from the heat.

3. In a salad bowl, combine the greens, tomatoes, onion, yellow pepper and pork. Drizzle with warm dressing and toss to coat; serve immediately.

PER SERVING *1 serving equals 229 cal., 9 g fat (2 g sat. fat), 63 mg chol., 274 mg sodium, 13 g carb., 3 g fiber, 25 g pro. Diabetic Exchanges: 3 lean meat, 2 vegetable.*

PEACHY HAM SLICE

Ham is wonderful with fruity flavors, so I decided to try it with peaches. I loved it! I have been making it this way for years.

—ERIKA KLOP AGASSIZ, BC

START TO FINISH: 30 MIN.
MAKES: 4-6 SERVINGS

- 1 can (15¼ ounces) sliced peaches
- 1 ham slice (about 1½ pounds)
- 1 tablespoon butter
- 1 tablespoon sugar
- 2 teaspoons cornstarch
- ⅛ teaspoon nutmeg
- ½ cup orange juice
- 1 tablespoon lemon juice
  Hot cooked rice

KIELBASA AND BOW TIES

This, like many of my recipes, was the result of a good refrigerator cleaning. The ingredients mix up into a quick, satisfying meal for one.

—SHIRLEY KACMARIK GLASGOW, SCOTLAND

START TO FINISH: 25 MIN.
MAKES: 1 SERVING

- ¾ cup uncooked bow tie pasta
- 1 bacon strip, diced
- 2 medium fresh mushrooms, sliced
- 6 spinach leaves
- 6 slices smoked kielbasa or Polish sausage (½ inch thick)
- 3 grape tomatoes, halved
- 3 pitted ripe olives, sliced
- 2 tablespoons mayonnaise
- 2 tablespoons sour cream

1. Cook pasta according to package directions. Meanwhile, in a small skillet, cook bacon over medium heat until crisp. Using a slotted spoon, remove to paper towels. In the drippings, cook mushrooms for 3-4 minutes or until tender. Stir in spinach and kielbasa; heat through.

2. Remove from the heat. Drain pasta; add to kielbasa mixture. Stir in the tomatoes, olives, mayonnaise, sour cream and bacon.

EAT SMART

SPICY PORK WITH NOODLES

Ginger and red pepper flakes perk up this flavorful pork dish. I've been making this quick pasta dish for years. It's convenient because the noodles don't need to be boiled separately.

—ANN VAN TASSELL ALBUQUERQUE, NM

START TO FINISH: 30 MIN.
MAKES: 3 CUPS

- ¼ cup plus 2 tablespoons sliced green onions, divided
- 2 teaspoons minced fresh gingerroot
- 1 tablespoon canola oil
- 3 garlic cloves, minced
- ⅓ pound ground pork
- 1 can (8 ounces) sliced water chestnuts, drained
- 3 tablespoons reduced-sodium soy sauce
- 1 teaspoon sesame oil
- ¼ teaspoon crushed red pepper flakes
- 2 cups uncooked egg noodles
- 1½ cups water

1. In a large skillet, saute ¼ cup green onions and ginger in canola oil until tender. Add the garlic; cook 1 minute longer. Add pork; cook until no longer pink. Drain.

2. Stir in water chestnuts, soy sauce, sesame oil and pepper flakes. Add noodles and water. Bring to a boil. Reduce heat; cover and simmer 5-7 minutes or until noodles are tender. Sprinkle with remaining onions.

PER SERVING *1 cup equals 315 cal., 15 g fat (4 g sat. fat), 58 mg chol., 645 mg sodium, 31 g carb., 3 g fiber, 15 g pro.* **Diabetic Exchanges:** *2 starch, 1½ lean meat, 1½ fat.*

SPICY PORK WITH NOODLES

PORK MEDALLIONS
IN MUSTARD SAUCE

PORK MEDALLIONS IN MUSTARD SAUCE

I like pairing pork medallions with apricot preserves and wondered how else I could dress them up. I played with different flavors until I found this combo. Wows 'em every time.

—**TAHNIA FOX** TRENTON, MI

START TO FINISH: 30 MIN.
MAKES: 4 SERVINGS

- ½ cup reduced-sodium chicken broth
- 2 tablespoons thawed apple juice concentrate
- 4½ teaspoons stone-ground mustard
- 1 pound pork tenderloin, cut into ½-inch slices
- ¼ teaspoon salt
- ¼ teaspoon pepper
- 1 tablespoon olive oil
- 2 garlic cloves, minced
- 1 teaspoon cornstarch
- 2 tablespoons cold water
- 1 tablespoon minced fresh parsley

1. In a small bowl, mix broth, apple juice concentrate and mustard. Sprinkle pork with salt and pepper. In a large nonstick skillet, heat oil over medium-high heat. Brown pork on both sides; remove from pan.
2. Add garlic to same pan; cook and stir for 1 minute. Add broth mixture, stirring to loosen browned bits from the pan. Bring to a boil. Reduce heat; simmer, uncovered, 6-8 minutes or until liquid is reduced to about ⅓ cup.
3. Return pork to pan; cook, covered, over low heat 3-4 minutes or until a thermometer inserted in pork reads 145°. Mix cornstarch and water until smooth; stir into pan. Bring to a boil; cook and stir for 2 minutes or until thickened. Sprinkle with parsley.
PER SERVING 3 ounces cooked pork equals 193 cal., 7 g fat (2 g sat. fat), 63 mg chol., 356 mg sodium, 6 g carb., 1 g fiber, 23 g pro. **Diabetic Exchanges:** 3 lean meat, ½ starch, ½ fat.

BARBECUE PORK AND PENNE SKILLET

I'm the proud mother of wonderful, active children. So, simple, delicious and quick meals like this are perfect for us to enjoy together after errands, school activities and soccer practice are over.

—**JUDY ARMSTRONG** PRAIRIEVILLE, LA

START TO FINISH: 25 MIN.
MAKES: 8 SERVINGS

- 1 package (16 ounces) penne pasta
- 1 cup chopped sweet red pepper
- ¾ cup chopped onion
- 1 tablespoon butter
- 1 tablespoon olive oil
- 3 garlic cloves, minced
- 1 carton (16 ounces) refrigerated fully cooked barbecued shredded pork
- 1 can (14½ ounces) diced tomatoes with mild green chilies, undrained
- ½ cup beef broth
- 1 teaspoon ground cumin
- 1 teaspoon pepper
- ¼ teaspoon salt
- 1¼ cups shredded cheddar cheese
- ¼ cup chopped green onions

1. Cook the pasta according to the package directions. Meanwhile, in a large skillet, saute red pepper and onion in butter and oil until tender. Add garlic; saute 1 minute longer. Stir in the pork, tomatoes, broth, cumin, pepper and salt; heat through.
2. Drain pasta. Add pasta and cheese to the pork mixture; stir until blended. Sprinkle with green onions.

FREEZE OPTION *Freeze cooled pasta mixture in freezer containers. To use, partially thaw in the refrigerator overnight. Place in a shallow microwave-safe dish. Cover and microwave on high until heated through.*

ASIAN PORK TENDERLOIN SALAD

This crisp, crunchy salad with succulent tenderloin is a nice change of pace. If you like a sweeter taste, add a little sweet-and-sour sauce to the soy sauce mixture.

—**GINA BERRY** CHANHASSEN, MN

START TO FINISH: 25 MIN.
MAKES: 2 SERVINGS

- ½ pound pork tenderloin, cut into ½-inch strips
- 2 teaspoons sesame oil
- 1 cup shredded red cabbage
- 1 cup fresh snow peas
- 1 snack-size cup (4 ounces) mandarin oranges, drained
- ½ small sweet yellow pepper, chopped
- 2 tablespoons reduced-sodium soy sauce
- 2 tablespoons reduced-sodium teriyaki sauce
- ½ cup chow mein noodles

1. In a small skillet, saute pork in oil until juices run clear. Meanwhile, combine the cabbage, peas, oranges and yellow pepper in a bowl.
2. Add soy sauce and teriyaki sauce; toss to coat. Divide between two salad plates. Arrange the pork on salads; sprinkle with chow mein noodles.

SEED AND SLICE PEPPERS

Holding the pepper by the stem, slice from the top of the pepper down using a chef's knife. Use this technique to slice around the seeds when a recipe calls for julienned or chopped peppers.

Fish & Seafood

SHRIMP JAMBALAYA

This delightfully different jambalaya is lighter than many of the traditional sausage varieties. Plus, it's a great way to use up leftover ham. I appreciate how easy it is to prepare, and I love the aroma while it's cooking.

—MARGUERITE SHAEFFER SEWELL, NJ

PREP: 15 MIN. • **COOK:** 25 MIN.
MAKES: 4 SERVINGS

- 1 **cup cubed fully cooked ham**
- ¾ **cup chopped onion**
- 1 **garlic clove, minced**
- 2 **tablespoons canola oil**
- 2 **cups chicken broth**
- 1 **can (14½ ounces) stewed tomatoes**
- 2 **tablespoons minced fresh parsley**
- ½ **teaspoon salt**
- ¼ **teaspoon dried thyme**
- ⅛ **teaspoon each cayenne pepper, chili powder and pepper**
- 1 **bay leaf**
- 1 **cup uncooked long grain rice**
- 1 **pound uncooked medium shrimp, peeled and deveined**

In a large skillet, cook the ham, onion and garlic in oil until onion is tender. Stir in the broth, tomatoes, parsley and seasonings. Bring to a boil. Stir in rice. Reduce heat; cover and simmer for 15 minutes. Add the shrimp; cook 5 minutes longer or until the shrimp turn pink and rice is tender. Discard the bay leaf.

PESTO FISH
WITH PINE NUTS

PESTO FISH WITH PINE NUTS

I love fish, and Italian flavors are my favorite. This is a simple, tasty way to get more healthy fish into your diet.

—VALERY ANDERSON STERLING HEIGHTS, MI

START TO FINISH: 15 MIN.
MAKES: 4 SERVINGS

- 2 **envelopes pesto sauce mix, divided**
- 4 **cod fillets (6 ounces each)**
- ¼ **cup olive oil**
- ½ **cup shredded Parmesan or Romano cheese**
- ½ **cup pine nuts, toasted**

1. Prepare one envelope pesto sauce mix according to package directions; set aside. Sprinkle fish fillets with the remaining pesto mix, patting to help adhere.

2. In a large skillet, heat olive oil over medium heat. Add the cod fillets; cook 4-5 minutes on each side or until fish just begins to flake easily with a fork. Remove from heat. Sprinkle with the cheese and pine nuts. Serve with the pesto sauce.

NOTE *To toast nuts, bake in a shallow pan in a 350° oven for 5-10 minutes or cook in a skillet over low heat until lightly browned, stirring occasionally.*

COCONUT-MANGO MAHI MAHI

Take a tropical taste trip in minutes with this special recipe. Whipping a bit of candied ginger into the sauce enhances its delicious flavor.

—**DON THOMPSON** HOUSTON, OH

START TO FINISH: 30 MIN.
MAKES: 6 SERVINGS (1½ CUPS SAUCE)

- ½ cup all-purpose flour
- 2 large eggs, lightly beaten
- 1 cup dry bread crumbs
- 1 cup flaked coconut
- 6 mahi mahi fillets (5 ounces each)
- 2 tablespoons peanut or canola oil
- 2 medium mangoes, peeled and cubed
- ¼ cup white wine or chicken broth
- 2 tablespoons brown sugar
- 1 garlic clove, halved
- 1 teaspoon finely chopped crystallized ginger
- 1 teaspoon reduced-sodium soy sauce
- ⅛ teaspoon pepper
- 2 tablespoons minced fresh basil

1. Place flour and eggs in separate shallow bowls. In another shallow bowl, combine bread crumbs and coconut. Dip fillets in flour, eggs, then bread crumb mixture.

2. In a large skillet over medium heat, cook fish in oil for 4-5 minutes on each side or until the fish is golden brown on the outside and just turns opaque in the center.

3. Meanwhile, in a food processor, combine the mangoes, wine, brown sugar, garlic, ginger, soy sauce and pepper; cover and process until blended. Stir in basil. Serve with fish.

PER SERVING *1 fillet with ¼ cup sauce equals 374 cal., 12 g fat (5 g sat. fat), 168 mg chol., 315 mg sodium, 35 g carb., 2 g fiber, 31 g pro.* **Diabetic Exchanges:** *4 lean meat, 2 fat, 1 starch, 1 fruit.*

SAVORY TOMATO-BRAISED TILAPIA

SAVORY TOMATO-BRAISED TILAPIA

I shared this recipe with my bunco group, and now one of my friends makes it all the time. I think that's the perfect testament to how good this dish is.

—**NANCY SHIVELY** SHOREWOOD, IL

START TO FINISH: 30 MIN.
MAKES: 4 SERVINGS

- 4 tilapia fillets (6 ounces each)
- ¼ teaspoon seasoned salt
- 1 tablespoon lemon juice
- 2 tablespoons olive oil
- 1 small red onion, chopped
- 1 can (10 ounces) diced tomatoes and green chilies, undrained
- ¾ cup chopped roasted sweet red peppers
- ½ cup chicken broth
- ¼ cup tomato paste
- 1 teaspoon garlic powder
- 1 teaspoon dried oregano
  Hot cooked pasta, optional

1. Sprinkle fillets with seasoned salt; drizzle with lemon juice. In a large skillet, heat oil over medium-high heat. Add onion; cook and stir until tender. Add tomatoes, peppers, broth, tomato paste, garlic powder and oregano; cook 2-3 minutes longer.

2. Place fillets over tomato mixture; cook, covered, 6-8 minutes or until fish flakes easily with a fork. If desired, serve with pasta.

PER SERVING *1 fillet with ½ cup sauce (calculated without pasta) equals 254 cal., 8 g fat (2 g sat. fat), 83 mg chol., 740 mg sodium, 10 g carb., 2 g fiber, 34 g pro.* **Diabetic Exchanges:** *5 lean meat, 1½ fat, 1 vegetable.*

TOP TIP

FREEZING FISH

Tilapia, catfish, haddock and other lean types of fish may be frozen for up to 6 months. Oily fish, such as mackerel and salmon, shouldn't be frozen for more than 3 months.

GRILLED SALMON SANDWICHES

When our family was all home, I made this recipe often. As the children grew up, it became more difficult to be together for a meal, but Sunday evenings were always ours. These delicious sandwiches helped make those meals special.

—JUNE FORMANEK BELLE PLAINE, IA

START TO FINISH: 20 MIN.
MAKES: 4 SANDWICHES

- 1 can (8 ounces) red or pink salmon, well drained
- ⅓ cup finely chopped celery
- 2 tablespoons sweet pickle relish, well drained
- ⅛ teaspoon ground pepper
- ¼ cup mayonnaise
- 8 slices white or Italian bread
- 1 large egg
- ⅔ cup milk

1. In a small bowl, combine the first five ingredients. Spread over 4 bread slices. Top with remaining bread.
2. Beat egg and milk; dip sandwiches in mixture. Brown on a well-greased griddle or skillet on both sides. Serve immediately.

TUNA SALAD WITH BASIL DRESSING

I came up with this simple but delicious salad one night when my husband and I decided it was time to eat light. It has become one of our favorites that we enjoy a few times each month.

—LAURA MCALLISTER MORGANTON, NC

START TO FINISH: 30 MIN.
MAKES: 2 SERVINGS

- ½ pound fresh asparagus, trimmed and cut into 2-inch pieces
- 1 tuna steak (8 ounces)
- ⅛ teaspoon salt
- ⅛ teaspoon pepper
- 2 tablespoons olive oil
- 4 cups torn romaine
- 2 medium navel oranges, peeled and sectioned
- 1 cup cherry tomatoes, halved

DRESSING
- ¼ cup minced fresh basil
- ¼ cup olive oil
- 1 tablespoon orange juice
- 1 tablespoon balsamic vinegar
- 1 teaspoon grated orange peel
- 1 garlic clove, minced
- ½ teaspoon Dijon mustard
- ¼ teaspoon sugar
- ⅛ teaspoon pepper
  Dash salt

1. In a large saucepan, bring 4 cups water to a boil. Add asparagus; cover and boil for 3 minutes. Drain and immediately place asparagus in ice water. Drain and pat dry; set aside.
2. Sprinkle tuna with salt and pepper. In a small skillet, cook tuna in oil over medium heat for 3-4 minutes on each side for medium-rare or until slightly pink in the center.
3. Meanwhile, in a bowl, combine the romaine, oranges, tomatoes and asparagus. In a small bowl, whisk the dressing ingredients. Divide romaine mixture between two serving plates. Slice tuna; arrange over salads. Serve with dressing.

PAN-FRIED CATFISH WITH SPICY PECAN GREMOLATA

PREP: 25 MIN. • **COOK:** 10 MIN./BATCH
MAKES: 4 SERVINGS

- ½ cup packed fresh parsley sprigs
- ½ cup glazed pecans
- 2 tablespoons grated lemon peel
- 1 tablespoon grated orange peel
- 1 garlic clove, halved
- 1 teaspoon brown sugar
- ¼ teaspoon cayenne pepper
- 1 cup buttermilk
- ¾ cup all-purpose flour
- ¾ cup cornmeal
- 1½ teaspoons Cajun seasoning
- 4 catfish fillets (6 ounces each)
- ½ cup canola oil

1. Place the first seven ingredients in a food processor. Cover and process until chunky; set aside.
2. Place buttermilk in a shallow bowl. In another shallow bowl, combine the flour, cornmeal and Cajun seasoning. Dip fish in buttermilk, then coat with cornmeal mixture.
3. In a large skillet, cook the fillets in oil in batches over medium heat for 4-5 minutes on each side or until the fish flakes easily with a fork. Serve with gremolata.

TUNA SALAD WITH BASIL DRESSING

"Gremolata, a citrusy minced herb mix, makes a flavorful garnish. This well-seasoned version, with pecans added, gives an unexpected nutty flavor to the catfish."
—**LAUREEN PITTMAN** RIVERSIDE, CA

PAN-FRIED CATFISH WITH
SPICY PECAN GREMOLATA

CILANTRO
SHRIMP & RICE

CILANTRO SHRIMP & RICE

I created this one-dish wonder for my son, who has the pickiest palate. The aroma of fresh herbs is so appetizing—even my son can't resist!

—**NIBEDITA DAS** FORT WORTH, TX

START TO FINISH: 30 MIN.
MAKES: 8 SERVINGS

- 2 **packages (8½ ounces each) ready-to-serve basmati rice**
- 2 **tablespoons olive oil**
- 2 **cups frozen corn, thawed**
- 2 **medium zucchini, quartered and sliced**
- 1 **large sweet red pepper, chopped**
- ½ **teaspoon crushed red pepper flakes**
- 3 **garlic cloves, minced**
- 1 **pound peeled and deveined cooked large shrimp, tails removed**
- ½ **cup chopped fresh cilantro**
- 1 **tablespoon grated lime peel**
- 2 **tablespoons lime juice**
- ¾ **teaspoon salt**
  Lime wedges, optional

1. Prepare basmati rice according to the package directions.

2. Meanwhile, in a large skillet, heat oil over medium-high heat. Add the corn, zucchini, red pepper and pepper flakes; cook and stir for 3-5 minutes or until the zucchini is crisp-tender. Add the garlic; cook 1 minute longer. Add shrimp; cook and stir 3-5 minutes or until heated through.

3. Stir in rice, cilantro, lime peel, lime juice and salt. If desired, serve with lime wedges.

PER SERVING *1½ cups equals 243 cal., 6 g fat (1 g sat. fat), 86 mg chol., 324 mg sodium, 28 g carb., 3 g fiber, 16 g pro. Diabetic Exchanges: 2 lean meat, 1½ starch, ½ fat.*

TILAPIA WITH GREEN BEANS AMANDINE

TILAPIA WITH GREEN BEANS AMANDINE

Japanese bread crumbs give tilapia a light, crispy coating that doesn't overpower the delicate fish. Lemony green beans are the ideal complement to this delightful entree.

—*TASTE OF HOME* **TEST KITCHEN**

PREP: 20 MIN. • **COOK:** 15 MIN.
MAKES: 4 SERVINGS

- 4 **tilapia fillets (6 ounces each)**
- ½ **teaspoon salt**
- 1 **large egg**
- 1¼ **cups panko (Japanese) bread crumbs**
- ¾ **teaspoon dried parsley flakes**
- ¾ **teaspoon dried thyme**
- 2 **tablespoons butter**
- 1 **tablespoon plus 2 teaspoons olive oil, divided**
- 1 **teaspoon cornstarch**
- 1 **can (14½ ounces) chicken broth**
- 4 **garlic cloves, minced**
- 4 **teaspoons lemon juice**
- ¾ **pound fresh green beans, trimmed**
- ¼ **cup slivered almonds, toasted**

1. Sprinkle tilapia fillets with salt. In a shallow bowl, whisk the egg. In another shallow bowl, combine the bread crumbs, parsley flakes and thyme. Dip fillets in egg, then coat with crumb mixture.

2. In a large skillet, cook the fillets in butter and 1 tablespoon olive oil over medium heat for 5-6 minutes on each side or until golden brown and fish flakes easily with a fork. Remove and keep warm.

3. In a bowl, combine the cornstarch, chicken broth, garlic and lemon juice until blended; set aside.

4. In the same skillet, saute beans in the remaining oil until crisp-tender. Stir the cornstarch mixture and pour over beans. Bring to a boil; cook and stir for 1-2 minutes or until slightly thickened. Sprinkle with almonds. Serve with fish.

CAROLINA CRAB CAKES

I think these little rounds are spiced just right, and the mustard sauce is the ideal accent. If you're a fan of crab cakes, these are a must-try!

—**KATIE SLOAN** CHARLOTTE, NC

PREP: 15 MIN. + CHILLING • **COOK:** 10 MIN.
MAKES: 2 SERVINGS

- 2 **tablespoons mayonnaise**
- 2 **tablespoons sour cream**
- 1 **tablespoon Dijon mustard**
- ½ **teaspoon lemon juice**
- ½ **teaspoon Worcestershire sauce**

CRAB CAKES

- 1 **large egg, lightly beaten**
- ½ **cup soft bread crumbs**
- ¼ **cup mayonnaise**
- 1 **teaspoon grated onion**
- ½ **teaspoon minced fresh parsley**
- ½ **teaspoon Worcestershire sauce**
- ⅛ **teaspoon seafood seasoning**
- ⅛ **teaspoon ground mustard**
  Dash pepper
  Dash hot pepper sauce
- 1 **can (6 ounces) crabmeat, drained, flaked and cartilage removed**
- 1 **tablespoon canola oil**

1. In a small bowl, combine first five ingredients. Cover and refrigerate.
2. In another bowl, combine the first 10 crab cake ingredients. Fold in crab. Refrigerate for 30 minutes.
3. In a large skillet, heat the canola oil over medium heat. Drop the crab mixture by ¼ cupfuls into the pan; cook crab cakes for 3-5 minutes on each side or until golden brown. Serve with sauce.

BAJA FISH TACOS

BAJA FISH TACOS

 Golden, crisp mahi mahi will pan out beautifully when you dress it up with fresh lime, cilantro and smoky adobo. Just one bite, and you'll be hooked!

—**BROOKE KELLER** LEXINGTON, KY

PREP: 30 MIN. • **COOK:** 5 MIN./BATCH
MAKES: 8 SERVINGS

- 1 **cup reduced-fat ranch salad dressing**
- 3 **tablespoons adobo sauce**
- 2 **tablespoons minced fresh cilantro**
- 2 **tablespoons lime juice**
- 2 **pounds mahi mahi, cut into 1-inch strips**
- ¼ **teaspoon salt**
- ¼ **teaspoon pepper**
- ⅔ **cup all-purpose flour**
- 3 **large eggs, beaten**
- 2 **cups panko (Japanese) bread crumbs**
- 1 **cup canola oil**
- 16 **corn tortillas (6 inches), warmed**
- 3 **cups shredded cabbage**
  Additional minced fresh cilantro and lime wedges

1. In a small bowl, combine the salad dressing, adobo sauce, cilantro and lime juice. Chill until serving.
2. Sprinkle the mahi mahi with salt and pepper. Place the flour, eggs and bread crumbs in separate shallow bowls. Coat mahi mahi with flour, then dip in eggs and coat with bread crumbs. In a large skillet, heat oil over medium heat; cook the fish in batches for 2-3 minutes on each side or until golden brown. Drain on paper towels.
3. Place the fish in tortillas; top with cabbage, sauce mixture and additional cilantro. Serve with lime wedges.

GLAZED SALMON WITH BRUSSELS SPROUTS

This saucy meal goes on the table in under 30 minutes and proves that dinner can be fancy and stress-free at the same time!

—**TASTE OF HOME** TEST KITCHEN

START TO FINISH: 25 MIN.
MAKES: 4 SERVINGS

- 1½ pounds Brussels sprouts, halved
- 4 salmon fillets (6 ounces each)
- 2 tablespoons olive oil, divided
- 2 garlic cloves, minced
- ¼ cup honey
- 2 teaspoons chili powder
- 1 teaspoon balsamic vinegar
- ½ teaspoon salt
- ¼ teaspoon pepper

1. Place Brussels sprouts in a large saucepan; cover with water. Bring to a boil. Reduce heat; cover and simmer for 7-9 minutes or until crisp-tender.
2. Meanwhile, in a large skillet, cook salmon over medium heat in 1 tablespoon oil for 4-5 minutes on each side or until fish flakes easily with a fork. Remove and keep warm.
3. Saute the garlic in remaining oil for 1 minute; add the honey, chili powder, vinegar, salt and pepper. Cook and stir until blended. Set aside 2 tablespoons glaze. Drain Brussels sprouts; add to the skillet. Cook and stir for 1-2 minutes or until tender. Serve with salmon; drizzle with reserved glaze.

CRAB ALFREDO

I improvised this cozy recipe when I was looking for quick Lenten dishes. It has since become a favorite that my husband and I enjoy all year.

—**ESTHER PITTELLO** CHICOPEE, MA

START TO FINISH: 25 MIN.
MAKES: 2 SERVINGS

- ¼ cup chopped onion
- 1 tablespoon butter
- 1 cup sliced fresh mushrooms
- 1 cup prepared Alfredo sauce
- 2 tablespoons chicken broth
- 1 package (8 ounces) imitation crabmeat, flaked
- 2 cups hot cooked fettuccine or pasta of your choice

In a small skillet, saute the onion in butter until tender. Add mushrooms; cook and stir for 3 minutes or until tender. Stir in the sauce and broth until blended. Add the crab. Reduce heat; cook for 10 minutes or until heated through, stirring occasionally. Serve over pasta.

SHRIMP LINGUINE WITH PARMESAN CREAM SAUCE

Easy and elegant, this creamy pasta dish with a hint of heat makes a weeknight dinner seem like a special affair.

—**ATHENA RUSSELL** GREENVILLE, SC

START TO FINISH: 25 MIN.
MAKES: 3 SERVINGS

- 6 ounces uncooked linguine
- ⅓ cup chopped onion
- ⅓ cup sliced fresh mushrooms
- 2 garlic cloves, minced
- ¼ cup butter, cubed
- 2 tablespoons olive oil
- ¼ cup heavy whipping cream
- 2 tablespoons grated Parmesan cheese
- ¼ teaspoon crushed red pepper flakes
- ½ pound uncooked medium shrimp, peeled and deveined
- ⅛ teaspoon salt
- ⅛ teaspoon pepper

1. Cook the linguine according to the package directions.
2. Meanwhile, in a large skillet, saute the chopped onion, mushrooms and garlic in butter and oil for 2-3 minutes or until vegetables are tender. Stir in the cream and cheese; sprinkle with pepper flakes.
3. Drain linguine. Add shrimp and linguine to skillet; cook over medium-low heat 5-7 minutes or until shrimp are no longer pink. Sprinkle with salt and pepper.

GLAZED SALMON WITH BRUSSELS SPROUTS

"These patties take the cake! The recipe starts off simple with canned tuna. If you'd like, add more kick to the creamy mustard-mayo sauce with prepared horseradish."
—*TASTE OF HOME* TEST KITCHEN

TUNA CAKES WITH
MUSTARD MAYO

TUNA CAKES WITH MUSTARD MAYO

START TO FINISH: 30 MIN.
MAKES: 4 SERVINGS

- 2 large eggs, beaten
- 3 tablespoons minced fresh parsley, divided
- ½ teaspoon seafood seasoning
- 2 cans (5 ounces each) light water-packed tuna, drained and flaked
- ½ cup seasoned bread crumbs
- ½ cup shredded carrot
- 2 tablespoons butter, divided
- 1 package (12 ounces) frozen peas
- ¼ teaspoon pepper
- ⅓ cup mayonnaise
- 1 tablespoon Dijon mustard
- 1 teaspoon 2% milk

1. In a large bowl, combine the eggs, 2 tablespoons minced parsley and seafood seasoning. Stir in the tuna, bread crumbs and carrot. Shape into eight patties.
2. In a large skillet, brown patties in 1 tablespoon butter for 3-4 minutes on each side or until golden brown.
3. Meanwhile, microwave peas according to package directions. Stir in the pepper and remaining butter and parsley. Combine the mayonnaise, mustard and milk. Serve with tuna cakes and peas.

TOP TIP

CALCULATE YOUR PROTEIN NEEDS

A good rule of thumb for calculating your daily protein need is to multiply your body weight in pounds by .4 grams. For example, a 150-pound person needs about 60 grams of protein daily. Three ounces (a serving the size of a deck of cards) of cooked tuna, sirloin steak, pork loin, chicken or turkey breast provides about 25 grams of protein.

SWEET 'N' SOUR HALIBUT

My mother shared this fabulous recipe with me several years ago. I've found that even my friends who aren't fond of fish enjoy this particular dish and find themselves taking seconds.

—KIMBERLIE SYLVESTER LITCHFIELD, PA

START TO FINISH: 25 MIN.
MAKES: 2 SERVINGS

- 4 to 6 tablespoons sugar
- 1 tablespoon cornstarch
- ⅓ cup white vinegar
- ¼ cup water
- 1 to 2 teaspoons soy sauce
- ¼ teaspoon hot pepper sauce
- 1 tablespoon all-purpose flour
- ¼ teaspoon salt
- ⅛ to ¼ teaspoon pepper
- ½ pound halibut or swordfish fillet, cut into 2-inch strips
- 2 tablespoons canola oil
- ½ cup green pepper chunks (1 inch)
- ½ cup sweet onion chunks (1 inch)
- ½ cup pineapple chunks
  Hot cooked rice

1. In a small bowl, combine sugar and cornstarch. Stir in the vinegar, water, soy sauce and hot pepper sauce until smooth; set aside.
2. In a small resealable plastic bag, combine the flour, salt and pepper. Add fish and shake to coat. In a small skillet, saute fish in oil for 4-6 minutes or until fish flakes easily with a fork; remove and keep warm.
3. In same skillet, saute green pepper and sweet onion for 3 minutes or until crisp-tender. Add the pineapple. Stir sauce and add to skillet. Bring to a boil; cook and stir for 2 minutes or until thickened. Return fish to skillet; heat through. Serve with rice.
PER SERVING *1 cup (calculated without rice) equals 436 cal., 16 g fat (2 g sat. fat), 36 mg chol., 517 mg sodium, 47 g carb., 2 g fiber, 25 g pro.*

SHRIMP SPINACH SALAD

Shrimp and garlic are sauteed in butter then set atop a bed of spinach. Almonds, tomatoes and a squeeze of lemon finish off this beauty. Perfecto!

—JAMIE LARSON DODGE CENTER, MN

START TO FINISH: 20 MIN.
MAKES: 4 SERVINGS

- 2 tablespoons butter
- 1 pound uncooked medium shrimp, peeled and deveined
- 3 garlic cloves, minced
- 2 tablespoons minced fresh parsley
- 4 cups fresh baby spinach
- ¾ cup cherry tomatoes, halved
- ¼ cup sliced almonds, toasted
- 1 medium lemon
- ¼ teaspoon salt
- ¼ teaspoon pepper

1. In a large nonstick skillet over medium heat, melt butter. Add the shrimp. Cook and stir for 3-4 minutes or until shrimp turn pink. Add garlic and parsley; cook 1 minute longer. Remove from the heat.
2. Place spinach in a salad bowl. Top with tomatoes, almonds and shrimp mixture. Squeeze juice from the lemon; drizzle over salad. Sprinkle with salt and pepper.
PER SERVING *1 serving equals 201 cal., 10 g fat (4 g sat. fat), 153 mg chol., 350 mg sodium, 6 g carb., 2 g fiber, 21 g pro. **Diabetic Exchanges:** 3 lean meat, 1½ fat, 1 vegetable.*

SHEPHERD'S PIE
PAGE 206

Oven Entrees

Bring your **family** rushing to the table with these **heartwarming dishes.** **Cozy** potpies, **homey** meat loaves, **savory** roasts and **special** lasagnas are some of the **100+ best-loved** entrees here. Plus, you can create **memorable meals** with 32 of our **favorite** sides, salads and breads.

Beef & Ground Beef

ITALIAN CRUMB-CRUSTED
BEEF ROAST

ITALIAN CRUMB-CRUSTED BEEF ROAST

Italian-style panko crumbs and seasoning give this roast beef a special touch—it's a nice, effortless weeknight meal.

—**MARIA REGAKIS** SAUGUS, MA

PREP: 10 MIN.
BAKE: 1¾ HOURS + STANDING
MAKES: 8 SERVINGS

- 1 beef sirloin tip roast (3 pounds)
- ¼ teaspoon salt
- ¾ cup Italian-style panko (Japanese) bread crumbs
- ¼ cup mayonnaise
- 3 tablespoons dried minced onion
- ½ teaspoon Italian seasoning
- ¼ teaspoon pepper

1. Preheat oven to 325°. Place roast on a rack in a shallow roasting pan; sprinkle with salt. In a small bowl, mix remaining ingredients; press onto top and sides of roast.

2. Roast 1¾-2¼ hours or until meat reaches desired doneness (for medium-rare, a thermometer should read 145°; medium, 160°; well-done, 170°). Remove roast from the oven; tent with foil. Let stand 10 minutes before slicing.

PER SERVING *5 ounces cooked beef equals 319 cal., 15 g fat (3 g sat. fat), 111 mg chol., 311 mg sodium, 7 g carb., trace fiber, 35 g pro.* **Diabetic Exchanges:** *5 lean meat, 1 fat, ½ starch.*

CAJUN BEEF CASSEROLE

Have little ones who won't eat veggies? They won't complain one bit when you bring this cheesy casserole with a corn bread crust to the table. For picky eaters, try using less Cajun seasoning.

—**KELLY CIEPLUCH** KENOSHA, WI

PREP: 15 MIN. • **BAKE:** 25 MIN.
MAKES: 6 SERVINGS

- 1 package (8½ ounces) corn bread/muffin mix
- 1 pound ground beef
- 2 cans (14½ ounces each) diced tomatoes, drained
- 2 cups frozen mixed vegetables, thawed
- 1 can (6 ounces) tomato paste
- 1 to 2 teaspoons Cajun seasoning
- 1 cup (4 ounces) shredded cheddar cheese
- 2 green onions, thinly sliced

1. Prepare corn bread batter according to package directions. Spread in greased 11x7-in. baking dish.
2. In a large skillet, cook beef over medium heat until no longer pink; drain. Add tomatoes, vegetables, tomato paste and seasoning. Bring to a boil. Reduce the heat; simmer, uncovered, 5 minutes. Pour over batter. Sprinkle with cheese.
3. Bake casserole, uncovered, at 350° for 25-30 minutes or until golden brown. Sprinkle with onions.

FREEZE OPTION *Omit onion topping. Cool baked casserole; wrap and freeze. To use, partially thaw in refrigerator overnight. Remove 30 minutes before baking. Preheat oven to 350°. Bake as directed, increasing time as necessary to heat through and for a thermometer inserted in center to read 165°. Sprinkle cooked casserole with onions.*

CAJUN BEEF CASSEROLE

HOT CORNED BEEF BUNS

It wouldn't be St. Patrick's Day without corned beef…and folks always love these savory sandwiches. I've also placed the filling between slices of bread and cooked the sandwiches like grilled cheese.

—**TONI KEYWORTH** YALE, MI

START TO FINISH: 30 MIN.
MAKES: 6 SERVINGS

- 1 pound deli corned beef, chopped
- 1 cup (4 ounces) shredded cheddar cheese
- ⅔ cup mayonnaise
- 2 tablespoons dried minced onion
- 1 tablespoon dill or sweet pickle relish
- 2 tablespoons butter, softened
- 6 hamburger buns, split

In a bowl, combine the corned beef, cheese, mayonnaise, onion and relish. Spread butter over buns. Spoon the corned beef mixture over bottoms of buns; replace tops. Place in an ungreased 13x9-in. baking pan. Cover with foil. Bake at 425° until heated through, 15-20 minutes.

CURRIED MEAT LOAF

This meat loaf has three things going for it: rich color, out-of-the-ordinary taste and a wonderful aroma when it's baking. Plus, it's so easy!

—**DENISE KILBACK** BALGONIE, SK

PREP: 15 MIN. • **BAKE:** 1 HOUR
MAKES: 6-8 SERVINGS

- 1 large egg, beaten
- ⅓ cup milk
- ½ cup dry bread crumbs or rolled oats
- 1 garlic clove, minced
- 1 to 2 teaspoons curry powder
- 1 teaspoon ground cumin
- ½ teaspoon salt
- ½ teaspoon pepper
- 1 cup shredded carrots
- 1 medium onion, chopped
- 1½ pounds lean ground beef

Combine egg, milk, bread crumbs, garlic, seasonings, carrots and onion. Add beef; mix well. Pat mixture into a 9x5-in. loaf pan. Bake meat loaf at 350° until a thermometer reads 160° and no pink remains, 1-1¼ hours.

PHILLY CHEESESTEAKS

Steak in any capacity pleases my husband. Philly Cheesesteaks are a great dinnertime alternative to the typical burger.

—SUSAN SEYMOUR VALATIE, NY

PREP: 30 MIN. + FREEZING • **BROIL:** 5 MIN.
MAKES: 4 SERVINGS

- 1 beef top sirloin steak (1½ pounds)
- 3 tablespoons butter, divided
- 4 medium onions, halved and sliced
- 2 small green peppers, cut into thin strips
- 2 small sweet red peppers, cut into thin strips
- 1 teaspoon hot pepper sauce
- 4 submarine buns, split and toasted
- ¾ teaspoon salt
- ½ teaspoon pepper
- 8 slices cheddar cheese

1. Freeze steak 1 hour until firm but not frozen.

2. In a large skillet, heat 2 tablespoons butter over medium heat. Add onions, peppers and pepper sauce; cook and stir 5 minutes or until tender; remove and keep warm.

3. Place bun bottoms on a baking sheet, cut side up. Remove steak from freezer; cut into thin slices. Sprinkle with salt and pepper. In same skillet, heat remaining butter over medium-high heat. Add beef in batches; cook and stir 1-2 minutes or until meat is no longer pink. Remove from pan.

4. Layer bun bottoms with meat, onion mixture and cheese. Broil 4 in. from heat for 2-3 minutes or until cheese is melted. Replace tops.

CHILI TORTILLA BAKE

PREP: 20 MIN. • **BAKE:** 25 MIN.
MAKES: 6 SERVINGS

- 1 pound extra-lean ground beef (95% lean)
- 2 cans (8 ounces each) no-salt-added tomato sauce
- 1 can (15 ounces) black beans, rinsed and drained
- 1 cup frozen corn
- 1 can (4 ounces) chopped green chilies
- 2 tablespoons dried minced onion
- 2 tablespoons chili powder
- 1 teaspoon ground cumin
- ½ teaspoon garlic powder
- ½ teaspoon dried oregano
- 6 whole wheat tortillas (8 inches)
- 1 cup (4 ounces) shredded reduced-fat cheddar cheese

1. In a large skillet, cook beef over medium heat until no longer pink. Stir in the tomato sauce, beans, corn, green chilies, onion, chili powder, cumin, garlic powder and oregano; heat through.

2. In an 11x7-in. baking dish coated with cooking spray, layer half of the tortillas, beef mixture and cheese. Repeat layers. Bake, uncovered, at 350° for 25-30 minutes or until bubbly.

FREEZE OPTION *Cool unbaked casserole; cover and freeze. To use, partially thaw in the refrigerator overnight. Remove from refrigerator 30 minutes before baking. Preheat oven to 350°. Bake casserole as directed, increasing time as necessary to heat through and for a thermometer inserted in center to read 165°.*

PER SERVING *1 serving equals 413 cal., 11 g fat (4 g sat. fat), 56 mg chol., 590 mg sodium, 47 g carb., 8 g fiber, 28 g pro.*

PHILLY CHEESESTEAKS

"A homestyle Tex-Mex casserole is all it takes to gather the whole family around the dinner table. With its popular flavors and bubbly cheese topping, there is never a need to worry about leftovers." —CELINE WELDY CAVE CREEK, AZ

CHILI TORTILLA BAKE

BROCCOLI
BISCUIT SQUARES

BROCCOLI BISCUIT SQUARES

With a cheesy biscuit-like crust, these pretty squares disappear quickly at our house. We enjoy them for dinner or breakfast.

—VI JANUS PELICAN LAKE, WI

PREP: 25 MIN. • **BAKE:** 25 MIN.
MAKES: 6 SERVINGS

- 1 **pound ground beef**
- 1 **can (4 ounces) mushroom stems and pieces, drained**
- 1 **small onion, chopped**
- 2 **cups biscuit/baking mix**
- 2 **cups (8 ounces) shredded cheddar cheese, divided**
- ¼ **cup grated Parmesan cheese**
- ½ **cup water**
- 3 **cups frozen chopped broccoli, thawed and drained**
- 4 **large eggs**
- ½ **cup milk**
- 1 **teaspoon salt**
  Dash pepper

1. In a large skillet, cook the beef, mushrooms and onion over medium heat until meat is no longer pink; drain. In a large bowl, combine the biscuit mix, ½ cup cheddar cheese, Parmesan cheese and water until a soft dough forms.
2. Press dough onto the bottom and ½ in. up the sides of a greased 13x9-in. baking dish. Stir remaining cheddar cheese into the beef mixture; spread over dough. Sprinkle with broccoli.
3. In a large bowl, beat eggs, milk, salt and pepper. Pour over the meat mixture. Bake, uncovered, at 400° for 25 minutes or until a knife inserted near the center comes out clean.

OLD-FASHIONED SWISS STEAK

My husband and I have enjoyed this standby for years. The rich tomato sauce is wonderful, and the dish always brings back memories.

—VERA KLEIBER RALEIGH, NC

PREP: 20 MIN. • **BAKE:** 1½ HOURS
MAKES: 4 SERVINGS

- 2 **tablespoons all-purpose flour**
- ½ **to 1 teaspoon salt**
- ¼ **teaspoon pepper**
- 1½ **pounds beef top round steak**
- 2 **tablespoons canola oil**
- 2 **medium onions, chopped**
- 2 **cans (5½ ounces each) tomato juice**
- 1 **cup diced tomatoes**
- 4 **teaspoons lemon juice**
- 4 **teaspoons Worcestershire sauce**
- 2 **to 3 teaspoons packed brown sugar**
- 1 **teaspoon prepared mustard**

1. In a large resealable plastic bag, combine the flour, salt and pepper. Cut steak into four pieces. Add beef to bag, a few pieces at a time, and shake to coat. Remove meat from bag and pound with a mallet to tenderize.
2. In a large skillet, brown the round steak in oil on both sides. Transfer to a shallow 2-qt. baking dish coated with cooking spray.
3. In the same skillet, saute onions in drippings until tender. Stir in the remaining ingredients. Pour over meat. Cover and bake at 350° for 1½ hours or until tender.

PER SERVING *1 serving equals 359 cal., 12 g fat (2 g sat. fat), 96 mg chol., 721 mg sodium, 20 g carb., 3 g fiber, 41 g pro.* **Diabetic Exchanges:** *5 lean meat, 2 vegetable, 1½ fat, ½ starch.*

OLD-FASHIONED SWISS STEAK

WILD WEST WELLINGTONS

Here's a spicy spin-off of traditional beef Wellington. If you like your food extra-spicy, choose a hot salsa rather than mild or medium.

—**JENNI DISE** PHOENIX, AZ

PREP: 15 MIN. • **BAKE:** 20 MIN.
MAKES: 2 SERVINGS

- 2 **beef tenderloin steaks (6 ounces each)**
- ¼ **teaspoon salt**
- ¼ **teaspoon ground cumin**
- ¼ **teaspoon pepper**
- 2 **ounces cream cheese, softened**
- ¼ **cup canned chopped green chilies**
- ½ **sheet frozen puff pastry, thawed**
- 2 **teaspoons beaten egg**
- ½ **teaspoon water**
  Salsa, optional

1. Sprinkle steaks with salt, cumin and pepper. In a large nonstick skillet coated with cooking spray, brown steaks on both sides; remove and keep warm. In a small bowl, combine cream cheese and chilies; set aside.
2. On a lightly floured surface, roll pastry into a 16x12-in. rectangle. Cut into two 12x8-in. rectangles. Place a steak on one side of each rectangle; top with cream cheese mixture. Fold pastry over meat; seal seams. Place seam side down on a lightly greased baking sheet.
3. Combine egg and water; brush over pastry. Bake at 400° for 18-22 minutes or until the meat reaches desired doneness (for medium-rare, a thermometer should read 145°; medium, 160°; well-done, 170°). Let stand for 5 minutes. Serve with salsa if desired.

EAT SMART

ITALIAN BURRITOS

My family is picky, so I created the Italian Burrito loaded with beef and cheeses to satisfy everyone. It turned out great! These are quick, easy and delicious.

—**DONNA HOLTER** CENTENNIAL, CO

PREP: 20 MIN. • **BAKE:** 20 MIN.
MAKES: 8 SERVINGS

- 1 **pound lean ground beef (90% lean)**
- 1 **cup marinara sauce**
- ½ **cup shredded part-skim mozzarella cheese**
- ¼ **cup grated Parmesan cheese**
- ¼ **teaspoon garlic powder**
- 8 **whole wheat tortillas (8 inches)**

1. Preheat oven to 375°. In a large skillet, cook beef over medium heat 6-8 minutes or until no longer pink, breaking into crumbles; drain. Stir in the marinara sauce, cheeses and garlic powder.
2. Spoon ⅓ cup filling near the center of each tortilla. Fold bottom and sides of tortilla over filling and roll up. Place on a baking sheet coated with cooking spray. Bake 18-20 minutes or until bottoms are light brown.
PER SERVING *1 burrito equals 275 cal., 10 g fat (3 g sat. fat), 42 mg chol., 326 mg sodium, 26 g carb., 3 g fiber, 18 g pro. **Diabetic Exchanges:** 2 starch, 2 lean meat.*

ITALIAN BURRITOS

**MEATBALLS IN
BARBECUE SAUCE**

MEATBALLS IN BARBECUE SAUCE

When I was in high school, we made these meatballs in my home economics class. I still enjoy making them today because they taste great and you can throw them in the oven and do other things while they are baking.
—**YVONNE NAVE** LYONS, KS

PREP: 20 MIN. • **BAKE:** 30 MIN.
MAKES: ABOUT 4 DOZEN

- 1 **large egg, lightly beaten**
- 1 **can (5 ounces) evaporated milk**
- 1 **cup quick-cooking oats**
- ½ **cup finely chopped onion**
- 1 **teaspoon salt**
- 1 **teaspoon chili powder**
- ¼ **teaspoon garlic powder**
- ¼ **teaspoon pepper**
- 1½ **pounds ground beef**

SAUCE

- 1 **cup ketchup**
- ¾ **cup packed brown sugar**
- ¼ **cup chopped onion**
- ½ **teaspoon Liquid Smoke, optional**
- ¼ **teaspoon garlic powder**

1. In a large bowl, combine the egg, milk, oats, onion and seasonings. Crumble beef over mixture and mix well. Shape into 1-in. balls.
2. Place the meatballs on a greased rack in a shallow baking pan. Bake, uncovered, at 350° for 18-20 minutes or until meat is no longer pink; drain.
3. Meanwhile, combine the sauce ingredients in a saucepan. Bring to a boil. Reduce heat and simmer for 2 minutes, stirring frequently. Pour sauce over the meatballs and bake 10-12 minutes longer.

TOMATO STEAK
SANDWICHES

TOMATO STEAK SANDWICHES

When we were light on groceries one day, my husband and I came up with steak and tomatoes over bagels. They've been a favorite ever since, particularly when we need a quick dinner.

—TESSA EDWARDS PROVO, UT

START TO FINISH: 20 MIN.
MAKES: 6 SERVINGS

- 2 teaspoons canola oil
- 1 pound beef top sirloin steak, cut into thin strips
- ⅛ teaspoon salt
  Dash pepper
- 3 plain bagels, split
- ⅓ cup cream cheese, softened
- 6 thick slices tomato
- 6 slices part-skim mozzarella cheese

1. Preheat broiler. In a large skillet, heat oil over medium heat. Add beef; cook and stir until browned; drain. Stir in salt and pepper.

2. Spread cut sides of bagels with cream cheese. Transfer bagels to an ungreased baking sheet; spoon beef over bagels. Top with the tomato and mozzarella cheese. Broil 4-6 in. from heat 3-5 minutes or until cheese is melted and lightly browned.

EAT SMART

SIRLOIN WITH MUSHROOM SAUCE

START TO FINISH: 30 MIN.
MAKES: 4 SERVINGS

- 1 boneless beef sirloin steak (1 pound and ¾ inch thick)
- 1 teaspoon coarsely ground pepper
- 2 teaspoons canola oil
- 1½ cups sliced fresh mushrooms
- ½ cup beef broth
- ½ cup dry red wine or additional beef broth

1. Preheat oven to 450°. Rub steak with pepper. In a heavy ovenproof skillet, heat oil over medium-high heat. Brown steak on both sides. Transfer to oven; roast 4 minutes or until meat reaches desired doneness (for medium-rare, a thermometer should read 145°; medium, 160°; well-done, 170°).

"At the end of a busy day, nothing's better than this mouthwatering dish with rich mushroom sauce and peppery steak. Whenever visitors drop in around dinnertime, I pull out this recipe and it's ready before we know it."
—JOE ELLIOTT WEST BEND, WI

SIRLOIN WITH MUSHROOM SAUCE

2. Remove the steak from pan; tent with foil. Let meat stand 10 minutes before slicing.

3. Add mushrooms to same pan; cook and stir over medium-high heat until golden brown. Add broth and wine, stirring to loosen browned bits from pan. Bring to a boil; cook until liquid is reduced by half. Thinly slice steak; serve with mushroom sauce.

PER SERVING 3 ounces cooked beef with ¼ cup mushroom sauce equals 214 cal., 9 g fat (3 g sat. fat), 77 mg chol., 161 mg sodium, 1 g carb., trace fiber, 27 g pro. **Diabetic Exchanges:** 3 lean meat, ½ fat.

VEGETABLE BEEF CASSEROLE

This easy one-dish recipe has been a favorite ever since my husband's aunt handed it down to me 35 years ago. Make it with whatever vegetables you have on hand. A simple salad goes nicely with this dish.

—**EVANGELINE REW** MANASSAS, VA

PREP: 20 MIN.
BAKE: 1¼ HOURS + STANDING
MAKES: 6-8 SERVINGS

- **3 medium potatoes, sliced**
- **3 carrots, sliced**
- **3 celery ribs, sliced**
- **2 cups cut fresh or frozen cut green beans**
- **1 medium onion, chopped**
- **1 pound lean ground beef (90% lean)**
- **1 teaspoon dried thyme**
- **1 teaspoon salt**
- **1 teaspoon pepper**
- **4 medium tomatoes, peeled, seeded and chopped**
- **1 cup (4 ounces) shredded cheddar cheese**

1. In a 3-qt. baking dish, layer half of the potatoes, carrots, celery, green beans and onion. Crumble half of the uncooked beef over vegetables. Sprinkle with ½ teaspoon each of thyme, salt and pepper. Repeat layers.
2. Top with tomatoes. Cover and bake at 400° for 15 minutes. Reduce heat to 350°; bake about 1 hour longer or until vegetables are tender and meat is no longer pink. Sprinkle with cheese; cover and let stand until cheese is melted.

VEGETABLE BEEF
CASSEROLE

SWEET-AND-SOUR MEAT LOAF

My husband and I like basic hearty meat-and-potatoes meals. The sweet-and-sour flavor adds a deliciously different twist to this longtime standby. I hardly ever make plain meat loaf anymore. You may not, either, once you've taste this one.

—**DEBBIE HANEKE** STAFFORD, KS

PREP: 15 MIN. • **BAKE:** 1 HOUR
MAKES: 6 SERVINGS

- **1 cup dry bread crumbs**
- **1 teaspoon salt**
- **¼ teaspoon pepper**
- **2 large eggs, lightly beaten**
- **1½ pounds ground beef**
- **1 teaspoon dried minced onion**
- **1 can (15 ounces) tomato sauce, divided**
- **½ cup sugar**
- **2 tablespoons brown sugar**
- **2 tablespoons cider vinegar**
- **2 teaspoons prepared mustard**

1. In a large bowl, combine the bread crumbs, salt, pepper and the eggs; crumble beef over top and mix well. Add onion and half of the tomato sauce. Press into a 9x5-in. loaf pan.
2. Bake at 350° for 50 minutes. In a saucepan, combine the sugars, vinegar, mustard and remaining tomato sauce; bring to a boil. Pour over the meat loaf; bake 10 minutes longer or until no pink remains and a thermometer reads 160°.
FREEZE OPTION *Securely wrap and freeze cooled meat loaf in plastic wrap and foil. To use, partially thaw in the refrigerator overnight. Unwrap meat loaf; reheat on a greased 15x10x1-in. baking pan in a preheated 350° oven until meat loaf is heated through and a thermometer inserted in center reads 165°.*

SWEET-AND-SOUR
MEAT LOAF

"Onion soup mix and stuffing add lots of flavor to these meat loaves. This recipe is also handy in summer when I don't want to turn on the oven."
—**NICOLE RUSSMAN** LINCOLN, NE

BARBECUED ONION
MEAT LOAVES

BARBECUED ONION MEAT LOAVES

PREP: 20 MIN. • **BAKE:** 35 MIN.
MAKES: 5 SERVINGS

- 1 large egg, lightly beaten
- ⅓ cup milk
- 2 tablespoons plus ¼ cup barbecue sauce, divided
- ½ cup crushed seasoned stuffing
- 1 tablespoon onion soup mix
- 1¼ pounds lean ground beef (90% lean)
  Minced fresh parsley, optional

1. In a large bowl, combine the egg, milk, 2 tablespoons barbecue sauce, stuffing and onion soup mix. Crumble beef over mixture and mix well. Shape into five loaves; place in a greased shallow baking dish.

2. Bake at 350° until no pink remains and a thermometer reads 160°, about 35-40 minutes . Top with remaining barbecue sauce. If desired, sprinkle with minced parsley.

PER SERVING *1 serving equals 234 cal., 10 g fat (4 g sat. fat), 100 mg chol., 451 mg sodium, 9 g carb., 1 g fiber, 25 g pro.*

TOP TIP

LEAN GROUND BEEF
Using lean ground beef in the meat loaf instead of beef that's 80% lean saves 45 calories per serving. Lean ground beef is also 29% lower in saturated fat.

JAPANESE STEAK SALAD

My family enjoys all kinds of ethnic foods. This beef entree is easy to make, and it's very tasty. With a sweet soy marinade and fresh veggies, there's lots to love in this main-dish salad.

—**DIANE HALFERTY** CORPUS CHRISTI, TX

PREP: 25 MIN. + MARINATING
COOK: 20 MIN. • **MAKES:** 4 SERVINGS

- 3 tablespoons sherry or reduced-sodium chicken broth
- 3 tablespoons rice vinegar
- 3 tablespoons reduced-sodium soy sauce
- 2 tablespoons hoisin sauce
- ½ teaspoon minced fresh gingerroot
- 1 boneless beef sirloin steak (1 inch thick and 1¼ pounds)
- 2 green onions, chopped
- 1 tablespoon sugar
- 1 tablespoon sesame oil
- ⅓ cup fresh snow peas
- 3 cups sliced Chinese or napa cabbage
- 3 cups torn romaine
- ⅓ cup uncooked instant rice
- ½ cup julienned carrot
- ½ cup thinly sliced cucumber
- ½ cup sliced radishes

1. In a small bowl, combine the first five ingredients. Pour ⅓ cup into a large resealable plastic bag; add beef. Seal bag and turn to coat; refrigerate for at least 2 hours. For dressing, add onions, sugar and sesame oil to the remaining marinade. Cover and refrigerate until serving.

2. Preheat the broiler. In a small saucepan, bring 1 in. of water to a boil. Add peas. Reduce heat; cover peas and simmer for 2-3 minutes or until crisp-tender. Drain and immediately place peas in ice water. Drain and pat dry. Combine the cabbage, romaine and peas; place on a serving platter.

3. Drain and discard marinade. Place beef on broiler pan. Broil beef 4-6 in. from the heat 8-10 minutes on each side or until meat reaches desired doneness (for medium-rare, a thermometer should read 145°; medium, 160°; well-done, 170°). Let stand 5 minutes before slicing.

4. Meanwhile, cook rice according to package directions. Arrange the carrot, cucumber and radishes on cabbage mixture. Top with rice and beef; drizzle with dressing.

PER SERVING *1 serving equals 298 cal., 10 g fat (3 g sat. fat), 80 mg chol., 438 mg sodium, 19 g carb., 3 g fiber, 30 g pro. Diabetic Exchanges: 4 lean meat, 1 vegetable, ½ starch, ½ fat.*

EASY MEAT LOAF WELLINGTON

My family would rather have this than plain meat loaf. It's a good way to dress up an ordinary dish for company. Many people have asked for the recipe.

—**WANDA ORTON** EMPORIA, KS

PREP: 15 MIN. • **BAKE:** 70 MIN.
MAKES: 6-8 SERVINGS

- 1 can (10¼ ounces) beef gravy, divided
- 1½ cups cubed day-old bread
- ¼ cup chopped onion
- 1 large egg, beaten
- 1 teaspoon salt
- 2 pounds ground beef
- 1 tube (8 ounces) refrigerated crescent rolls

1. In a bowl, combine ¼ cup gravy, bread cubes, onion, egg and salt. Crumble beef over mixture and mix well.

2. Press into a greased 9x5-in. loaf pan. Bake, uncovered, at 375° until meat is no longer pink and a thermometer reads 160°, about 1 hour.

3. Remove loaf from pan; drain on paper towels. Place in a greased 13x9-in. baking pan. Unroll crescent dough; seal seams and perforations. Cover top and sides of meat loaf with dough; trim excess.

4. Bake until pastry is golden brown, 10-15 minutes. Heat the remaining gravy; serve with meat loaf.

SPUD-STUFFED PEPPERS

We don't care for rice, so I created a yummy stuffed pepper recipe that uses fresh potatoes from my garden.

—**JOYCE JANDERA** HANOVER, KS

PREP: 25 MIN. • **BAKE:** 40 MIN.
MAKES: 2 SERVINGS

- 2 **medium green peppers**
- ½ **pound lean ground beef (90% lean)**
- 1 **medium potato, peeled and grated**
- 1½ **teaspoons chili powder**
- ¼ **teaspoon salt**
  Dash coarsely ground pepper
- ¼ **cup shredded reduced-fat cheddar cheese**

1. Cut tops off peppers and remove seeds. In a large saucepan, cook the peppers in boiling water for 4-5 minutes. Drain and rinse in cold water; invert on paper towels.
2. In a nonstick skillet, cook beef and potato over medium heat until meat is no longer pink; drain. Stir in the chili powder, salt and pepper. Spoon into the peppers.
3. Place peppers in a small baking pan coated with cooking spray. Cover and bake at 350° 35 minutes. Sprinkle with cheese. Bake, uncovered, for 5-10 minutes longer or until the cheese is melted.

PER SERVING *1 stuffed pepper equals 332 cal., 12 g fat (6 g sat. fat), 66 mg chol., 487 mg sodium, 28 g carb., 5 g fiber, 29 g pro.* **Diabetic Exchanges:** *3 lean meat, 2 vegetable, 1 starch, 1 fat.*

BALSAMIC BRAISED POT ROAST

BALSAMIC BRAISED POT ROAST

Pot roast can be an easy, elegant way to serve a relatively inexpensive cut of meat, so I have spent years perfecting this recipe. Believe it or not, there is an art to perfect pot roast, and every time I make this dish, parents and kids alike gobble it up.

—**KELLY ANDERSON** GLENDALE, CA

PREP: 40 MIN. • **BAKE:** 2½ HOURS
MAKES: 8 SERVINGS

- 1 **boneless beef chuck roast (3 to 4 pounds)**
- 1 **teaspoon salt**
- ½ **teaspoon pepper**
- 2 **tablespoons olive oil**
- 3 **celery ribs with leaves, cut into 2-inch pieces**
- 2 **medium carrots, cut into 1-inch pieces**
- 1 **medium onion, coarsely chopped**
- 3 **medium turnips, peeled and quartered**
- 1 **large sweet potato, peeled and cubed**
- 3 **garlic cloves, minced**
- 1 **cup dry red wine or beef broth**
- 1 **can (14½ ounces) beef broth**
- ½ **cup balsamic vinegar**
- 1 **small bunch fresh thyme sprigs**
- 4 **fresh sage leaves**
- 2 **bay leaves**
- ¼ **cup cornstarch**
- ¼ **cup cold water**

1. Preheat oven to 325°. Sprinkle the roast with salt and pepper. In a Dutch oven, heat the oil over medium heat. Brown roast on all sides. Remove meat from pan.
2. Add celery, carrots and onion to the pan; cook and stir 3-4 minutes or until fragrant. Add turnips, sweet potato and garlic; cook 1 minute longer.
3. Add the wine, stirring to loosen browned bits from pan. Stir in broth, vinegar and herbs. Return roast to pan; bring to a boil. Bake, covered, 2½-3 hours or until meat is tender.
4. Remove beef and vegetables; keep warm. Discard herbs from cooking juices; skim fat. In a small bowl, mix cornstarch and water until smooth; stir into cooking juices. Bring to a boil; cook and stir for 2 minutes or until thickened. Serve with the pot roast and vegetables.

STEAK AND POTATO PIE

This hearty delight will warm you up on a chilly evening. It's the perfect comfort food for my family after a long day.
—**DOROTHEA COE** PORT ANGELES, WA

PREP: 30 MIN. • **BAKE:** 20 MIN.
MAKES: 6 SERVINGS

- ¼ cup all-purpose flour
- 2 teaspoons salt
- ½ teaspoon pepper
- ½ teaspoon paprika
  - Dash ground ginger
  - Dash ground allspice
- 1 pound beef top round steak
- 2 tablespoons canola oil
- 1 cup sliced onion
- 2 cups diced peeled potatoes
- 2 cups water

PASTRY

- 1 cup all-purpose flour
- ½ teaspoon salt
- ⅓ cup shortening
- 3 tablespoons cold water
- 1 large egg, lightly beaten

1. In a large resealable plastic bag, combine the flour, salt, pepper, paprika, ginger and allspice; set aside 2 tablespoons. Add meat to bag; seal and toss to coat.

2. In a large skillet, cook meat and onions in oil over medium-high heat until meat is no longer pink and onion is tender. Gradually stir in reserved flour mixture. Add potatoes and water; bring to a boil. Cook and stir until thickened, 1-2 minutes. Reduce heat; simmer, uncovered, potatoes are tender, 20 minutes.

3. Meanwhile, for pastry, in a large bowl, combine flour and salt. Cut in shortening. Gradually add water, tossing with a fork until dough forms a ball.

4. Divide pastry in half so one ball is slightly larger than the other. On a lightly floured surface, roll out larger ball to fit a 9-in. deep-dish pie plate. Transfer pastry to pie plate. Trim pastry even with edge of plate. Add filling. Roll out remaining pastry to fit top of pie; place over filling. Trim, seal and flute edges. Cut slits in top.

5. Brush top with egg. Bake at 450° until golden brown, 20-25 minutes. Serve immediately.

MEATBALL PIE

I grew up on a farm, so I took part in 4-H Club cooking activities. I still love to prepare and serve classic, wholesome recipes like this meat and veggie pie.
—**SUSAN KEITH** FORT PLAIN, NY

PREP: 50 MIN. • **BAKE:** 45 MIN. + STANDING
MAKES: 6 SERVINGS

- 1 pound ground beef
- ¾ cup soft bread crumbs
- ¼ cup chopped onion
- 2 tablespoons minced fresh parsley
- 1 teaspoon salt
- ½ teaspoon dried marjoram
- ⅛ teaspoon pepper
- ¼ cup milk
- 1 large egg, lightly beaten
- 1 can (14½ ounces) stewed tomatoes
- 1 tablespoon cornstarch
- 2 teaspoons beef bouillon granules
- 1 cup frozen peas
- 1 cup sliced carrots, cooked

CRUST

- 2⅔ cups all-purpose flour
- ½ teaspoon salt
- 1 cup shortening
- 7 to 8 tablespoons ice water
  - Half-and-half cream

1. In a large bowl, combine the first nine ingredients (mixture will be soft). Divide into fourths; shape each portion into 12 small meatballs. Brown meatballs in batches in a large skillet; drain and set aside.

2. Drain tomatoes, reserving liquid. Combine liquid with cornstarch; pour into skillet. Add tomatoes and bouillon; bring to a boil over medium heat, stirring constantly. Stir in peas and carrots. Remove from heat and set aside.

3. Preheat oven to 400°. For crust, in a large bowl, combine flour and salt. Cut in shortening until mixture resembles coarse crumbs. Add water, 1 tablespoon at a time, tossing lightly with a fork. Transfer to a lightly floured surface. Knead gently to form a dough. (Mixture will be very crumbly at first, but will come together and form a dough as it's kneaded.) Divide dough in half.

4. Roll each half of dough between two pieces of lightly floured waxed paper to a ⅛-in.-thick circle. Remove top piece of waxed paper from one pastry circle; invert onto a 9-in. deep-dish pie plate. Remove the remaining waxed paper. Trim pastry even with rim. Add the meatballs; spoon tomato mixture over top.

5. Remove top piece of waxed paper from remaining pastry circle; invert onto pie. Remove remaining waxed paper. Trim, seal and flute edge. Cut slits in top; brush with cream.

6. Bake until crust is golden brown, 45-50 minutes. Cover edges loosely with foil during the last 10 minutes if needed to prevent overbrowning. Let stand 10 minutes before cutting.

MEATBALL PIE

BEEF AND
MUSHROOM POTPIES

FREEZE IT
ITALIAN BEEF PATTIES

START TO FINISH: 25 MIN.
MAKES: 6 SERVINGS

- ⅔ **cup pizza sauce, divided**
- 1 **large egg, beaten**
- ⅓ **cup dry bread crumbs**
- 2 **teaspoons dried minced onion**
- ½ **teaspoon dried oregano**
- ¼ **teaspoon salt**
- ⅛ **teaspoon pepper**
- 1½ **pounds ground beef**
- 3 **slices part-skim mozzarella cheese, halved**

1. In a large bowl, combine ⅓ cup pizza sauce, egg, bread crumbs, onion, oregano, salt and pepper. Crumble beef over mixture and mix well. Shape into six patties. Place on a broiler pan coated with cooking spray.

2. Broil 6 in. from the heat for 5-6 minutes on each side or until juices run clear, basting frequently with remaining pizza sauce. Top with cheese. Broil 1 minute longer or until cheese is melted.

FREEZE OPTION *Prepare uncooked patties and freeze, covered, on a plastic wrap-lined baking sheet until firm. Transfer patties to a large resealable plastic bag; return to freezer. To use, cook frozen patties and top with cheese as directed, increasing cooking time as necessary for a thermometer to read 160°.*

BEEF AND
MUSHROOM POTPIES

My husband and I absolutely love potpies, and preparing them together makes them even more enjoyable! Skip the homemade pie dough and let a package of crescent rolls fill in. You can double the recipe and make it in a large casserole so it's even easier.

—**MACEY ALLEN** GREEN FOREST, AR

PREP: 40 MIN. • **BAKE:** 20 MIN.
MAKES: 4 SERVINGS

- 1½ **cups cubed peeled potatoes**
- 1 **pound beef top sirloin steak, cut into ¼-inch pieces**
- 2 **tablespoons olive oil, divided**
- 1 **large red onion, chopped**
- 2 **cups sliced fresh mushrooms**
- 1 **cup frozen sliced carrots**
- 1 **cup frozen peas**
- 2 **tablespoons ketchup**
- 1 **teaspoon pepper**
- 1 **tablespoon cornstarch**
- 1 **cup sour cream**
- 1 **cup beef gravy**
- 1 **tube (8 ounces) refrigerated crescent rolls**

1. Place potatoes in a microwave-safe dish; cover with water. Cover and microwave on high for 7-8 minutes or until tender; drain and set aside.

2. In a large skillet, saute beef in 1 tablespoon oil in batches until no longer pink. Remove and set aside.

3. In the same pan, saute onion and mushrooms in remaining oil until tender; add the carrots, peas, ketchup and pepper. Combine the cornstarch, sour cream and gravy until blended; stir into pan and heat through. Stir in potatoes and beef. Divide mixture among four greased 16-oz. ramekins.

4. Remove crescent roll dough from tube, but do not unroll; cut dough into 16 slices. Cut each slice in half. Arrange seven pieces, curved sides out, around the edge of each ramekin. Press the dough slightly to secure in place. Place remaining pieces on the center of each. Place the ramekins on a baking sheet.

5. Bake at 375° for 17-20 minutes or until filling is bubbly and crusts are golden brown.

> **TOP TIP**
>
> ## DRIED MINCED ONION
> You can substitute dried minced onion from the spice aisle for chopped onion in casseroles, soups, meat loaves and other cooked recipes. One tablespoon of dried minced onion equals ¼ cup minced raw onion.

"Make these pizza-flavored patties and watch the kids devour dinner! Give them a try on rice or with a side of deli pasta salad for a super-fast fix."
—**DEANNA MACIEJEWSKI** BRIDGETON, MO

ITALIAN BEEF PATTIES

BEEF & MUSHROOM
BRAISED STEW

BEEF & MUSHROOM BRAISED STEW

Every spring, my family heads out to our timber acreage to collect morel mushrooms, and then we cook up this stew. We use morels, of course, but baby portobellos or button mushrooms will work, too.

—AMY WERTHEIM ATLANTA, IL

PREP: 35 MIN. • **BAKE:** 1½ HOURS
MAKES: 6 SERVINGS

- 1 boneless beef chuck roast (2 to 3 pounds), cut into 1-inch cubes
- ¼ teaspoon salt
- ¼ teaspoon pepper
- 3 tablespoons olive oil
- 1 pound sliced fresh mushrooms
- 2 medium onions, sliced
- 2 garlic cloves, minced
- 1 carton (32 ounces) beef broth
- 1 cup dry red wine or additional beef broth
- ½ cup brandy
- 1 tablespoon tomato paste
- ¼ teaspoon each dried parsley flakes, rosemary, sage leaves, tarragon and thyme
- 3 tablespoons all-purpose flour
- 3 tablespoons water
  Hot mashed potatoes

1. Preheat oven to 325°. Sprinkle beef with salt and pepper. In an ovenproof Dutch oven, heat oil over medium heat; brown beef in batches. Remove from pan.

2. Add mushrooms and onions to pan; cook and stir until tender. Add garlic; cook 1 minute longer. Stir in broth, wine, brandy, tomato paste and herbs. Return beef to the pan. Bring to a boil.

3. Bake, covered, 1 hour. In a small bowl, mix the flour and water until smooth; gradually stir into stew. Bake, covered, 30 minutes longer or until stew is thickened and beef is tender. Skim fat. Serve stew with potatoes.

FREEZE OPTION *Freeze cooled stew in freezer containers. To use, partially thaw stew in refrigerator overnight. Heat through in a saucepan, stirring occasionally and adding a little broth or water if necessary.*

TEXAS-STYLE LASAGNA

With its spicy flavor, this dish is a real crowd-pleaser. It goes great with side servings of picante sauce, guacamole and tortilla chips.

—EFFIE GISH FORT WORTH, TX

PREP: 40 MIN. • **BAKE:** 30 MIN. + STANDING
MAKES: 12 SERVINGS

- 1½ pounds ground beef
- 1 teaspoon seasoned salt
- 1 package (1¼ ounces) taco seasoning
- 1 can (14½ ounces) diced tomatoes, undrained
- 1 can (15 ounces) tomato sauce
- 1 can (4 ounces) chopped green chilies
- 2 cups (16 ounces) 4% cottage cheese
- 2 large eggs, lightly beaten
- 12 corn tortillas (6 inches), torn
- 3½ to 4 cups shredded Monterey Jack cheese
  Optional toppings: crushed tortilla chips, salsa and cubed avocado

1. In a large skillet, cook beef over medium heat until no longer pink; drain. Add the seasoned salt, taco seasoning mix, tomatoes, tomato sauce and chilies. Reduce heat; simmer mixture, uncovered, for 15-20 minutes. In a small bowl, combine cottage cheese and eggs.

2. In a greased 13x9-in. baking dish, layer half of each of the following: meat sauce, tortillas, the cottage cheese mixture and Monterey Jack cheese. Repeat layers.

3. Bake lasagna, uncovered, at 350° for 30 minutes or until bubbly. Let stand 10 minutes before serving. Garnish with toppings if desired.

FREEZE OPTION *Before baking, cover and freeze the lasagna up to 3 months. Thaw in the refrigerator overnight. Remove from refrigerator 30 minutes before baking. Bake as directed, increasing time as necessary for a thermometer to read 160°.*

WHISKEY SIRLOIN STEAK

Tender and slightly sweet from the marinade, this juicy steak boasts wonderful flavor and oh-so-easy preparation. Serve with potatoes and a green vegetable for a complete meal.

—TASTE OF HOME TEST KITCHEN

PREP: 10 MIN. + MARINATING
BROIL: 15 MIN. • **MAKES:** 4 SERVINGS

- ¼ cup whiskey or apple cider
- ¼ cup reduced-sodium soy sauce
- 1 tablespoon sugar
- 1 garlic clove, thinly sliced
- ½ teaspoon ground ginger
- 1 beef top sirloin steak (1 pound and 1 inch thick)

1. In a large resealable plastic bag, combine the first five ingredients; add the beef. Seal bag and turn to coat; refrigerate for 8 hours or overnight.

2. Drain and discard marinade. Place beef on a broiler pan coated with cooking spray. Broil 4-6 in. from the heat for 7-8 minutes on each side or until meat reaches desired doneness (for medium-rare, a thermometer should read 145°; medium, 160°; well-done, 170°).

PER SERVING *3 ounces cooked beef equals 168 cal., 5 g fat (2 g sat. fat), 46 mg chol., 353 mg sodium, 2 g carb., trace fiber, 25 g pro.* **Diabetic Exchange:** *3 lean meat.*

ITALIAN MEATBALL TORTES

With classic Italian flavor, these hearty dinner pies filled with tomatoes, mozzarella and savory homemade meatballs will be a hit with your family. Preparation takes some time, but the results are well worth it.

—**SANDY BLESSING** OCEAN SHORES, WA

PREP: 1¼ HOURS + RISING • **BAKE:** 30 MIN.
MAKES: 2 TORTES (6 SERVINGS EACH)

- 1 package (¼ ounce) active dry yeast
- ¼ cup warm water (110° to 115°)
- ¾ cup warm milk (110° to 115°)
- ¼ cup sugar
- ¼ cup shortening
- 1 large egg
- 1 teaspoon salt
- 3½ to 3¾ cups all-purpose flour

MEATBALLS

- 1 can (5 ounces) evaporated milk
- 2 large eggs, lightly beaten
- 1 cup quick-cooking oats
- 1 cup crushed saltines
- ½ cup chopped onion
- ½ cup chopped celery
- 2 teaspoons salt
- 2 teaspoons chili powder
- ½ teaspoon garlic powder
- ½ teaspoon pepper
- 3 pounds ground beef

FILLING

- 1 can (15 ounces) crushed tomatoes
- ½ cup chopped onion
- ⅓ cup grated Parmesan cheese
- 1½ teaspoons dried basil
- 1½ teaspoons dried oregano
- 1 teaspoon minced fresh parsley
- 1 teaspoon salt
- 1½ cups (6 ounces) shredded part-skim mozzarella cheese

1. In a large bowl, dissolve yeast in warm water. Add the milk, sugar, shortening, egg, salt and 2 cups flour. Beat until smooth. Stir in enough remaining flour to form a soft dough.

2. Turn dough onto a floured surface; knead until smooth and elastic, about 6-8 minutes. Place in a greased bowl, turning once to grease the top. Cover and let rise in a warm place until doubled, 1-1½ hours.

3. In a large bowl, combine the milk, eggs, oats, saltines, onion, celery and seasonings. Crumble beef over the mixture and mix well. Shape into 1½-in. balls. In a large skillet over medium heat, cook meatballs in batches until no longer pink.

4. Meanwhile, place tomatoes and onion in a small saucepan. Bring to a boil. Reduce heat; simmer, uncovered, for 10 minutes or until the mixture is slightly thickened. Stir in Parmesan cheese, herbs and salt.

5. Punch dough down. Divide into three portions. Roll two portions into 11-in. circles; line the bottoms and press partially up the sides of two greased 9-in. springform pans. Roll the third portion of dough into a 12x10-in. rectangle; cut into twelve 10x1-in. strips.

6. Place meatballs in prepared crusts; top with the tomato mixture and the mozzarella cheese. Make lattice crusts with strips of dough; trim and seal edges. Cover and let rise 30 minutes.

7. Preheat oven to 350°. Bake tortes 30-35 minutes or until golden brown. Cut into wedges.

ROADSIDE DINER CHEESEBURGER QUICHE

Here is an unforgettable quiche that tastes just like its burger counterpart. Easy and appealing, it's perfect for guests and fun for the whole family.

—**BARB MILLER** OAKDALE, MN

PREP: 20 MIN. • **BAKE:** 50 MIN. + STANDING
MAKES: 8 SERVINGS

- 1 sheet refrigerated pie pastry
- ¾ pound ground beef
- 2 plum tomatoes, seeded and chopped
- 1 medium onion, chopped
- ½ cup dill pickle relish
- ½ cup crumbled cooked bacon
- 5 large eggs
- 1 cup heavy whipping cream
- ½ cup 2% milk
- 2 teaspoons prepared mustard
- 1 teaspoon hot pepper sauce
- ½ teaspoon salt
- ¼ teaspoon pepper
- 1½ cups (6 ounces) shredded cheddar cheese
- ½ cup shredded Parmesan cheese
  Optional garnishes: mayonnaise, additional pickle relish, crumbled cooked bacon, and chopped onion and tomato

1. Unroll pastry into a 9-in. deep-dish pie plate; flute edges and set aside. In a large skillet, cook beef over medium heat until no longer pink; drain. Stir in the tomatoes, onion, relish and bacon. Transfer to prepared pastry.

2. In a large bowl, whisk eggs, cream, milk, mustard, pepper sauce, salt and pepper. Pour over the beef mixture. Sprinkle with cheeses.

3. Bake at 375° for 50-60 minutes or until a knife inserted in center comes out clean. Cover edges with foil during last 15 minutes if necessary to prevent overbrowning. Let stand 10 minutes before cutting. If desired, garnish with optional ingredients.

BAKED SPAGHETTI

It takes a little longer to make baked spaghetti, but the difference in taste, texture and richness is well worth the time. I serve this lasagna-style dish with a tossed green salad and breadsticks for a hearty, healthy meal.

—**BETTY RABE** MAHTOMEDI, MN

PREP: 20 MIN. • **BAKE:** 30 MIN. + STANDING
MAKES: 6 SERVINGS

- 8 **ounces uncooked spaghetti, broken into thirds**
- 1 **large egg**
- ½ **cup fat-free milk**
- ½ **pound lean ground beef (90% lean)**
- ½ **pound Italian turkey sausage links, casings removed**
- 1 **small onion, chopped**
- ¼ **cup chopped green pepper**
- 1 **jar (14 ounces) meatless spaghetti sauce**
- 1 **can (8 ounces) no-salt-added tomato sauce**
- ½ **cup shredded part-skim mozzarella cheese**

1. Cook spaghetti according to package directions; drain. In a large bowl, beat egg and milk. Add the spaghetti; toss to coat. Transfer to a 13x9-in. baking dish coated with cooking spray.

2. In a large skillet, cook the beef, sausage, onion and green pepper over medium heat until meat is no longer pink; drain. Stir in spaghetti sauce and tomato sauce. Spoon over the spaghetti mixture.

3. Bake casserole, uncovered, at 350° for 20 minutes. Sprinkle with the cheese. Bake 10 minutes longer or until cheese is melted. Let stand for 10 minutes before cutting.

PER SERVING *1 serving equals 343 cal., 10 g fat (3 g sat. fat), 87 mg chol., 616 mg sodium, 39 g carb., 3 g fiber, 23 g pro.* **Diabetic Exchanges:** *2 starch, 2 medium-fat meat, 1 vegetable.*

BAKED SPAGHETTI

Poultry

TURKEY SAUSAGE-STUFFED ACORN SQUASH

Finding healthy recipes the family will eat is a challenge. This elegant squash is one we love, and it works with pork, turkey and chicken sausage.

—**MELISSA PELKEY-HASS** WALESKA, GA

PREP: 30 MIN. • **BAKE:** 50 MIN.
MAKES: 8 SERVINGS

- 4 **medium acorn squash (about 1½ pounds each)**
- 1 **cup cherry tomatoes, halved**
- 1 **pound Italian turkey sausage links, casings removed**
- ½ **pound sliced fresh mushrooms**
- 1 **medium apple, peeled and finely chopped**
- 1 **small onion, finely chopped**
- 2 **teaspoons fennel seed**
- 2 **teaspoons caraway seeds**
- ½ **teaspoon dried sage leaves**
- 3 **cups fresh baby spinach**
- 1 **tablespoon minced fresh thyme**
- ¼ **teaspoon salt**
- ⅛ **teaspoon pepper**
- 8 **ounces fresh mozzarella cheese, chopped**
- 1 **tablespoon red wine vinegar**

TURKEY SAUSAGE-STUFFED ACORN SQUASH

1. Preheat oven to 400°. Cut squash lengthwise in half; remove and discard seeds. Using a sharp knife, cut a thin slice from bottom of each half to allow them to lie flat. Place the squash in a shallow roasting pan, hollow side down; add ¼ in. of hot water and halved tomatoes. Bake, uncovered, 45 minutes.

2. Meanwhile, in a large skillet, cook sausage, mushrooms, apple, onion and dried seasonings over medium heat 8-10 minutes or until sausage is no longer pink, breaking up sausage into crumbles; drain. Add spinach, thyme, salt and pepper; cook and stir 2 minutes. Remove from heat.

3. Carefully remove squash from roasting pan. Drain cooking liquid, reserving tomatoes. Return squash to pan, hollow side up.

4. Stir the cheese, vinegar and reserved tomatoes into the sausage mixture. Spoon into squash cavities. Bake 5-10 minutes longer or until heated through and squash is easily pierced with a fork.

PER SERVING *1 stuffed squash half equals 302 cal., 10 g fat (5 g sat. fat), 43 mg chol., 370 mg sodium, 42 g carb., 7 g fiber, 15 g pro.* **Diabetic Exchanges:** *2½ starch, 2 medium-fat meat.*

TROPICAL LIME CHICKEN

TROPICAL LIME CHICKEN

This recipe has long been a family favorite. I found it many years ago in a recipe book and altered it to fit what we like. Every time I make it, I change up the salsa. You can add papaya, green pepper or any other good-for-you ingredients.

—JENNIFER EILTS LINCOLN, NE

PREP: 20 MIN. + MARINATING
COOK: 10 MIN.
MAKES: 4 SERVINGS (1 CUP SALSA)

SALSA
- ½ cup pineapple tidbits
- 1 medium kiwifruit, peeled and chopped
- ¼ cup chopped sweet red pepper
- 1 tablespoon lime juice
- 1 tablespoon white wine vinegar
- 1 tablespoon honey
- 1 teaspoon crushed red pepper flakes

CHICKEN
- 3 tablespoons plus 1½ teaspoons lime juice
- 1 tablespoon canola oil

- 1 teaspoon grated lime peel
- ⅛ teaspoon salt
- ⅛ teaspoon pepper
- 4 boneless skinless chicken breast halves (4 ounces each)
- 1 cup uncooked couscous

1. In a small bowl, combine the salsa ingredients; cover and refrigerate until serving.
2. In a large resealable plastic bag, combine the lime juice, oil, lime peel, salt and pepper; add chicken. Seal bag and turn to coat; refrigerate for 2-4 hours.
3. Drain and discard marinade. Place chicken on a broiler pan coated with cooking spray. Broil 3 in. from the heat for 5-6 minutes on each side or until juices run clear. Meanwhile, cook the couscous according to package directions. Serve with the chicken and salsa.

ALMOND TURKEY CASSEROLE

My husband and I have enjoyed cooking together since we were married more than 40 years ago. We love this one. We make it whenever we have leftover turkey or chicken.

—LUCILLE ROWLAND STILLWATER, MN

PREP: 20 MIN. • **BAKE:** 20 MIN.
MAKES: 4 SERVINGS

- 2 cups uncooked egg noodles
- 1 package (9 ounces) frozen broccoli cuts
- 2 tablespoons butter
- 2 tablespoons all-purpose flour
- 1 teaspoon salt
- ½ teaspoon ground mustard
- ¼ teaspoon pepper
- 1½ cups milk
- 1 cup (4 ounces) shredded Swiss cheese
- 2 cups cubed cooked turkey
- ½ cup slivered almonds, toasted

1. Cook the noodles according to package directions; drain. Cook the broccoli according to package directions; drain. Place noodles and broccoli in a large bowl; set aside.
2. In a large saucepan, melt the butter. Stir in the flour, salt, mustard and pepper until smooth. Gradually stir in milk. Bring to a boil; cook and stir for 2 minutes or until thickened. Remove from the heat; stir in cheese until melted. Add the turkey; pour over noodle mixture.
3. Transfer to a greased 1½-qt. baking dish. Sprinkle with almonds. Bake, uncovered, at 350° for 20-25 minutes or until heated through.

FREEZE IT
TURKEY MEAT LOAF

I switched up my mom's classic meat loaf recipe with ground turkey instead of beef, and added chopped bell peppers. My turkey loaf is a favorite at church potlucks.
—**JOHN COTTI-DIAZ** DEL RIO, TX

PREP: 20 MIN. • **BAKE:** 50 MIN.
MAKES: 6 SERVINGS

- 1 large egg, lightly beaten
- 1 can (8 ounces) tomato sauce, divided
- 1 cup soft bread crumbs
- ¼ cup finely chopped onion
- ¼ cup finely chopped green pepper
- ¼ cup finely chopped sweet red pepper
- 1½ teaspoons garlic powder
- ¼ teaspoon salt
- ⅛ teaspoon pepper
- 1½ pounds lean ground turkey
- 1 can (10¾ ounces) reduced-sodium condensed tomato soup, undiluted
- 2 tablespoons brown sugar
- 2 tablespoons cider vinegar
- 2 tablespoons ketchup
- 2 tablespoons prepared mustard

1. In a large bowl, combine the egg, ½ cup tomato sauce, bread crumbs, onion, peppers, garlic powder, salt and pepper. Crumble turkey over mixture and mix well.

2. In an 11x7-in. baking dish coated with cooking spray, pat the turkey mixture into a 9x4-in. loaf. Bake, uncovered, at 350° for 30 minutes; drain if necessary.

3. Meanwhile, combine the soup, brown sugar, vinegar, ketchup, mustard and remaining tomato sauce. Pour ½ cup over meat loaf. Bake for 20-30 minutes longer or until a thermometer reads 165° and juices run clear. Warm remaining sauce; serve with meat loaf.

FREEZE OPTION *Cover and freeze unbaked meat loaf and remaining sauce in separate freezer containers for up to 3 months. Thaw in refrigerator overnight. Bake as directed.*

TURKEY MEAT LOAF

CHICKEN CAESAR PIZZA

Dressed greens on top of pizza may sound strange, but trust me when I say the result is fantastic!
—**TRACY YOUNGMAN** POST FALLS, ID

START TO FINISH: 30 MIN.
MAKES: 6 SERVINGS

- 1 tube (13.8 ounces) refrigerated pizza crust
- 1 tablespoon olive oil
- 1 pound boneless skinless chicken breasts, cut into ½-inch cubes
- 1½ teaspoons minced garlic, divided
- 6 tablespoons creamy Caesar salad dressing, divided
- 2 cups (8 ounces) shredded Monterey Jack cheese
- ½ cup grated Parmesan cheese
- 2 cups hearts of romaine salad mix
- 2 green onions, thinly sliced
- 2 plum tomatoes, chopped

1. Preheat oven to 400°. Unroll pizza crust and press to fit into a greased 15x10x1-in. baking pan, pinching edges to form a rim. Bake 10 minutes or until edges are lightly browned.

2. Meanwhile, in a large skillet, heat oil over medium-high heat. Add the chicken and ½ teaspoon garlic; cook and stir until chicken is no longer pink. Remove from the heat; stir in 2 tablespoons salad dressing. Spread the crust with 3 tablespoons salad dressing; sprinkle with remaining garlic. Top with half of the cheeses and all of the chicken. Sprinkle with the remaining cheeses. Bake pizza for 10-15 minutes or until crust is golden brown and cheese is melted.

3. Toss the salad mix and green onions with remaining dressing. Just before serving, top pizza with salad and tomatoes.

READER RAVE

"I made this with ready-made chicken and garlic flatbread to save time on a busy day. It turned out fabulous."
—**ALISAHINTON**
FROM TASTEOFHOME.COM

CHICKEN
CAESAR PIZZA

CHICKEN TACO PIE

HONEY-BRINED TURKEY BREAST

This recipe will give you a beautiful, lightly salted turkey roast. I prefer to use cider or apple juice instead of water for my brine.

—**DEIRDRE COX** KANSAS CITY, MO

PREP: 50 MIN. + CHILLING
BAKE: 1¾ HOURS • **MAKES:** 8 SERVINGS

- 2 quarts apple cider or juice
- ½ cup kosher salt
- ⅓ cup honey
- 2 tablespoons Dijon mustard
- 1½ teaspoons crushed red pepper flakes
- 1 fresh rosemary sprig
- 2 large oven roasting bags
- 1 bone-in turkey breast (4 to 5 pounds)
- 1 tablespoon olive oil

1. In a Dutch oven, bring the first five ingredients to a boil. Cook and stir until salt and honey are dissolved. Stir in rosemary. Remove from the heat; cool to room temperature. Refrigerate until chilled.
2. Place a large oven roasting bag inside a second roasting bag; add the turkey breast. Carefully pour brine into bag. Squeeze out as much air as possible; seal bags and turn to coat. Place in a roasting pan. Refrigerate for 8 hours or overnight, turning occasionally.
3. Line the bottom of a large shallow roasting pan with foil. Drain turkey and discard brine; place on a rack in prepared pan. Pat dry.
4. Bake, uncovered, at 325° for 30 minutes. Brush with oil. Bake for 1½-2 hours longer or until a thermometer reads 170°. (Cover loosely with foil if the turkey browns too quickly.) Cover and let stand for 15 minutes before carving.
NOTE *This recipe was tested with Morton brand kosher salt. It is best not to use a prebasted turkey breast for this recipe. However, if you do, omit the salt in the recipe.*
PER SERVING *6 ounces cooked turkey equals 208 cal., 3 g fat (1 g sat. fat), 117 mg chol., 131 mg sodium, trace carb., trace fiber, 43 g pro.* **Diabetic Exchange:** *6 lean meat.*

CHICKEN TACO PIE

I turn to this taco pie meal on busy nights when we've been rushing to soccer, swimming lessons or Scouts. I put it together in the morning and just pop it in the oven when we get home.

—**KAREN LATIMER** WINNIPEG, MB

PREP: 20 MIN. • **BAKE:** 30 MIN.
MAKES: 6 SERVINGS

- 1 tube (8 ounces) refrigerated crescent rolls
- 1 pound ground chicken
- 1 envelope taco seasoning
- 1 can (4 ounces) chopped green chilies
- ½ cup water
- ½ cup salsa
- ½ cup shredded Mexican cheese blend
- 1 cup shredded lettuce
- 1 small sweet red pepper, chopped
- 1 small green pepper, chopped
- 1 medium tomato, seeded and chopped
- 1 green onion, thinly sliced
- 2 tablespoons pickled jalapeno slices
  Sour cream and additional salsa

1. Preheat oven to 350°. Unroll the crescent dough and separate into triangles. Press onto bottom of a greased 9-in. pie plate to form a crust, sealing seams. Bake 18-20 minutes or until golden brown.
2. Meanwhile, in a large skillet, cook the chicken over medium heat for 6-8 minutes or until no longer pink, breaking into crumbles; drain. Stir in taco seasoning, green chilies, water and salsa; bring to a boil.
3. Spoon into crust; sprinkle with cheese. Bake 8-10 minutes or until cheese is melted.
4. Top pie with lettuce, peppers, tomato, green onion and pickled jalapeno. Serve with sour cream and additional salsa.

CHICKEN 'N' BISCUITS

Give my chicken with biscuits a try when you need a down-home meal. The golden homemade biscuits on top make this a comforting choice when the weather turns cool.

—MARILYN MINNICK HILLSBORO, IN

PREP: 25 MIN. • **BAKE:** 30 MIN.
MAKES: 8 SERVINGS

- 1 medium onion, chopped
- 2 teaspoons canola oil
- ¼ cup all-purpose flour
- ½ teaspoon dried basil
- ½ teaspoon dried thyme
- ¼ teaspoon pepper
- 2½ cups fat-free milk
- 1 tablespoon Worcestershire sauce
- 1 package (16 ounces) frozen mixed vegetables
- 2 cups cubed cooked chicken
- 2 tablespoons grated Parmesan cheese

BISCUITS
- 1 cup all-purpose flour
- 1 tablespoon sugar
- 1½ teaspoons baking powder
- ¼ teaspoon salt
- ⅓ cup fat-free milk
- 3 tablespoons canola oil
- 1 tablespoon minced fresh parsley

1. In a large saucepan, saute the onion in oil until tender. Stir in the flour, basil, thyme and pepper until blended. Gradually stir in milk and Worcestershire sauce until smooth. Bring to a boil; cook and stir for 2 minutes or until thickened. Stir in the vegetables, chicken and cheese; reduce heat to low.

2. Meanwhile, in a large bowl, combine the flour, sugar, baking powder and salt. In a small bowl, combine the milk, oil and parsley; stir into dry ingredients just until combined.

3. Transfer hot chicken mixture to a greased 2½-qt. baking dish. Drop biscuit batter by rounded tablespoonfuls onto chicken mixture.

4. Bake, uncovered, at 375° for 30-40 minutes or until biscuits are lightly browned.

PER SERVING *One serving equals 246 cal., 8 g fat (0 g sat. fat), 24 mg chol., 284 mg sodium, 31 g carb., 0 g fiber, 13 g pro.* **Diabetic Exchanges:** *2 starch, 1 meat, ½ fat.*

OVEN-FRIED CHICKEN WITH CRANBERRY SAUCE

Pair crispy oven-fried chicken with tangy cranberry sauce for a tempting entree.

—DONNA NOEL GRAY, ME

START TO FINISH: 30 MIN.
MAKES: 4 SERVINGS (1 CUP SAUCE)

- ½ cup dry bread crumbs
- 2 tablespoons grated Parmesan cheese
- 2 tablespoons toasted wheat germ
- 2 garlic cloves, minced
- ½ teaspoon paprika
- ¼ teaspoon each dried oregano, thyme and rosemary, crushed
- ¼ teaspoon pepper
- 4 boneless skinless chicken breast halves (4 ounces each)

SAUCE
- 1 cup jellied cranberry sauce
- 2 tablespoons lime juice
- 1 tablespoon balsamic vinegar
- 1½ teaspoons Dijon mustard

1. In a large resealable plastic bag, combine the bread crumbs, cheese, wheat germ, garlic and seasonings. Add chicken, one piece at a time, and shake to coat. Place on a baking sheet coated with cooking spray.

2. Bake at 375° for 20-25 minutes or until a thermometer reads 170°, turning once.

3. Meanwhile, in a small saucepan, bring cranberry sauce to a boil. Remove from the heat; whisk in the lime juice, vinegar and mustard. Serve with chicken.

OVEN-FRIED CHICKEN
WITH CRANBERRY SAUCE

"This chunky stew makes a hearty supper, especially in the fall and winter. Plus, it's a great way to use extra turkey during the holidays."
—LORI SCHLECHT WIMBLEDON, ND

TURKEY
BISCUIT STEW

TURKEY BISCUIT STEW

PREP: 15 MIN. • **BAKE:** 20 MIN.
MAKES: 6-8 SERVINGS

- ⅓ cup chopped onion
- ¼ cup butter, cubed
- ⅓ cup all-purpose flour
- ½ teaspoon salt
- ⅛ teaspoon pepper
- 1 can (10½ ounces) condensed chicken broth, undiluted
- ¾ cup milk
- 2 cups cubed cooked turkey
- 1 cup cooked peas
- 1 cup cooked whole baby carrots
- 1 tube (10 ounces) refrigerated buttermilk biscuits

1. In a 10-in. ovenproof skillet, saute onion in butter until tender. Stir in the flour, salt and pepper until blended. Gradually add broth and milk. Bring to a boil. Cook and stir for 2 minutes or until thickened and bubbly. Add the turkey, peas and carrots; heat through. Separate the biscuits and arrange over the stew.
2. Bake at 375° for 20-25 minutes or until biscuits are golden brown.

MEXICAN MANICOTTI

Combining Italian pasta and Mexican ingredients creates an exceptional dish. This recipe is well-liked, even in Cajun country Louisiana!

—**LARRY PHILLIPS** SHREVEPORT, LA

PREP: 25 MIN. • **BAKE:** 25 MIN.
MAKES: 2 SERVINGS

- 4 uncooked manicotti shells
- 1 cup cubed cooked chicken breast
- 1 cup salsa, divided
- ½ cup ricotta cheese
- 2 tablespoons sliced ripe olives
- 4 teaspoons minced fresh parsley
- 1 tablespoon diced pimientos
- 1 green onion, thinly sliced
- 1 small garlic clove, minced
- ¼ to ½ teaspoon hot pepper sauce
- ⅓ cup shredded Monterey Jack cheese

1. Cook manicotti according to package directions. In a small bowl, combine the chicken, ¼ cup salsa, ricotta cheese, olives, parsley, pimientos, green onion, garlic and

SOUTHWEST CHICKEN POCKETS

pepper sauce. Drain the manicotti; fill with chicken mixture.
2. Spread ¼ cup salsa in an 8-in. square baking dish coated with cooking spray. Top with manicotti shells and remaining salsa.
3. Cover and bake at 400° for 20 minutes. Uncover; sprinkle with Monterey Jack cheese and bake 5-10 minutes longer or until cheese is melted and filling is heated through.

SOUTHWEST CHICKEN POCKETS

Black beans, convenient chicken strips and chilies star in these loaded pockets. Eat them out by hand or with a fork. Serve salsa on the side for an extra flavor burst.

—**TASTE OF HOME** TEST KITCHEN

PREP: 15 MIN. • **BAKE:** 20 MIN.
MAKES: 4 SERVINGS

- 1 medium onion, chopped
- 2 teaspoons olive oil
- 1 package (9 ounces) ready-to-serve roasted chicken breast strips
- 1 can (15 ounces) black beans, rinsed and drained
- 1 medium tomato, seeded and chopped
- 1 can (4 ounces) chopped green chilies, divided
- 1 sheet frozen puff pastry, thawed
- ¼ cup shredded cheddar cheese
- 1 large egg, beaten
- ½ cup sour cream

1. In a large skillet, saute onion in oil until tender. Remove from the heat; stir in the chicken, beans, tomato and ¼ cup chilies.
2. On a lightly floured surface, roll puff pastry into a 14-in. square. Cut into four squares. Spoon chicken mixture into a center of each square; sprinkle with cheese.
3. Brush egg over edges. Fold the dough over filling, forming a triangle; pinch seams to seal. Transfer to a greased baking sheet and brush with remaining egg. Bake at 400° for 18-22 minutes or until golden brown.
4. Meanwhile, in a small bowl, combine sour cream and remaining chilies. Serve with pockets.

BISTRO TURKEY CALZONE

Turkey, cheddar, bacon and apple harmonize well in this unique sandwich perfect for a harvest meal.

—**DONNA MARIE RYAN** TOPSFIELD, MA

PREP: 25 MIN. • **BAKE:** 20 MIN.
MAKES: 6 SERVINGS

- 1 **tablespoon cornmeal**
- 1 **loaf (1 pound) frozen pizza dough, thawed**
- ¾ **pound thinly sliced cooked turkey**
- 8 **slices cheddar cheese**
- 5 **bacon strips, cooked and crumbled**
- 1 **small tart apple, peeled and thinly sliced**
- 1 **large egg, beaten**
- ½ **teaspoon Italian seasoning**

1. Sprinkle cornmeal over a greased baking sheet. On a lightly floured surface, roll dough into a 15-in. circle. Transfer to prepared pan. Arrange half of turkey over half of the dough; top with cheese, bacon, apple and the remaining turkey. Fold dough over filling and pinch edges to seal.
2. With a sharp knife, cut three slashes in the top. Brush with egg and sprinkle with Italian seasoning. Bake at 400° for 20-25 minutes or until golden brown. Let stand for 5 minutes before cutting into wedges.

BISTRO
TURKEY CALZONE

TURKEY BREAST FLORENTINE

A lovely dish for guests, this spinach-stuffed turkey breast looks beautiful when you slice it for serving. I've also spooned the filling into a pocket slit in a boneless center-cut pork roast.

—**SHIRLEY GOEHRING** LODI, CA

PREP: 30 MIN.
BAKE: 1 HOUR 25 MIN. + STANDING
MAKES: 6-8 SERVINGS

- 1 **boneless skinless turkey breast half (3 to 4 pounds)**
- 5 **bacon strips, divided**
- ¾ **cup chopped onion**
- 3 **tablespoons all-purpose flour**
- ¾ **teaspoon dried tarragon**
- ½ **teaspoon salt**
- ¼ **teaspoon pepper**
- 1½ **cups milk**
- 1 **package (10 ounces) frozen chopped spinach, thawed and squeezed dry**
- 1 **jar (4½ ounces) sliced mushrooms, drained**
- 1 **tablespoon butter, melted**
- ⅓ **cup shredded Swiss cheese**

1. Make a lengthwise slit down center of turkey breast to within ½ in. of bottom. Open meat so it lies flat; cover with plastic wrap. Flatten to ½-in. thickness. Remove plastic; set aside.
2. In a large skillet, cook two bacon strips until crisp. Drain, reserving drippings. Crumble bacon; set aside. In the drippings, saute onion until tender. Stir in the flour, tarragon, salt and pepper until blended. Gradually stir in milk. Bring to a boil; cook and stir for 2 minutes or until thickened. Remove from heat.
3. Refrigerate ½ cup sauce. Add the spinach, mushrooms and crumbled bacon to the remaining sauce; spread over turkey breast. Starting at a short end, roll up and tuck in ends; tie with kitchen string. Place on a rack in a greased shallow roasting pan. Brush with butter. Cover loosely with foil.
4. Bake at 350° for 1 hour. Remove foil. Cut remaining bacon strips in half; place over the turkey. Bake the 25-35 minutes longer or until turkey is no longer pink.
5. Discard string. Let turkey stand for 10 minutes before slicing. Meanwhile, heat the reserved sauce; stir in cheese until melted. Serve with turkey.

BLACKENED CHICKEN SALAD

I'm always in need of quick recipes, so I like to serve this easy, healthy salad with garlic cheese bread and peanut butter cookies for dessert. I'll sometimes make a big batch of seasoning to keep on hand.

—**TANYA BRADY** MONTAGUE, MI

START TO FINISH: 25 MIN.
MAKES: 4 SERVINGS

- 2 teaspoons paprika
- 1 teaspoon onion powder
- 1 teaspoon garlic powder
- ½ teaspoon salt
- ½ teaspoon pepper
- ½ teaspoon dried oregano
- ½ teaspoon dried thyme
- ¼ teaspoon cayenne pepper
- 1½ pounds boneless skinless chicken breasts
- 1 package (10 ounces) Italian-blend salad greens
- 4 plum tomatoes, thinly sliced
- 1 medium sweet red pepper, julienned
- 1 cup seasoned salad croutons
- ½ to ¾ cup salad dressing of your choice

1. Combine the seasonings; rub over chicken. Broil or grill, uncovered, over medium heat for 5-7 minutes on each side or until juices run clear.
2. On a serving platter or individual plates, arrange the salad greens, tomatoes and red pepper. Slice the chicken; place over salad. Top with croutons and dressing.

HOW-TO

MAKE HERBS LAST

1. Because dried herbs don't spoil but do lose flavor over time, replace any herbs you've had more than 1 year.

2. Store dried herbs in airtight containers and away from heat and light. This will help them keep their potency longer.

EAT SMART

CRISPY BUFFALO CHICKEN ROLL-UPS FOR TWO

These winning chicken rolls with a crispy crust are both impressive and simple to make. My family and friends absolutely love them!

—**LISA KEYS** KENNETT SQUARE, PA

PREP: 15 MIN. • **BAKE:** 30 MIN.
MAKES: 2 SERVINGS

- 2 boneless skinless chicken breast halves (6 ounces each)
- ¼ teaspoon salt
- ¼ teaspoon pepper
- 2 tablespoons crumbled blue cheese
- 2 tablespoons hot pepper sauce
- 1 tablespoon mayonnaise
- ½ cup crushed cornflakes

1. Preheat oven to 400°. Flatten the chicken breasts to ¼-in. thickness. Season with salt and pepper; sprinkle with blue cheese. Roll up each from a short side and secure with toothpicks.
2. In a shallow bowl, combine the pepper sauce and mayonnaise. Place cornflakes in a separate shallow bowl. Dip chicken in the pepper sauce mixture, then coat with cornflakes. Place seam side down in a greased 11x7-in. baking dish.
3. Bake, uncovered, 30-35 minutes or until chicken is no longer pink. Discard toothpicks.

PER SERVING *1 serving equals 270 cal., 8 g fat (3 g sat. fat), 101 mg chol., 617 mg sodium, 10 g carb., trace fiber, 37 g pro.* **Diabetic Exchanges:** *5 lean meat, ½ starch, ½ fat.*

CRISPY BUFFALO CHICKEN ROLL-UPS FOR TWO

ROASTED CHICKEN WITH LEMON SAUCE

We love chicken cooked many ways, but this roasted version with a homemade sauce is tops for us.

—GENEVA GARRISON JACKSONVILLE, FL

PREP: 20 MIN.
BAKE: 2 HOURS + STANDING
MAKES: 6 SERVINGS

- 1 roasting chicken (6 to 7 pounds)
- 1 medium lemon
- 1 garlic clove, minced
- ½ teaspoon salt
- ½ teaspoon pepper
- 6 medium carrots, cut into chunks
- 1 large onion, quartered

LEMON SAUCE
- ½ cup sugar
- 4½ teaspoons cornstarch
- 1 cup cold water
- 2 tablespoons lemon juice
- 2 tablespoons grated lemon peel
- 1 to 2 drops yellow food coloring, optional
- 1 green onion, sliced

1. Preheat oven to 350°. Pat chicken dry. Cut lemon in half; squeeze juice over chicken. Place lemon in cavity. Rub garlic over chicken; sprinkle with salt and pepper.

2. Place chicken on a rack in a shallow roasting pan. Roast 2-2½ hours or until a thermometer inserted into thickest part of thigh reads 170°-175°, basting occasionally with pan juices and adding carrots and onion during the last hour. Cover loosely with foil if chicken browns too quickly.

3. Remove the chicken from oven; tent with foil. Let stand 15 minutes before carving.

4. Meanwhile, in a small saucepan, combine the sugar and cornstarch. Stir in water until smooth. Bring to a boil; cook and stir 2 minutes or until thickened. Remove from heat. Stir in the lemon juice, lemon peel and, if desired, food coloring.

5. Serve sauce with chicken and vegetables. Sprinkle with green onion.

FREEZE OPTION *Cool chicken, vegetables and sauce. Cut chicken into parts and freeze along with vegetables and sauce in freezer containers. To use, partially thaw in refrigerator overnight. Heat through slowly in a covered skillet until a thermometer inserted in chicken reads 165°, stirring occasionally and adding a little broth or water if necessary. Serve as directed.*

POPPY SEED CREAMED CHICKEN

A dear friend gave me this recipe, and it's been so popular with my family that I'm passing it along. A few years back, it won a blue ribbon in a chicken recipe contest.

—JUNE SHEAFFER FREDERICKSBURG, PA

PREP: 10 MIN. • **BAKE:** 30 MIN.
MAKES: 2 SERVINGS

- 2 cups cubed cooked chicken
- 1 can (10¾ ounces) condensed cream of chicken soup, undiluted
- ½ cup sour cream
- 1 teaspoon poppy seeds
- ¾ cup crushed Ritz crackers (about 18 crackers)
- 2 tablespoons butter
  Hot cooked noodles

1. In a large bowl, combine chicken, soup, sour cream and poppy seeds. Pour mixture into a greased shallow 3-cup baking dish. In a small bowl, combine cracker crumbs and butter; sprinkle over top.

2. Bake casserole, uncovered, at 350° for 30-35 minutes or until bubbly. Serve with noodles.

ROASTED CHICKEN WITH LEMON SAUCE

2-FOR-1 CHICKEN TETRAZZINI

A good friend shared a version of this recipe with me 35 years ago. I pay it forward by bringing the second casserole to friends.

—HELEN MCPHEE SAVOY, IL

PREP: 30 MIN. • **BAKE:** 20 MIN.
MAKES: 2 CASSEROLES
(3-4 SERVINGS EACH)

- 1 **package (12 ounces) spaghetti**
- ⅓ **cup butter, cubed**
- ⅓ **cup all-purpose flour**
- ¾ **teaspoon salt**
- ¼ **teaspoon white pepper**
- 1 **can (14½ ounces) chicken broth**
- 1½ **cups half-and-half cream**
- 1 **cup heavy whipping cream**
- 4 **cups cubed cooked chicken**
- 3 **cans (4 ounces each) mushroom stems and pieces, drained**
- 1 **jar (4 ounces) sliced pimientos, drained**
- ½ **cup grated Parmesan cheese**

1. Cook the spaghetti according to package directions. Meanwhile, in a Dutch oven, melt butter. Stir in the flour, salt and pepper until smooth. Gradually add the broth, half-and-half and whipping cream. Bring to a boil; cook and stir for 2 minutes or until thickened.

2. Remove from the heat. Stir in the chicken, mushrooms and pimientos. Drain spaghetti; add to the chicken mixture and toss to coat.

3. Transfer to two greased 11x7-in. baking dishes. Sprinkle with cheese. Cover and freeze one casserole for up to 2 months. Bake second casserole, uncovered, at 350° for 20-25 minutes or until heated through.

TO USE FROZEN CASSEROLE *Thaw in the refrigerator overnight. Cover and bake at 350° for 30 minutes. Uncover; bake 15-20 minutes longer or until heated through. Stir before serving.*

SPINACH-STUFFED
CHICKEN WITH LINGUINE

SPINACH-STUFFED CHICKEN WITH LINGUINE

Worthy of a special occasion, this elegant stuffed and rolled chicken looks gorgeous and tastes delicious.

—TASTE OF HOME TEST KITCHEN

PREP: 20 MIN. • **BAKE:** 25 MIN.
MAKES: 4 SERVINGS

- 3 **garlic cloves, minced**
- ⅓ **cup butter, divided**
- 1 **package (6 ounces) fresh baby spinach**
- ¼ **cup shredded Parmesan cheese**
- ¼ **teaspoon salt**
- 4 **boneless skinless chicken breast halves (6 ounces each)**
- ½ **cup ricotta cheese**
- 1 **large egg, beaten**
- ¾ **cup seasoned bread crumbs**
- 8 **ounces uncooked linguine**
- ½ **cup salsa**

1. In a large skillet, saute garlic in 1 tablespoon butter until tender. Add spinach and cook just until wilted. Remove from heat; stir in Parmesan cheese and salt.

2. Flatten chicken to ¼-in. thickness. Spread ricotta cheese and spinach mixture over the center of each chicken breast. Roll up and secure with toothpicks.

3. Place egg in a shallow bowl. Place bread crumbs in a separate shallow bowl. Dip chicken in egg, then coat with crumbs. In a large skillet, brown chicken in 2 tablespoons butter. Place chicken, seam side down, in a greased 11x7-in. baking dish.

4. Bake chicken, uncovered, at 375° for 25-30 minutes or until a thermometer reads 170°.

5. Meanwhile, cook the linguine according to package directions. Drain linguine; toss with remaining butter and salsa. Discard toothpicks from chicken. Serve with linguine.

CHERRY-GLAZED CHICKEN WITH TOASTED PECANS

START TO FINISH: 30 MIN.
MAKES: 4 SERVINGS

- 4 **boneless skinless chicken breast halves (4 ounces each)**
- ¾ **cup cherry preserves**
- 1 **teaspoon onion powder**
- 2 **ounces fontina cheese, thinly sliced**
- 2 **tablespoons chopped pecans, toasted**

1. Preheat oven to 375°. Place the chicken in an ungreased 11x7-in. baking dish. Top with preserves; sprinkle with onion powder. Bake, uncovered, 18-22 minutes or until a thermometer reads 165°.

2. Top with cheese; bake 5 minutes longer or until the cheese is melted. Sprinkle with pecans.

NOTE *To toast nuts, bake in a shallow pan in a 350° oven for 5-10 minutes or cook in a skillet over low heat until lightly browned, stirring occasionally.*

PER SERVING *1 chicken breast half equals 354 cal., 10 g fat (4 g sat. fat), 79 mg chol., 168 mg sodium, 40 g carb., trace fiber, 27 g pro.*

> "What started out as a way to use up some leftover preserves and cheese turned out to be a winning family dinner that I now make often."
> —**KERI COTTON** LAKEVILLE, MN

CHERRY-GLAZED CHICKEN
WITH TOASTED PECANS

CHICKEN-STUFFED CUBANELLE PEPPERS

Here's a new take on traditional stuffed peppers. I substituted chicken for the beef and used Cubanelle peppers in place of the usual green peppers.

—**BEV BURLINGAME** CANTON, OH

PREP: 20 MIN. • **BAKE:** 55 MIN.
MAKES: 6 SERVINGS

- 6 **Cubanelle peppers or mild banana peppers**
- 2 **large eggs**
- 1 **cup salsa**
- 3 **cups shredded cooked chicken breast**
- ¾ **cup soft bread crumbs**
- ½ **cup cooked long grain rice**
- 2 **cups meatless spaghetti sauce, divided**

1. Cut tops off peppers and remove seeds. In a large bowl, combine the eggs, salsa, chicken, bread crumbs and rice. Spoon into peppers.

2. Coat a 13x9-in. baking dish with cooking spray. Spread spaghetti sauce in dish. Place peppers over sauce. Spoon the remaining spaghetti sauce over the peppers.

3. Cover and bake at 350° for 60-65 minutes or until the peppers are tender and a thermometer inserted in stuffing reads at least 165°.

PER SERVING *1 stuffed pepper equals 230 cal., 4 g fat (1 g sat. fat), 125 mg chol., 661 mg sodium, 22 g carb., 7 g fiber, 28 g pro.* **Diabetic Exchanges:** *3 lean meat, 2 vegetable, 1 starch.*

TOP TIP

STUFFED PEPPERS SWITCH

Want to change up the rice in Chicken-Stuffed Cubanelle Peppers, too? Try using cooked barley or whole kernel corn instead.

CHICKEN-STUFFED
CUBANELLE PEPPERS

ROASTED CHICKEN WITH GARLIC-SHERRY SAUCE

This garlic-kissed chicken is delicious, plain or fancy. It's an elegant entree for guests and my husband, and I'll use leftovers in rice casseroles and hot open-faced sandwiches.

—**SHERI SIDWELL** ALTON, IL

PREP: 30 MIN. + MARINATING
BAKE: 20 MIN. • **MAKES:** 4 SERVINGS

- 2 **quarts water**
- ½ **cup salt**
- 4 **bone-in chicken breast halves (12 ounces each)**
- ¾ **teaspoon pepper, divided**
- 2 **teaspoons canola oil**
- 8 **garlic cloves, peeled and thinly sliced**
- 1 **cup reduced-sodium chicken broth**
- ½ **cup sherry or additional reduced-sodium chicken broth**
- 3 **fresh thyme sprigs**
- ¼ **cup butter, cubed**
- 1 **teaspoon lemon juice**

1. For brine, in a large saucepan, bring water and salt to a boil. Cook and stir until salt is dissolved. Remove from heat; cool to room temperature.
2. Place a large heavy-duty resealable plastic bag inside a second large resealable plastic bag; add chicken. Carefully pour cooled brine into bag. Squeeze out as much air as possible; seal bags and turn to coat. Refrigerate 1-2 hours, turning several times.
3. Preheat oven to 400°. Drain and discard brine. Rinse the chicken with cold water; pat dry. Sprinkle with ½ teaspoon pepper. In a large ovenproof skillet, brown the chicken in oil over medium heat.
4. Bake, uncovered, 20-25 minutes or until a thermometer reads 170°. Remove the chicken and keep warm. Drain the drippings, reserving 1 tablespoon.
5. Saute garlic in reserved drippings for 1 minute. Add the broth, sherry or additional broth and thyme. Bring to a boil; cook until liquid is reduced to 1 cup. Discard thyme. Stir in the butter, lemon juice and remaining pepper. Serve with chicken.

EAT SMART

SAUSAGE SPINACH PIZZA

My husband loves this pizza, and it's the best way for him to get his fix while staying in his carb range. Putting Asiago cheese in the crust lets you get by with less cheese on top.

—**ELENA FALK** VERSAILLES, OH

PREP: 35 MIN. + RISING • **BAKE:** 10 MIN.
MAKES: 2 PIZZAS (8 SLICES EACH)

- 1 **package (¼ ounce) active dry yeast**
- 1 **cup warm water (110° to 115°)**
- 2¼ **cups all-purpose flour**
- 2 **tablespoons olive oil**
- 1 **tablespoon sugar**
- 2 **teaspoons Italian seasoning**
- ½ **teaspoon salt**
- ½ **cup shredded Asiago cheese**
- ¾ **pound Italian turkey sausage links, thinly sliced**
- 1 **can (14½ ounces) Italian diced tomatoes, undrained**
- 2 **cups fresh baby spinach**
- 6 **slices reduced-fat provolone cheese, halved**

1. In a large bowl, dissolve yeast in water. Add flour, oil, sugar, Italian seasoning and salt; beat on medium speed for 3 minutes or until smooth. Stir in Asiago cheese.
2. Turn onto a lightly floured surface; knead until smooth and elastic, about 5-6 minutes. Place in a bowl coated with cooking spray, turning once to coat top. Cover and let rise in a warm place until doubled, about 1 hour.
3. Preheat oven to 425°. Punch the dough down; divide in half. On a floured surface, roll each portion into a 13-in. circle. Transfer to two 12-in. pizza pans coated with cooking spray. Build up edges slightly. Prick the dough thoroughly with a fork. Bake 5-8 minutes or until the edges are lightly browned.
4. Meanwhile, in a large nonstick skillet, cook sausage over medium heat until no longer pink; drain. Place tomatoes in a food processor; cover and pulse until finely chopped.
5. Spread tomatoes over crusts; layer with spinach, sausage and provolone cheese. Bake 8-12 minutes or until crusts and cheese are lightly browned.
PER SERVING *2 slices equals 314 cal., 12 g fat (4 g sat. fat), 39 mg chol., 729 mg sodium, 34 g carb., 2 g fiber, 17 g pro. **Diabetic Exchanges:** 2 starch, 2 lean meat, 1 vegetable, ½ fat.*

SAUSAGE SPINACH PIZZA

JERK TURKEY
TENDERLOINS

JERK TURKEY TENDERLOINS

The salsa for the tenderloins is best with fresh pineapple; however, on particularly busy days, I have used canned pineapple tidbits in an effort to speed up the preparation.

—**HOLLY BAUER** WEST BEND, WI

START TO FINISH: 30 MIN.
MAKES: 5 SERVINGS (2 CUPS SALSA)

- 1 package (20 ounces) turkey breast tenderloins
- ½ teaspoon seasoned salt
- 2 tablespoons olive oil
- 1 tablespoon dried rosemary, crushed
- 1 tablespoon Caribbean jerk seasoning
- 1 tablespoon brown sugar

SALSA
- 1½ cups cubed fresh pineapple
- 1 medium sweet red pepper, chopped
- ¼ cup chopped red onion
- ¼ cup minced fresh cilantro
- 1 jalapeno pepper, seeded and minced
- 2 tablespoons lime juice
- 2 garlic cloves, minced
- ¼ teaspoon salt
- ⅛ teaspoon pepper

1. Sprinkle the tenderloins with seasoned salt. Combine the oil, rosemary, jerk seasoning and brown sugar. Rub over tenderloins. Broil 3-4 in. from the heat for 7-9 minutes on each side or until a thermometer reads 170°.

2. Meanwhile, in a large bowl, combine the salsa ingredients. Serve with turkey.

FREEZE OPTION *Season turkey as directed. Transfer to a resealable plastic freezer bag; freeze. To use, completely thaw in refrigerator. Broil tenderloins and prepare salsa as directed.*

NOTE *Wear disposable gloves when cutting hot peppers; the oils can burn skin. Avoid touching your face.*

PER SERVING *3 ounces cooked turkey with ⅓ cup salsa equals 216 cal., 7 g fat (1 g sat. fat), 56 mg chol., 503 mg sodium, 12 g carb., 2 g fiber, 27 g pro.* **Diabetic Exchanges:** *3 lean meat, 1 vegetable, 1 fat, ½ fruit.*

LEMON FETA CHICKEN

You just just need five ingredients to get this flavorful chicken oven-ready. My husband and I prepare the dish often, and it's a hit every time.

—**ANN CAIN** MORRILL, NE

START TO FINISH: 25 MIN.
MAKES: 4 SERVINGS

- 4 boneless skinless chicken breast halves (4 ounces each)
- 2 to 3 tablespoons lemon juice
- ¼ cup crumbled feta cheese
- 1 teaspoon dried oregano
- ¼ to ½ teaspoon pepper

1. Place chicken in a 13x9-in. baking dish coated with cooking spray. Pour lemon juice over chicken; sprinkle with feta cheese, oregano and pepper.

2. Bake chicken, uncovered, at 400° for 20-25 minutes or until a thermometer reads 170°.

PER SERVING *1 chicken breast half equals 143 cal., 4 g fat (1 g sat. fat), 66 mg chol., 122 mg sodium, 1 g carb., trace fiber, 24 g pro.* **Diabetic Exchanges:** *3 lean meat, ½ fat.*

Pork

RIBS WITH
PLUM SAUCE

RIBS WITH PLUM SAUCE

I found this tangy-sweet basting sauce recipe when a surplus of plums sent me searching for new ideas to use all the fruit. In summer, I like to finish the ribs on the grill, brushing on the sauce, after first baking them in the oven. Depending on how many people you are serving, consider making a double batch.

—**MARIE HOYER** HODGENVILLE, KY

PREP: 10 MIN. • **BAKE:** 1½ HOURS
MAKES: 6 SERVINGS

>   5 **to 6 pounds pork spareribs**
>   ¾ **cup reduced-sodium soy sauce**
>   ¾ **cup plum jam or apricot preserves**
>   ¾ **cup honey**
>   2 **to 3 garlic cloves, minced**

1. Cut ribs into serving-size pieces; place with bone side down on a rack in a shallow roasting pan. Cover and bake at 350° for 1 hour or until ribs are tender; drain.
2. In a small bowl, combine the remaining ingredients; brush some of sauce over ribs. Bake at 350° or grill over medium heat, uncovered, 30 minutes longer, turning and basting occasionally.

HAM & NOODLE BAKE

CIDER-MOLASSES PORK TENDERLOIN WITH PEARS

I think this is perfect for entertaining. Drizzling the pork tenderloin with a robust molasses sauce and serving it with tender, sweet baked pears will have everyone asking for more.

—**LISA RENSHAW** KANSAS CITY, MO

PREP: 25 MIN. • **BAKE:** 25 MIN.
MAKES: 6 SERVINGS

- 2 **pork tenderloins (1 pound each)**
- 3 **tablespoons olive oil**
- 4 **teaspoons minced fresh rosemary or 1 teaspoon dried rosemary, crushed**
- 1 **teaspoon salt**
- 1 **teaspoon pepper**
- 6 **medium pears, peeled, halved and cored**
- 1 **cup apple cider or juice**
- ½ **cup molasses**
- ¼ **cup balsamic vinegar**

1. Preheat oven to 425°. Place pork on a rack in a shallow roasting pan. Combine the oil, rosemary, salt and pepper; rub over pork. Arrange pears around pork. In a small bowl, combine the remaining ingredients; pour over the top.
2. Bake for 25-30 minutes or until a thermometer reads 145°, basting occasionally with pan juices. Let stand 5 minutes before slicing.
PER SERVING *4 ounces cooked pork with 2 pear halves and 3 tablespoons sauce equals 437 cal., 12 g fat (3 g sat. fat), 84 mg chol., 472 mg sodium, 53 g carb., 5 g fiber, 31 g pro.*

TOP TIP

TENDERLOIN LEFTOVERS

If you end up with extra pork tenderloin, try using it in place of beef or chicken in some of your favorite recipes. You might find a new winning dish!

HAM & NOODLE BAKE

Bored by leftovers? Time to stir things up! Toss extra cooked ham, Mexican cheese and green chilies into a rich sauce. With oodles of noodles and lots of crunch, it'll be a party in your kitchen tonight.

—**GLENDA WATTS** TACOMA, WA

PREP: 20 MIN. • **BAKE:** 15 MIN.
MAKES: 5 SERVINGS

- 5⅔ **cups uncooked egg noodles**
- 2 **cups cubed fully cooked ham**
- 2 **cups (8 ounces) shredded Mexican cheese blend**
- 1 **can (10¾ ounces) condensed cream of mushroom soup, undiluted**
- 1 **cup frozen peas**
- ½ **cup sour cream**
- 1 **can (4 ounces) chopped green chilies**
- ⅓ **cup heavy whipping cream**
- ¼ **teaspoon pepper**
- 1 **can (6 ounces) french-fried onions, divided**

1. Cook noodles according to package directions. Meanwhile, in a large saucepan, combine ham, cheese, soup, peas, sour cream, chilies, cream and pepper. Cook and stir over medium heat until cheese is melted. Drain noodles. Add noodles and half of the onions to ham mixture.
2. Transfer to a greased 13x9-in. baking dish. Sprinkle remaining onions over top. Bake, uncovered, at 375° for 15-20 minutes or until golden brown.

"Colorful mango relish is a cool counterpoint to the heat in the meat rub. I use the rub on many of my pork dishes. These roasted tenderloins are sure to turn out nice and juicy."

—GLORIA BRADLEY NAPERVILLE, IL

PORK TENDERLOIN
WITH MANGO RELISH

PORK TENDERLOIN WITH MANGO RELISH

PREP: 15 MIN. • **BAKE:** 45 MIN.
MAKES: 6 SERVINGS

- 1½ teaspoons ground coriander
- 1 teaspoon ground cumin
- ½ teaspoon salt
- ½ teaspoon sugar
- ½ teaspoon ground chipotle pepper
- ½ teaspoon smoked Spanish paprika
- 2 pork tenderloins (¾ pound each)

MANGO RELISH

- 1 medium mango, peeled and chopped
- 2 plum tomatoes, seeded and chopped
- ⅓ cup chopped onion
- ⅓ cup chopped seeded peeled cucumber
- ¼ cup minced fresh cilantro
- 1 jalapeno pepper, seeded and chopped
- 3 tablespoons lime juice

1. In a bowl, combine the first six ingredients. Set aside ½ teaspoon for relish; rub the remaining spice mixture over tenderloins. Place in a lightly greased 13x9-in. baking pan. Bake, uncovered, at 350° for 45-50 minutes or until thermometer reads 160°. Let stand for 5 minutes.
2. Meanwhile, in a small bowl, combine mango, tomatoes, onion, cucumber, cilantro and jalapeno. Combine lime juice and reserved spice mixture; add to mango mixture and toss to coat. Slice pork; serve with relish.
NOTE *Wear disposable gloves when cutting hot peppers; the oils can burn skin. Avoid touching your face.*
PER SERVING *3 ounces cooked pork with ⅓ cup relish equals 171 cal., 4 g fat (1 g sat. fat), 63 mg chol., 245 mg sodium, 9 g carb., 2 g fiber, 23 g pro. Diabetic Exchanges: 3 lean meat, ½ starch.*

LINGUINE WITH
HAM & SWISS CHEESE

LINGUINE WITH HAM & SWISS CHEESE

This version of a classic linguine casserole recipe eliminates nearly half the saturated fat from the original without losing the creamy texture or distinctive Swiss cheese flavor.
—**MIKE TCHOU** PEPPER PIKE, OH

PREP: 15 MIN. • **BAKE:** 45 MIN.
MAKES: 8 SERVINGS

- 8 ounces uncooked whole wheat linguine, broken in half
- 2 cups cubed fully cooked ham
- 1¾ cups (7 ounces) shredded Swiss cheese, divided
- 1 can (10¾ ounces) reduced-fat reduced-sodium condensed cream of mushroom soup, undiluted
- 1 cup (8 ounces) reduced-fat sour cream
- 1 medium onion, chopped
- 1 small green pepper, finely chopped

1. Cook the linguine according to package directions. Meanwhile, in a large bowl, combine ham, 1½ cups cheese, soup, sour cream, onion and green pepper. Drain pasta; add to ham mixture and stir to coat.
2. Transfer to a 13x9-in. baking dish coated with cooking spray. Cover and bake at 350° for 35 minutes. Uncover; sprinkle with remaining cheese. Bake 10-15 minutes longer or until the cheese is melted.
PER SERVING *1 cup equals 293 cal., 12 g fat (7 g sat. fat), 47 mg chol., 665 mg sodium, 29 g carb., 4 g fiber, 19 g pro. Diabetic Exchanges: 2 starch, 2 lean meat, 1 fat.*

SAUSAGE & SWISS CHARD LASAGNA

SAUSAGE & SWISS CHARD LASAGNA

Rustic and comforting, this rich lasagna is a great way to get kids to eat healthy greens. It's such a tasty casserole they'll never know the Swiss chard is there!
—**CANDACE MOREHOUSE** SHOW LOW, AZ

PREP: 45 MIN. • **BAKE:** 55 MIN. + STANDING
MAKES: 6 SERVINGS

- 1 pound bulk Italian sausage
- 1¾ cups sliced fresh mushrooms
- 2 garlic cloves, minced
- 1 bunch Swiss chard (10 ounces)
- 3 tablespoons butter
- ¼ cup all-purpose flour
- 3 cups 2% milk
- 1 cup (4 ounces) shredded Gruyere or Swiss cheese, divided
- 1 tablespoon minced fresh parsley or 1 teaspoon dried parsley flakes
- 1 tablespoon minced fresh oregano or 1 teaspoon dried oregano
- 1 teaspoon grated lemon peel
- ½ teaspoon salt
- ⅛ teaspoon pepper
- 6 no-cook lasagna noodles

1. Preheat the oven to 350°. In a large skillet, cook sausage, mushrooms and garlic over medium heat 8-10 minutes or until sausage is no longer pink and mushrooms are tender, breaking up sausage into crumbles. Remove from pan with a slotted spoon. Remove drippings.

2. Remove the stems from Swiss chard; coarsely chop leaves. In same skillet, heat butter over medium heat. Stir in flour until smooth; gradually whisk in milk. Bring to a boil, stirring constantly; cook and stir 1-2 minutes or until thickened. Add ¾ cup cheese, parsley, oregano, lemon peel, salt and pepper; stir until cheese is melted. Stir in Swiss chard leaves.

3. Spread one-fourth of the cheese sauce into a greased 8-in. square baking dish. Layer with each of the following: two noodles, one-third of the meat mixture and one-fourth of the cheese sauce. Repeat layers twice. Sprinkle with remaining cheese.

4. Bake, covered, 45 minutes. Bake, uncovered, 8-10 minutes longer or until cheese is melted. Let stand 10 minutes before serving.

GLAZED HAM WITH SWEET POTATOES

I took a class at a local junior college on cooking. This recipe is the perfect size for me, and I can reheat the second serving for lunch the next day.

—ELOISE SMITH WILLOWBROOK, IL

START TO FINISH: 15 MIN.
MAKES: 2 SERVINGS

- 2 **tablespoons apricot jam**
- 1 **teaspoon Dijon mustard**
- 1 **boneless fully cooked ham steak (about 8 ounces)**
- 1 **can (15¾ ounces) sweet potatoes, drained**
- 1 **can (8½ ounces) sliced peaches, drained**
- 2 **tablespoons maple syrup, divided**

1. In a small microwave-safe bowl, combine the jam and the mustard. Microwave, uncovered, on high for 15-30 seconds or until jam is melted; stir until blended. Set aside.

2. Place ham steak in an ovenproof skillet. Arrange sweet potatoes and peaches around ham. Drizzle with 1 tablespoon syrup. Broil 3-4 in. from the heat for 5 minutes. Turn ham, peaches and potatoes. Brush ham with jam mixture; drizzle peaches and potatoes with remaining syrup. Broil 5 minutes longer or until heated through.

ONION-APPLE PORK CHOPS

TOP TIP

SUBSTITUTE PINEAPPLE

Instead of peaches, prep the ham steak with a small can of crushed pineapple. Add a bit more maple syrup or a dash of cinnamon to sweeten it up.

EAT SMART

ONION-APPLE PORK CHOPS

You couldn't ask for a better entree to serve on a fall evening. The apple, pork and maple flavors complement each other perfectly. Rice and steamed broccoli make nice accompaniments.

—TRISHA KRUSE EAGLE, ID

PREP: 25 MIN. • **BAKE:** 15 MIN.
MAKES: 2 SERVINGS

- 2 **boneless pork loin chops (4 ounces each)**
- ¼ **teaspoon garlic salt**
- ¼ **teaspoon lemon-pepper seasoning**
- 2 **teaspoons olive oil**
- 1 **medium apple, peeled and thinly sliced**
- 1 **small onion, thinly sliced**
- ⅓ **cup reduced-sodium chicken broth**
- 2 **tablespoons maple syrup**

1. Sprinkle chops with garlic salt and lemon pepper. In a large ovenproof skillet, brown chops in oil. Remove and keep warm.

2. In the same skillet, saute apple and onion in drippings until tender. Stir in broth and syrup. Bring to a boil. Reduce heat; simmer, uncovered, for 5-7 minutes or until liquid is almost evaporated. Return chops to pan.

3. Cover and bake at 350° for 15-20 minutes or until a thermometer reads 145°.

PER SERVING *1 pork chop with ½ cup apple mixture equals 291 cal., 11 g fat (3 g sat. fat), 55 mg chol., 414 mg sodium, 25 g carb., 2 g fiber, 23 g pro.* **Diabetic Exchanges:** *3 lean meat, 1 starch, 1 fat, ½ fruit.*

SAUSAGE PIZZA

Make two of these fully-loaded pizzas, then keep one in the freezer for busy nights. If making them for kids, try using a less spicy sausage, such as chicken or turkey sausage.

—TASTE OF HOME TEST KITCHEN

PREP: 20 MIN. • **BAKE:** 15 MIN.
MAKES: 8 SLICES

- 1 loaf (1 pound) frozen bread dough, thawed
- ¾ pound bulk hot Italian sausage
- ½ cup sliced onion
- ½ cup sliced fresh mushrooms
- ½ cup chopped green pepper
- ½ cup pizza sauce
- 2 cups (8 ounces) shredded part-skim mozzarella cheese

1. With greased fingers, pat dough onto an ungreased 12-in. pizza pan. Prick dough thoroughly with a fork. Bake at 400° for 10-12 minutes or until lightly browned. Meanwhile, in a large skillet, cook the sausage, onion, mushrooms and green pepper over medium heat until sausage is no longer pink; drain.

2. Spread pizza sauce over crust. Top with sausage mixture; sprinkle with cheese. Bake at 400° for 12-15 minutes or until golden brown, or wrap pizza and freeze for up to 2 months.

TO USE FROZEN PIZZA *Unwrap and place on a pizza pan; thaw in the refrigerator. Bake at 400° for 18-22 minutes or until golden brown.*

BACON QUICHE

With a quiche like this, you don't need a lot of heavy side dishes. It has a little of everything—eggs, bacon, cheese and a touch of apple juice for a salty-sweet fix. Serve fresh berries or a simple green salad on the side to round it out.

—COLLEEN BELBEY WARWICK, RI

PREP: 15 MIN. • **BAKE:** 40 MIN. + STANDING
MAKES: 6 SERVINGS

- 1 sheet refrigerated pie pastry
- ¼ cup sliced green onions
- 1 tablespoon butter
- 6 large eggs
- 1½ cups heavy whipping cream
- ¼ cup unsweetened apple juice
- 1 pound sliced bacon, cooked and crumbled
- ⅛ teaspoon salt
- ⅛ teaspoon pepper
- 2 cups (8 ounces) shredded Swiss cheese

1. Preheat oven to 350°. Line a 9-in. pie plate with pastry; trim and flute edges. Set aside. In a skillet, saute green onions in butter until tender.

2. In a large bowl, whisk eggs, cream and juice. Stir in bacon, salt, pepper and green onions. Pour into pastry; sprinkle with cheese.

3. Bake 40-45 minutes or until a knife inserted near center comes out clean. Let stand 10 minutes before cutting.

FREEZE OPTION *Securely wrap the individual portions of cooled quiche in plastic wrap and foil; freeze. To use, partially thaw in the refrigerator overnight. Remove from refrigerator 30 minutes before baking. Preheat oven to 350°. Unwrap quiche; reheat in oven until heated through and a thermometer inserted in center reads 165°.*

HAM QUICHE *Omit the apple juice. Increase heavy whipping cream to 1¾ cup. Substitute 3 cups diced cooked ham for bacon and cheddar cheese for the Swiss cheese. Proceed as directed.*

HAM BROCCOLI QUICHE *Follow directions for Ham Quiche. Add 1 cup chopped broccoli florets to the egg mixture.*

SHEPHERD'S PIE

PREP: 30 MIN. • **BAKE:** 45 MIN.
MAKES: 6 SERVINGS

PORK LAYER
- 1 pound ground pork
- 1 small onion, chopped
- 2 garlic cloves, minced
- 1 cup cooked rice
- ½ cup pork gravy or ¼ cup chicken broth
- ½ teaspoon salt
- ½ teaspoon dried thyme

CABBAGE LAYER
- 1 medium carrot, diced
- 1 small onion, chopped
- 2 tablespoons butter or margarine
- 6 cups chopped cabbage
- 1 cup chicken broth
- ½ teaspoon salt
- ¼ teaspoon pepper

POTATO LAYER
- 2 cups mashed potatoes
- ¼ cup shredded cheddar cheese

In a skillet over medium heat, brown pork until no longer pink. Add onion and garlic. Cook until vegetables are tender; drain. Stir in rice, gravy, salt and thyme. Spoon into a greased 11x7-in. baking dish. In the same skillet, saute the carrot and onion in butter over medium heat for 5 minutes. Stir in cabbage; cook for 1 minute. Add broth, salt and pepper; cover and cook for 10 minutes. Spoon over the pork layer. Spoon or pipe mashed potatoes on top; sprinkle with cheese. Bake, uncovered, at 350° for 45 minutes or until browned.

TOP TIP

CHIPS ADD CRUNCH

Looking to add a crunch to your meat pie? I'll often top mine with crushed barbecue potato chips.

—LORRAINE D.
MOUNTAIN CITY, TN

"Of all the shepherd's pie recipes I've tried through the years, this one is definitely the best. I enjoy cooking for friends and family, who agree this meat pie is a keeper."
—**MARY ARTHURS** ETOBICOKE, ON

SHEPHERD'S PIE

CRANBERRY-STUFFED
PORK CHOPS

CRANBERRY-STUFFED PORK CHOPS

A moist corn bread-cranberry stuffing complements these tender chops. The recipe easily can be doubled for company.
—**LOREE REININGER** POLK CITY, FL

PREP: 15 MIN. • **BAKE:** 25 MIN.
MAKES: 2 SERVINGS

- 3 **tablespoons chopped onion**
- 1 **tablespoon chopped pecans**
- 1 **small garlic clove, minced**
- ½ **teaspoon butter**
- ¼ **cup corn bread stuffing mix**
- 3 **tablespoons dried cranberries**
- 2 **tablespoons hot water**
- 2 **boneless pork loin chops (5 ounces each)**
- 4 **teaspoons red currant jelly, warmed**

1. In a small nonstick skillet coated with cooking spray, saute the onion, pecans and garlic in butter until the onion is tender. Stir in the stuffing mix, cranberries and water. Remove from the heat.

2. Carefully cut a pocket in each pork chop; stuff with cranberry mixture. Place on a baking sheet coated with cooking spray. Bake at 350° for 22-28 minutes or until thermometer reads 160°. Brush with jelly.
PER SERVING *1 pork chop equals 326 cal., 12 g fat (4 g sat. fat), 71 mg chol., 177 mg sodium, 26 g carb., 1 g fiber, 29 g pro.* **Diabetic Exchanges: 4 lean meat, 1½ starch.**

ROSEMARY PORK ROAST WITH VEGETABLES

I found this recipe in a friend's collection many years ago. Since then, my family has requested it more times than I can count.
—**SUZANNE STROCSHER** BOTHELL, WA

PREP: 10 MIN.
BAKE: 2 HOURS + STANDING
MAKES: 8 SERVINGS

- 2 **garlic cloves, minced**
- 5 **teaspoons dried rosemary, crushed**
- 4 **teaspoons dried marjoram**
- ½ **teaspoon pepper**
- 1 **boneless pork loin roast (2½ pounds), trimmed**
- 8 **small red potatoes, quartered**
- 1 **pound fresh baby carrots**
- 1 **tablespoon canola oil**

In a small bowl, combine the garlic, rosemary, marjoram and pepper; set aside 1 tablespoon. Rub remaining mixture over roast; place in a shallow roasting pan. Combine potatoes, carrots and oil in a large resealable plastic bag; add reserved spice mixture and toss to coat. Arrange vegetables around the roast. Cover and bake at 325° for 1 hour. Uncover and bake for 1 hour longer or until a thermometer reads 160°-170°. Let stand for 10 minutes before slicing.
PER SERVING *1 serving equals 283 cal., 12 g fat (0 sat. fat), 84 mg chol., 92 mg sodium, 12 g carb., 0 fiber, 31 g pro.* **Diabetic Exchanges: 4 lean meat, 1 vegetable, ½ starch.**

PARMESAN-PORK ZUCCHINI BOATS

My father-in-law grows zucchini, so we highlight it in as many recipes as we can. Stuffed with a sausage-cheese filling, these zucchini boats are hearty enough to be a main dish.

—**MICHELLE MASCIARELLI** TORRINGTON, CT

PREP: 25 MIN. • **BAKE:** 30 MIN.
MAKES: 4 SERVINGS

- 4 medium zucchini
- 1 pound bulk pork sausage
- 1 small onion, chopped
- 1 garlic clove, minced
- ⅔ cup seasoned bread crumbs
- ½ cup plus 2 tablespoons shredded Parmesan cheese, divided
- 1 large egg, beaten
- ¼ teaspoon salt
- ½ cup water

1. Cut zucchini in half lengthwise. Scoop out seeds and pulp from each, leaving a ¼-in. shell; set aside. Chop pulp; set aside.
2. In a large skillet, cook sausage and onion over medium heat until meat is no longer pink; drain. Add garlic and zucchini pulp; saute for 3-5 minutes or until pulp is tender. Remove from the heat. Stir in the bread crumbs, ½ cup Parmesan cheese and egg.
3. Sprinkle salt inside zucchini shells. Fill each with 3 tablespoons meat mixture. Sprinkle with remaining Parmesan cheese.
4. Place in ungreased 13x9-in. baking dish. Pour water into dish. Cover and bake at 350° for 15 minutes. Uncover; bake 15 minutes longer or until the zucchini is tender and the filling is heated through.

EAT SMART

APPLE-STUFFED PORK TENDERLOINS

This impressive entree is oven-ready in just 25 minutes! Garnish with extra sliced apple and fresh parsley for a dish that's sure to impress.

—**SUZANNE EARL** SPRING, TX

PREP: 25 MIN. • **BAKE:** 25 MIN. + STANDING
MAKES: 8 SERVINGS

- 1 medium apple, peeled and chopped
- 1 small onion, chopped
- 1 tablespoon olive oil
- 1 garlic clove, minced
- ½ teaspoon salt
- ¼ teaspoon pepper
- 2 pork tenderloins (1 pound each)

SAUCE
- 1 cup unsweetened apple juice
- 1 cup pomegranate juice
- 1 tablespoon Dijon mustard
- 2 tablespoons cornstarch
- 2 tablespoons cold water
- 1 tablespoon minced fresh parsley

1. In a small skillet, saute apple and onion in oil until tender. Add garlic, salt and pepper; cook 1 minute longer. Remove from the heat.

2. Make a lengthwise slit down the center of each tenderloin to within ½ in. of bottom. Open tenderloins so they lie flat; cover with plastic wrap. Flatten to ¾-in. thickness.
3. Remove plastic wrap; spread apple mixture over meat. Close tenderloins; tie with kitchen string, secure ends with toothpicks. Place in an ungreased 13x9-in. baking dish. Bake, uncovered, at 425° for 15 minutes.
4. Meanwhile, in a small saucepan, combine the juices and mustard. Bring to a boil; cook for 5 minutes, stirring occasionally. Combine cornstarch and water until smooth; gradually stir into juice mixture. Bring to a boil; cook and stir for 2 minutes or until thickened. Stir in parsley.
5. Pour ¾ cup sauce over tenderloins. Bake 10-15 minutes longer or until a thermometer reads 160°. Let stand for 10 minutes before slicing. Serve with remaining sauce.

PER SERVING *3 ounces cooked stuffed pork with 3 tablespoons sauce equals 200 cal., 6 g fat (2 g sat. fat), 63 mg chol., 243 mg sodium, 13 g carb., trace fiber, 23 g pro.* **Diabetic Exchanges:** *3 lean meat, 1 fruit.*

APPLE-STUFFED PORK TENDERLOINS

LEMON-MUSTARD PORK CHOPS

OKTOBERFEST STRUDELS

PREP: 30 MIN. • **BAKE:** 25 MIN. + STANDING
MAKES: 2 STRUDELS (3 SERVINGS EACH)

- 1 tablespoon butter
- 5 fully cooked bratwurst links, chopped
- 1 medium onion, chopped
- 1 can (14 ounces) sauerkraut, rinsed and well-drained
- ½ cup sour cream
- 3 tablespoons Dijon mustard
- 2½ teaspoons caraway seeds, divided
- 1 package (17.3 ounces) frozen puff pastry, thawed
- 1 cup (4 ounces) shredded Muenster cheese
- 1 cup (4 ounces) shredded sharp cheddar cheese

1. Preheat oven to 400°. In a large skillet, heat the butter over medium heat. Add the bratwurst and onion; cook and stir 8-10 minutes or until onion is tender. Stir in sauerkraut; cool slightly.

2. In a small bowl, mix sour cream, mustard and ½ teaspoon caraway seeds. Unfold one sheet of puff pastry. Spread with ⅓ cup sour cream mixture to within ½ in. of edges. Spoon 2½ cups sausage mixture down center of the pastry; sprinkle with ½ cup each Muenster and cheddar cheeses.

3. Lightly brush edges of pastry with water; bring edges together, pinching to seal. Transfer to an ungreased baking sheet, seam side down; pinch ends and fold under. Repeat with remaining ingredients.

4. Brush tops with water; sprinkle with remaining caraway seeds. Cut slits in pastry. Bake 25-30 minutes or until golden brown. Let stand 10 minutes before slicing.

EAT SMART

LEMON-MUSTARD PORK CHOPS

These savory chops are lip-smackin' tangy good! The recipe combines fresh lemon, Dijon, garlic and herbs—simple ingredients that work well together.

—**KATHY SPECHT** CLINTON, MT

START TO FINISH: 20 MIN.
MAKES: 4 SERVINGS

- 4 boneless pork loin chops (6 ounces each)
- 2 tablespoons lemon juice
- 2 tablespoons minced fresh parsley
- 2 tablespoons Dijon mustard
- 1 garlic clove, minced
- 1 teaspoon grated lemon peel
- ½ teaspoon dried rosemary, crushed
- ¼ teaspoon salt
  Lemon wedges

1. Drizzle pork chops with lemon juice. Combine the parsley, mustard, garlic, lemon peel, rosemary and salt; brush over both sides of chops.

2. Place pork on a greased broiler pan. Broil 4-5 in. from the heat for 4-5 minutes on each side or until a thermometer reads 145°. Let stand for 5 minutes before serving. Serve with lemon wedges.

PER SERVING *1 pork chop equals 239 cal., 10 g fat (4 g sat. fat), 82 mg chol., 376 mg sodium, 3 g carb., trace fiber, 33 g pro.* **Diabetic Exchange:** *5 lean meat.*

MEATY CORN BREAD CASSEROLE

Indulgently delicious, this down-home casserole is comfort food at its finest.

—JUSTINA WILSON WEST SALEM, WI

PREP: 20 MIN. • **BAKE:** 15 MIN.
MAKES: 6 SERVINGS

- ½ pound ground beef
- ½ pound bulk pork sausage
- 1¾ cups frozen corn, thawed
- 1 cup water
- 1 envelope brown gravy mix
- 1 package (8½ ounces) corn bread/muffin mix
- 1 tablespoon bacon bits
- 1½ teaspoons pepper
- ⅛ teaspoon garlic powder
- 1 envelope country gravy mix

1. In a large skillet, cook beef and sausage over medium heat until no longer pink; drain. Stir in the corn, water and brown gravy mix. Bring to a boil; cook and stir for 1 minute or until thickened. Spoon into a greased 8-in. square baking dish.

2. Prepare the corn bread batter according to package directions; stir in the bacon bits, pepper and garlic powder. Spread over meat mixture.

3. Bake, uncovered, at 400° for 15-20 minutes or until toothpick inserted into corn bread layer comes out clean. Meanwhile, prepare the country gravy mix according to package directions; serve with casserole.

"My husband was born and raised in Wisconsin, and he loves bratwurst. I tweaked this strudel filling to include some of his favorite hometown ingredients. Serve the strudel with extra mustard for dipping."
—CLEO GONSKE REDDING, CA

OKTOBERFEST
STRUDELS

SOUTHERN
PINWHEEL PIE

SAUSAGE AND PEPPERONI PIZZA PASTA

Spaghetti sauce mix helps get this meat-lover's pizza casserole on the table fast. It's great for potlucks, too, because it's inexpensive to double the recipe.

—JULIE GLISSON ZDERO RACINE, WI

PREP: 25 MIN. • **BAKE:** 25 MIN.
MAKES: 8 SERVINGS

- 4 **cups uncooked penne pasta**
- 3 **Italian sausage links, cut into ½-inch slices**
- 1 **cup sliced fresh mushrooms**
- 1 **medium green pepper, chopped**
- 1 **medium onion, chopped**
- 1 **package (3½ ounces) sliced pepperoni**
- 3½ **cups water**
- 2 **cans (6 ounces each) tomato paste**
- 2 **envelopes thick and zesty spaghetti sauce mix**
- 1 **can (2¼ ounces) sliced ripe olives, drained**
- ¼ **cup olive oil**
- ½ **teaspoon garlic salt**
- 1 **cup (4 ounces) shredded part-skim mozzarella cheese**

1. Cook penne according to package directions. Meanwhile, in a Dutch oven, cook the sausage, mushrooms, pepper and onion over medium heat until meat is no longer pink and the vegetables are tender; drain and remove from pan.

2. Cook pepperoni in the same pan until heated through. Return sausage mixture to the pan.

3. Stir in the water, tomato paste, spaghetti sauce mix, olives, oil and garlic salt. Bring to a boil. Reduce the heat; simmer, uncovered, for 4-5 minutes to allow flavors to blend.

4. Drain the pasta; stir into sausage mixture. Transfer to a greased 13x9-in. baking dish. Sprinkle with the cheese.

5. Bake, uncovered, at 350° for 25-30 minutes or until bubbly.

SOUTHERN PINWHEEL PIE

Pretty parsley pinwheels top this hearty casserole filled with a saucy mixture of broccoli, ham and onion. If you prefer, you can use asparagus instead of broccoli.

—SHARON WHITE MORDEN, MB

PREP: 20 MIN. • **BAKE:** 20 MIN.
MAKES: 6 SERVINGS

- 4 **cups cubed fully cooked ham (2 pounds)**
- 1 **medium onion, chopped**
- 2 **tablespoons butter**
- 2 **cans (10¾ ounces each) condensed cream of chicken soup, undiluted**
- 1 **cup 2% milk**
- 2 **cups fresh or frozen broccoli florets**
- 2 **cups biscuit/baking mix**
- ½ **cup water**
- ½ **cup minced fresh parsley**

1. In a large skillet, saute ham and onion in butter until onion is tender. Combine soup and milk; stir into ham mixture. Add broccoli; heat through. Pour into an ungreased shallow 2½-qt. baking dish.

2. Combine biscuit mix and water until a soft dough forms. On a lightly floured surface, knead dough 10 times. Roll out into a 12-in. square; sprinkle with parsley.

3. Roll up jelly-roll style. Cut into 12 pieces; place over ham mixture. Bake, uncovered, at 425° for 20-25 minutes or until biscuits are golden and ham mixture is bubbly.

SAUSAGE RAVIOLI LASAGNA

You can easily alter this lasagna to please any palate—substitute ground beef or turkey for the sausage or include beef ravioli instead of cheese ravioli.

—NICOLE GAZZO BONDURANT, IA

PREP: 20 MIN. • **BAKE:** 35 MIN. + STANDING
MAKES: 8 SERVINGS

- 1 **package (25 ounces) frozen cheese ravioli**
- 1½ **pounds bulk Italian sausage**
- 1 **container (15 ounces) ricotta cheese**
- 1 **large egg, lightly beaten**
- 1 **teaspoon dried basil**
- ½ **teaspoon Italian seasoning**
- 2 **jars (one 26 ounces, one 14 ounces) spaghetti sauce**
- 2 **cups (8 ounces) shredded Italian cheese blend**

1. Cook ravioli according to package directions.

2. Meanwhile, preheat oven to 350°. In a large skillet, cook sausage over medium heat until no longer pink; drain. In a small bowl, combine ricotta cheese, egg, basil and Italian seasoning; set aside. Drain ravioli.

3. Spoon 1⅓ cups spaghetti sauce into a greased 13x9-in. baking dish. Layer with half of the ravioli and sausage. Spoon ricotta mixture over sausage; top with 1⅓ cups sauce. Layer with remaining ravioli and sausage. Spread remaining sauce over the top; sprinkle with cheese.

4. Cover and bake 30 minutes. Uncover and bake 5-10 minutes longer or until cheese is melted. Let stand 10 minutes before cutting.

READER RAVE

"Family really liked this. I used turkey Italian sausage."

—LMMANDA
FROM TASTEOFHOME.COM

SAUSAGE RAVIOLI LASAGNA

"This golden loaf relies on the convenience of refrigerated dough that's stuffed with ham and cheese. I created the recipe by experimenting with a few simple ingredients my family loves. It makes a delicious hot sandwich in no time."
—**GLORIA LINDELL** WELCOME, MN

THREE-CHEESE
HAM STROMBOLI

THREE-CHEESE HAM STROMBOLI

PREP: 15 MIN. • **BAKE:** 30 MIN.
MAKES: 6 SERVINGS

- 1 tube (13.8 ounces) refrigerated pizza crust
- 10 slices deli ham
- ¼ cup sliced green onions
- 1 cup (4 ounces) shredded part-skim mozzarella cheese
- 1 cup (4 ounces) shredded cheddar cheese
- 4 slices provolone cheese
- 1 tablespoon butter, melted

1. Unroll dough onto a greased baking sheet; top with the ham, onions and cheeses. Roll up tightly jelly-roll style, starting with a long side; pinch seam to seal and tuck ends under. Brush with butter.
2. Bake at 350° for 30-35 minutes or until golden brown. Let stand for 5 minutes; cut into 1-in. slices.
FREEZE OPTION *Cool unsliced loaf on a wire rack. Spray a large piece of foil with cooking spray. Wrap loaf in prepared foil and freeze for up to 3 months. To use, thaw loaf at room temperature fo2 hours. Preheat oven to 350°. Unwrap and place on a greased baking sheet. Bake for 15-20 minutes or until heated through. Let stand for 5 minutes; cut into 1-in. slices.*

HOW-TO

MEASURE BUTTER

When a recipe such as Three-Cheese Ham Loaf calls for butter to be melted, you should measure the butter first, then melt that portion.

MEDITERRANEAN PIZZAS

Have only 15 minutes before dinner needs to be ready? These smothered English muffin pizzas are a snap to assemble before you pop them in the oven for a few minutes.
—**JENNIFER ANDRZEJEWSKI** GRIZZLY FLATS, CA

START TO FINISH: 15 MIN.
MAKES: 2 SERVINGS

- 2 English muffins, split and toasted
- 2 tablespoons prepared pesto
- 4 slices deli ham (¾ ounce each)
- ¼ cup julienned roasted sweet red peppers
- ¼ cup crumbled feta cheese
- 2 teaspoons minced fresh basil or ½ teaspoon dried basil

Spread cut sides of muffins with pesto; layer with ham and peppers. Sprinkle with cheese. Place on an ungreased baking sheet. Broil 4-6 in. from the heat for 2-4 minutes or until heated through. Sprinkle with basil.

PORK CHOP DINNER FOR TWO

I've doubled or tripled this dish when necessary for a tableful of people, but it's also perfect for just two. Have extra veggies on hand? Toss them in!
—**SHIRLEY LAZOR** COLORADO SPRINGS, CO

PREP: 10 MIN. • **BAKE:** 55 MIN.
MAKES: 2 SERVINGS

- 2 pork loin chops (¾ inch thick)
- 1 tablespoon canola oil
- 2 medium potatoes, peeled and sliced
- 1 medium onion, sliced
- 1 medium carrot, sliced
- 1 tablespoon butter
- ½ teaspoon salt
- ¼ teaspoon pepper

1. In a large skillet, brown pork chops in oil. Place in a greased 8-in. square baking pan. Layer potatoes, onion and carrot over chops. Dot with butter. Sprinkle with salt and pepper.
2. Cover and bake at 350° for 55-60 minutes or until pork chops and vegetables are tender.

HAM MAC AND CHEESE

You can switch up this family-pleasing dish in many ways. I sometimes use turkey or chicken instead of ham, and I like to use different types and flavors of mac and cheese. It's always popular with the kids.
—**SUSAN TAUL** BIRMINGHAM, AL

PREP: 30 MIN. • **BAKE:** 35 MIN.
MAKES: 4 SERVINGS

- 1 package (7¼ ounces) macaroni and cheese dinner mix
- ¾ cup soft bread crumbs
- 2 tablespoons grated Parmesan cheese
- 1 tablespoon minced fresh parsley
- 1 tablespoon butter, melted
- 1 cup cubed fully cooked ham
- 1 cup (8 ounces) cream-style cottage cheese
- ½ cup sour cream
- 2 tablespoons sliced green onion
- 1 tablespoon diced pimientos, optional
- ¼ teaspoon salt
- ¼ teaspoon ground mustard

1. Prepare macaroni and cheese according to package directions. Meanwhile, in a small bowl, combine bread crumbs, Parmesan cheese, parsley and butter; set aside.
2. In a large bowl, combine macaroni and cheese, ham, cottage cheese, sour cream, green onion, the pimientos if desired, salt and mustard. Pour into a greased 1½ qt. baking dish. Sprinkle with bread crumb mixture.
3. Bake, uncovered, at 350° for 35-40 minutes or until mixture is heated through.

Fish & Seafood

FISH & CHIPS WITH DIPPING SAUCE

My husband and I really like fish and chips but not all the grease that typically comes along with it. I decided to give the classic dinner a makeover. Turns out the pickle dip is healthier than tartar sauce, and we like it a lot better—who knew?

—MICHELLE LUCAS COLD SPRING, KY

PREP: 30 MIN. • **BAKE:** 30 MIN.
MAKES: 4 SERVINGS

- ½ **cup reduced-fat sour cream**
- 2 **tablespoons chopped dill pickle**
- 1 **tablespoon dill pickle juice**
- ⅛ **teaspoon pepper**

FRIES

- 4 **large potatoes (about 2 pounds)**
- 2 **tablespoons olive oil**
- ½ **teaspoon salt**
- ¼ **teaspoon pepper**

FISH

- 1½ **cups panko (Japanese) bread crumbs**
- 1 **teaspoon garlic powder**
- 1 **teaspoon onion powder**
- ½ **teaspoon salt**
- ½ **teaspoon pepper**
- 2 **large egg whites, beaten**
- 4 **cod fillets (4 ounces each)**
  Cooking spray
  Lemon wedges

1. Arrange one oven rack at lowest rack setting; place second rack in the middle of the oven. Preheat oven to 425°. In a small bowl, mix the sour cream, chopped pickle, pickle juice and pepper. Refrigerate, covered, until serving.

FISH & CHIPS WITH
DIPPING SAUCE

2. Cut potatoes into ¼-in. julienne strips. Rinse well and pat dry. In a large bowl, toss with oil, salt and pepper; transfer to a baking sheet coated with cooking spray. Bake on bottom oven rack 30-35 minutes or until golden brown and tender, turning once.

3. For fish, in a shallow bowl, mix bread crumbs, garlic powder, onion powder, salt and pepper. Place egg whites in a separate shallow bowl. Dip fish in egg whites, then in crumb mixture, patting to help coating adhere.

4. Transfer to a baking sheet coated with cooking spray. Spritz fish with cooking spray. Bake on top oven rack 14-16 minutes or until fish just begins to flake easily with a fork. Serve fish with fries, sour cream mixture and lemon wedges.

PER SERVING *1 serving equals 402 cal., 11 g fat (3 g sat. fat), 53 mg chol., 667 mg sodium, 48 g carb., 4 g fiber, 27 g pro. **Diabetic Exchanges:** 3 starch, 3 lean meat, 2 fat.*

CREAMY SEAFOOD ENCHILADAS

Shrimp and crab plus a flavorful sauce make these enchiladas outstanding. I made them for an annual fundraiser, and now they're always in demand. Spice up the recipe to your taste by adding more green chilies and salsa.

—EVELYN GEBHARDT KASILOF, AK

PREP: 20 MIN. • **BAKE:** 30 MIN.
MAKES: 6 SERVINGS

- ¼ cup butter
- ¼ cup all-purpose flour
- 1 cup chicken broth
- 1 can (10¾ ounces) condensed cream of chicken soup, undiluted
- 1 cup (8 ounces) sour cream
- ½ cup salsa
- ⅛ teaspoon salt
- 1 cup (8 ounces) 4% cottage cheese
- 1 pound small shrimp, cooked, peeled and deveined
- 1 cup cooked or canned crabmeat, drained, flaked and cartilage removed
- 1½ cups (6 ounces) shredded Monterey Jack cheese
- 1 can (4 ounces) chopped green chilies
- 1 tablespoon dried cilantro flakes
- 12 flour tortillas (6 inches)
  Additional salsa

1. In a saucepan over low heat, melt the butter; stir in flour until smooth. Gradually stir in broth and soup until blended. Bring to a boil; cook and stir 2 minutes or until slightly thickened. Remove from the heat. Stir in sour cream, salsa and salt; set aside.
2. Place cottage cheese in a blender; cover and process until smooth. Transfer to a bowl; add the shrimp, crab, Monterey Jack cheese, chilies and cilantro.
3. Spread ¾ cup sauce in a greased 13x9-in. baking dish. Place about ⅓ cup seafood mixture down the center of each tortilla. Roll up and place seam side down over sauce. Top with the remaining sauce. Bake, uncovered, at 350° for 30-35 minutes or until heated through. Serve with additional salsa.

HONEY-PECAN BAKED COD

HONEY-PECAN BAKED COD

While vacationing in the Blue Ridge Mountains, we tried pecan-crusted fish one night at dinner. We were able to re-create the entree and now enjoy this tasty version often. You can use fresh or frozen cod.

—LANA GERMAN LENOIR, NC

START TO FINISH: 30 MIN.
MAKES: 6 SERVINGS

- 3 tablespoons honey
- 2 tablespoons butter, melted
- 1 tablespoon reduced-sodium soy sauce
- 1½ teaspoons lemon-pepper seasoning
- ½ teaspoon garlic powder
- ½ teaspoon paprika
- ¼ teaspoon seasoned salt
- 1½ cups finely chopped pecans
- 6 cod fillets (6 ounces each)

1. Preheat oven to 400°. In a shallow bowl, combine first seven ingredients. Place pecans in another shallow bowl. Dip the fillets in honey mixture, then coat with pecans.
2. Place in a greased 13x9-in. baking dish. Bake, uncovered, 15-20 minutes or until fish flakes easily with a fork.
PER SERVING *1 fillet equals 330 cal., 19 g fat (4 g sat. fat), 75 mg chol., 398 mg sodium, 12 g carb., 2 g fiber, 29 g pro. Diabetic Exchanges: 4 lean meat, 3 fat, ½ starch.*

MEDITERRANEAN TILAPIA

I recently became a fan of tilapia. Its mild taste makes it easy to top with my favorite ingredients. Plus, it's low in calories and fat. What's not to love?

—**ROBIN BRENNEMAN** HILLIARD, OH

START TO FINISH: 20 MIN.
MAKES: 6 SERVINGS

- 6 **tilapia fillets (6 ounces each)**
- 1 **cup canned Italian diced tomatoes**
- ½ **cup water-packed artichoke hearts, chopped**
- ½ **cup sliced ripe olives**
- ½ **cup crumbled feta cheese**

Preheat oven to 400°. Place fillets in a 15x10x1-in. baking pan coated with cooking spray. Top with tomatoes, artichoke hearts, olives and cheese. Bake, uncovered, 15-20 minutes or until fish flakes easily with a fork.

ITALIAN TILAPIA *Follow method as directed, but top fillets with 1 cup canned diced tomatoes with roasted garlic, ½ cup each julienned roasted sweet red pepper, sliced mushrooms and diced fresh mozzarella cheese, and ½ teaspoon dried basil.*

SOUTHWEST TILAPIA *Follow method as directed, but top fillets with 1 cup canned diced tomatoes with mild green chilies, ½ cup each cubed avocado, frozen corn (thawed), cubed cheddar cheese and ½ teaspoon dried cilantro.*

PER SERVING *1 fillet equals 197 cal., 4 g fat (2 g sat. fat), 88 mg chol., 446 mg sodium, 5 g carb., 1 g fiber, 34 g pro.* **Diabetic Exchanges:** *5 lean meat, ½ fat.*

FISH & VEGGIE PACKETS

Try this traditional cooking technique to keep the fish moist while sealing in vitamins. I like to serve fish still wrapped in parchment for each person to open.

—**JILL ANDERSON** SLEEPY EYE, MN

START TO FINISH: 25 MIN.
MAKES: 4 SERVINGS

- 1½ **cups julienned carrots**
- 1½ **cups fresh snow peas**
- 2 **green onions, cut into 2-inch pieces**
- 4 **cod fillets (6 ounces each)**
- 2 **teaspoons lemon juice**
- ¼ **teaspoon salt**
- ¼ **teaspoon dried thyme**
- ¼ **teaspoon crushed red pepper flakes**
- ¼ **teaspoon pepper**
- 4 **teaspoons butter**

1. Combine carrots, snow peas and green onions. Cut parchment paper or heavy-duty foil into four 18x12-in. pieces; place a fish fillet off center on each. Drizzle with lemon juice and top with carrot mixture. Sprinkle with seasonings; dot with butter.

2. Fold parchment paper over fish. Bring edges of paper together on all sides and crimp to seal, forming packets. Place on baking sheets.

3. Bake at 450° for 10-15 minutes or until fish just begins to flake easily with a fork. Open packets carefully to allow steam to escape.

PER SERVING *1 serving equals 206 cal., 5 g fat (3 g sat. fat), 75 mg chol., 301 mg sodium, 10 g carb., 3 g fiber, 29 g pro.* **Diabetic Exchanges:** *3 lean meat, 1 vegetable, 1 fat.*

MEDITERRANEAN TILAPIA

READER RAVE

"It had a light lemon flavor and perfect texture. Cleanup was virtually nonexistent, a plus for those nights I have to work."

—**FOOTSIE**
FROM TASTEOFHOME.COM

FISH & VEGGIE
PACKETS

"Tiny and tender bay scallops take center stage in these miniature dishes. They're reminiscent of potpies, very creamy and packed with flavorful veggies in every bite."
—**VIVIAN MANARY** NEPEAN, ON

MINI SCALLOP CASSEROLES

EAT SMART

MINI SCALLOP CASSEROLES

PREP: 30 MIN. • **BAKE:** 20 MIN.
MAKES: 4 SERVINGS

- 3 **celery ribs, chopped**
- 1 **cup sliced fresh mushrooms**
- 1 **medium green pepper, chopped**
- 1 **small onion, chopped**
- 2 **tablespoons butter**
- ⅓ **cup all-purpose flour**
- ¼ **teaspoon salt**
- ¼ **teaspoon pepper**
- 2 **cups fat-free milk**
- 1 **pound bay scallops**

TOPPING

- 1 **cup soft bread crumbs**
- 1 **tablespoon butter, melted**
- ¼ **cup shredded cheddar cheese**

1. In a large skillet, saute the celery, mushrooms, green pepper and onion in butter until tender. Stir in flour, salt and pepper until blended; gradually add the milk. Bring to a boil; cook and stir 2 minutes or until thickened.

2. Reduce heat; add scallops. Cook, stirring occasionally, 3-4 minutes or until scallops are firm and opaque.

3. Preheat oven to 350°. Divide the mixture among four 10-oz. ramekins or custard cups. In a bowl, combine crumbs and butter; sprinkle over the scallop mixture.

4. Bake, uncovered, 15-20 minutes or until bubbly. Sprinkle with cheddar cheese; bake 5 minutes longer or until cheese is melted.

PER SERVING *1 serving equals 332 cal., 12 g fat (7 g sat. fat), 70 mg chol., 588 mg sodium, 27 g carb., 2 g fiber, 28 g pro.*
Diabetic Exchanges: 3 lean meat, 2 fat, 1 starch, 1 vegetable, ½ fat-free milk.

"WHAT'S IN THE FRIDGE" FRITTATA

This is great for a last-minute breakfast, brunch or lunch. Guests rave about the crab and Swiss combination. I also like to use sausage and cheddar with asparagus or whatever seasonal veggies I picked up at the farmers market.

—DEBORAH POSEY VIRGINIA BEACH, VA

START TO FINISH: 25 MIN.
MAKES: 4 SERVINGS

- 6 **large eggs**
- ⅓ **cup chopped onion**
- ⅓ **cup chopped sweet red pepper**
- ⅓ **cup chopped fresh mushrooms**
- 1 **tablespoon olive oil**
- 1 **can (6 ounces) lump crabmeat, drained**
- ¼ **cup shredded Swiss cheese**

1. In a small bowl, whisk eggs; set aside. In an 8-in. ovenproof skillet, saute the chopped onion, pepper and mushrooms in oil until tender. Reduce heat; sprinkle with crab. Top with eggs. Cover and cook for 5-7 minutes or until nearly set.
2. Uncover skillet; sprinkle with cheese. Broil 3-4 in. from the heat for 2-3 minutes or until the eggs are completely set. Let stand for 5 minutes. Cut into wedges.
PER SERVING *1 wedge equals 215 cal., 13 g fat (4 g sat. fat), 361 mg chol., 265 mg sodium, 3 g carb., 1 g fiber, 21 g pro.* **Diabetic Exchanges:** *3 lean meat, 1½ fat.*

BROILED SALMON WITH MEDITERRANEAN LENTILS

I used to weight-train to keep myself in shape for my work as a volunteer firefighter, and I often prepared this dish. It's loaded with fiber, protein and antioxidants. Now that I'm a stay-at-home mom, I make it to give myself energy to chase the kids.

—DAWN E. BRYANT THEDFORD, NE

PREP: 15 MIN. • **COOK:** 55 MIN.
MAKES: 4 SERVINGS

- 1 **small carrot, julienned**
- ¼ **cup chopped onion**
- 1 **tablespoon olive oil**
- ½ **cup dried lentils, rinsed**
- ½ **cup dried green split peas**
- 2 **garlic cloves, minced**
- 2 **teaspoons capers, drained**
- 2½ **cups water**
- ½ **teaspoon salt**
- ½ **teaspoon pepper**
- 2 **tablespoons lemon juice**

SALMON
- 4 **salmon fillets (4 ounces each)**
  Butter-flavored cooking spray
- ¼ **teaspoon salt**
- ⅛ **teaspoon pepper**

1. In a small saucepan, saute carrot and onion in oil until tender. Add the lentils, peas, garlic and capers; cook and stir 3 minutes longer.
2. Add water, salt and pepper. Bring to a boil. Reduce the heat; cover and simmer for 45-50 minutes or until tender. Stir in lemon juice.
3. Spritz fillets with butter-flavored spray; sprinkle with salt and pepper. Broil 4-6 in. from the heat for 7-9 minutes or until fish flakes easily with a fork. Serve with lentil mixture.

BROILED SALMON WITH
MEDITERRANEAN LENTILS

SHRIMP AND FONTINA CASSEROLE

Looking for a seafood casserole that tastes gourmet? Try this one. The Cajun flavor comes through the cheese topping, and the confetti of green onions and red peppers makes it pretty enough for a dinner party.

—EMORY DOTY JASPER, GA

PREP: 35 MIN. • **BAKE:** 15 MIN. + STANDING
MAKES: 8 SERVINGS

- ½ cup all-purpose flour
- 1 tablespoon Cajun seasoning
- ½ teaspoon pepper
- 2 pounds uncooked large shrimp, peeled and deveined
- 2 tablespoons olive oil
- 4 thin slices prosciutto or deli ham, cut into thin strips
- ½ pound medium fresh mushrooms, quartered
- 2 tablespoons butter
- 4 green onions, chopped
- 2 garlic cloves, minced
- 1 cup heavy whipping cream
- 8 ounces fontina cheese, cubed
- 1 jar (7 ounces) roasted sweet red peppers, drained and chopped
- ¼ cup grated Parmigiano-Reggiano cheese
- ¼ cup grated Romano cheese

1. Preheat oven to 350°. In a large resealable plastic bag, combine the flour, Cajun seasoning and pepper. Add the shrimp, a few at a time, and shake to coat.

2. In a large skillet over medium heat, cook the shrimp in oil in batches until golden brown. Drain on paper towels. Transfer to an ungreased 13x9-in. baking dish and top with prosciutto. Set aside.

3. In same skillet, saute mushrooms in butter until tender. Add onions and garlic; cook 1 minute longer. Add the cream and fontina cheese; cook and stir until cheese is melted. Remove from heat; stir in chopped peppers. Pour over prosciutto. Sprinkle with remaining cheeses.

4. Bake, uncovered, 15-20 minutes or until bubbly and cheese is melted. Let stand 10 minutes before serving.

SALMON WITH
BROWN SUGAR GLAZE

SALMON WITH BROWN SUGAR GLAZE

Need a simple way to serve a whole salmon fillet to a group of friends? Here's the super-easy recipe that finally made me a fan of the fish.

—RACHEL GARCIA COLORADO SPRINGS, CO

PREP: 15 MIN. • **BAKE:** 20 MIN.
MAKES: 8 SERVINGS

- 1 tablespoon brown sugar
- 2 teaspoons butter
- 1 teaspoon honey
- 1 tablespoon olive oil
- 1 tablespoon Dijon mustard
- 1 tablespoon reduced-sodium soy sauce
- ½ to ¾ teaspoon salt
- ¼ teaspoon pepper
- 1 salmon fillet (2½ pounds)

1. In a small saucepan over medium heat, cook and stir brown sugar, butter and honey until melted. Remove from the heat; whisk in the olive oil, Dijon mustard, soy sauce, salt and pepper. Cool for 5 minutes.

2. Place salmon in a large foil-lined baking pan; spoon the brown sugar mixture over top. Bake, uncovered, at 350° for 20-25 minutes or until fish flakes easily with a fork.

YUMMY TUNA PITAS

I like to tuck this cheesy tuna filling into pita pockets for a fun grab-and-go lunch. Celery adds a nice crunch.

—MARGE NICOL SHANNON, IL

START TO FINISH: 20 MIN.
MAKES: 2 SERVINGS

- 1 can (6 ounces) light water-packed tuna, drained and flaked
- ½ cup shredded cheddar cheese
- ⅓ cup chopped celery
- 2 tablespoons chopped onion
- ¼ cup mayonnaise
- 2 pita pocket halves

In a small bowl, combine the tuna, cheddar cheese, celery, onion and mayonnaise. Spoon into pita halves. Place on an ungreased baking sheet. Bake at 400° for 8-10 minutes or until heated through and cheese is melted.

LEMON-CAPER BAKED COD

START TO FINISH: 20 MIN.
MAKES: 4 SERVINGS

- ¼ **cup butter, cubed**
- 2 **tablespoons lemon juice**
- ¼ **teaspoon garlic pepper blend**
- ¼ **teaspoon grated lemon peel**
- 2 **tablespoons capers, drained**
- 4 **cod or haddock fillets (6 ounces each)**
- ½ **teaspoon seafood seasoning**
- 1 **tablespoon crumbled feta cheese**

1. In a small microwave-safe bowl, combine butter, lemon juice, garlic pepper and lemon peel. Microwave, uncovered, on high for 45-60 seconds or until butter is melted. Stir in capers.
2. Place cod in an ungreased 13x9-in. baking dish; sprinkle with the seafood seasoning. Spoon butter mixture over fillets. Sprinkle with the cheese. Bake, uncovered, at 425° for 10-15 minutes or until fish flakes easily with a fork.

> "Capers, lemon and feta cheese give this easy seafood dish a fabulous Greek flavor."
> —**CAROLYN SCHMELING** BROOKFIELD, WI

BROILED PARMESAN TILAPIA

Even picky eaters might just find a way to love fish when you plate up this toasty Parmesan-coated dish. I serve it with mashed cauliflower and a green salad for a low-calorie meal everyone can enjoy.

—**TRISHA KRUSE** EAGLE, ID

START TO FINISH: 20 MIN.
MAKES: 6 SERVINGS

- 6 **tilapia fillets (6 ounces each)**
- ¼ **cup grated Parmesan cheese**
- ¼ **cup reduced-fat mayonnaise**
- 2 **tablespoons lemon juice**
- 1 **tablespoon butter, softened**
- 1 **garlic clove, minced**
- 1 **teaspoon minced fresh basil or ¼ teaspoon dried basil**
- ½ **teaspoon seafood seasoning**

1. Place fillets on a broiler pan coated with cooking spray. In a small bowl, combine the remaining ingredients; spread over fillets.
2. Broil fillets 3-4 in. from the heat for 10-12 minutes or until fish flakes easily with a fork.
PER SERVING *1 fillet equals 207 cal., 8 g fat (3 g sat. fat), 94 mg chol., 260 mg sodium, 2 g carb., trace fiber, 33 g pro.* ***Diabetic Exchanges:*** *5 lean meat, 1 fat.*

LEMON-CAPER BAKED COD

HALIBUT WITH ORANGE SALSA

Crispy orange halibut is topped with a homemade salsa featuring tomatoes, oranges, kalamata olives and basil for a company-worthy dish that'll bring raves.

—**GLORIA BRADLEY** NAPERVILLE, IL

PREP: 35 MIN. • **COOK:** 20 MIN.
MAKES: 4 SERVINGS

- 1 cup orange juice
- 1¼ teaspoons Caribbean jerk seasoning, divided
- 4 halibut fillets (6 ounces each)
- ½ cup panko (Japanese) bread crumbs
- 2 teaspoons grated orange peel
- ½ teaspoon salt

SALSA
- 2 plum tomatoes, seeded and chopped
- 1 large navel orange, peeled, sectioned and chopped
- ¼ cup pitted Greek olives, chopped
- 2 tablespoons minced fresh basil
- 1 tablespoon olive oil
- 1 garlic clove, minced
- ⅛ teaspoon salt
- ⅛ teaspoon pepper

1. In a large resealable plastic bag, combine orange juice and 1 teaspoon jerk seasoning. Add the halibut; seal bag and turn to coat. Set aside for 15 minutes.
2. Meanwhile, in a shallow bowl, combine the bread crumbs, grated orange peel, salt and remaining jerk seasoning. Drain and discard the marinade. Coat halibut with bread crumb mixture. Place on a greased baking sheet.
3. Bake at 400° for 15 minutes. Broil 5-6 in. from the heat for 4-6 minutes or until lightly browned and the fish flakes easily with a fork.
4. In a small bowl, combine the salsa ingredients. Serve with halibut.

HALIBUT WITH
ORANGE SALSA

CREAMY SEAFOOD CASSEROLE

I love this recipe from my mother. It's easy and delicious. Even better: You can make it the night before. If you're out of buttery crackers, try topping it with french-fried onions or crushed potato chips—they'll give it a different kind of crunch.

—**MARY BROWN** WHITMAN, MA

PREP: 15 MIN. • **BAKE:** 25 MIN.
MAKES: 8 SERVINGS

- 1 pound flounder fillets, cut into 1½-inch pieces
- 1 pound uncooked medium shrimp, peeled and deveined
- 1 can (10¾ ounces) condensed cream of shrimp soup, undiluted
- ¼ cup 2% milk
- 1 cup crushed Ritz crackers (about 25 crackers)
- ¼ cup grated Parmesan cheese
- 1 teaspoon paprika
- 2 tablespoons butter, melted

1. Place fish and shrimp in a greased 11x7-in. baking dish. Combine soup and milk; pour over seafood. Combine the cracker crumbs, cheese, paprika and butter; sprinkle over top.
2. Bake, uncovered, at 350° for 25-30 minutes or until fish flakes easily with a fork and shrimp turn pink.
PER SERVING *1 serving equals 217 cal., 9 g fat (4 g sat. fat), 126 mg chol., 607 mg sodium, 11 g carb., trace fiber, 22 g pro. Diabetic Exchanges: 3 lean meat, 2 fat, 1 starch.*

READER RAVE

"This was excellent! I could not find the cream of shrimp soup in my local store. I substituted cream of celery, and it was delicious."

—**KATLAYDEE3**
FROM TASTEOFHOME.COM

BALSAMIC-SALMON
SPINACH SALAD

BALSAMIC-SALMON SPINACH SALAD

This healthy and tasty dish is a cinch to make after a hard day of work.

—KAREN1969
TASTE OF HOME ONLINE COMMUNITY

START TO FINISH: 20 MIN.
MAKES: 2 SERVINGS

- 1 **salmon fillet (6 ounces)**
- 2 **tablespoons reduced-fat balsamic vinaigrette, divided**
- 3 **cups fresh baby spinach**
- ¼ **cup cubed avocado**
- 1 **tablespoon chopped walnuts, toasted**
- 1 **tablespoon sunflower kernels, toasted**
- 1 **tablespoon dried cranberries**

1. Drizzle salmon with 1 tablespoon balsamic vinaigrette. Place on a broiler pan coated with cooking spray. Broil 3-4 in. from the heat for 10-15 minutes or until fish flakes easily with a fork. Cut salmon into two pieces.

2. Meanwhile, in a large bowl, toss spinach with remaining vinaigrette. Divide between two plates. Top with salmon, avocado, walnuts, sunflower kernels and cranberries.

PER SERVING *1 serving equals 283 cal., 19 g fat (3 g sat. fat), 50 mg chol., 219 mg sodium, 9 g carb., 3 g fiber, 21 g pro.* **Diabetic Exchanges:** *2 medium-fat meat, 2 fat, 1 vegetable.*

SWISS 'N' CRAB TART

I often make this delightful tart with fresh crab, which is plentiful here in Alaska. I hope your family enjoys it as much as mine does!

—KATHY CROW CORDOVA, AK

PREP: 15 MIN. • **BAKE:** 45 MIN. + STANDING
MAKES: 6-8 SERVINGS

- 1 **refrigerated pie pastry**
- 1 **can (6 ounces) lump crabmeat, drained**
- 1 **cup (4 ounces) shredded Swiss cheese**
- 2 **green onions, thinly sliced**
- 3 **large eggs, beaten**
- 1 **cup half-and-half cream**
- ½ **teaspoon salt**
- ½ **teaspoon grated lemon peel**
- ¼ **teaspoon ground mustard**
  Dash mace
- ¼ **cup sliced almonds**

1. Line a 9-in. tart pan with unpricked pastry shell; line pastry with heavy-duty foil. Bake at 450° for 5 minutes. Remove foil.

2. Arrange crabmeat evenly in baked crust. Top with the Swiss cheese and green onions. Combine the remaining ingredients except almonds; pour into tart shell. Top with almonds.

3. Bake tart at 325° for 45 minutes or until set. Let stand for 10 minutes before serving.

CLASSIC
CRAB CAKES

CLASSIC CRAB CAKES

Our region is known for good seafood, and crab cakes are a traditional favorite. I learned to make them from a chef in a restaurant where they were a best-seller. The crabmeat's sweet and mild flavor is sparked by the blend of other ingredients.
—**DEBBIE TERENZINI** LUSBY, MD

START TO FINISH: 20 MIN.
MAKES: 8 SERVINGS

- 1 **pound fresh or canned crabmeat, drained, flaked and cartilage removed**
- 2 **to 2½ cups soft bread crumbs**
- 1 **large egg, beaten**
- ¾ **cup mayonnaise**
- ⅓ **cup each chopped celery, green pepper and onion**
- 1 **tablespoon seafood seasoning**
- 1 **tablespoon minced fresh parsley**
- 2 **teaspoons lemon juice**
- 1 **teaspoon Worcestershire sauce**
- 1 **teaspoon prepared mustard**
- ¼ **teaspoon pepper**
- ⅛ **teaspoon hot pepper sauce**
- 2 **to 4 tablespoons vegetable oil, optional**
  Lemon wedges, optional

In a large bowl, combine the crabmeat, soft bread crumbs, egg, mayonnaise, vegetables and seasonings. Shape into eight patties. Broil patties or cook in a skillet in oil for 4 minutes on each side or until golden brown. Serve with the lemon if desired.
FREEZE OPTION *Freeze cooled crab cakes in freezer containers, separating layers with waxed paper. To use, reheat the crab cakes on a baking sheet in a preheated 325° oven until heated through.*

TERIYAKI SALMON WITH SESAME GINGER RICE

This delicious recipe is lower in fat, super fast and elegant enough for company. It's packed full of vitamins and antioxidants, so not only is it good for your waistline, it's heart-healthy, too!
—**KATRINA LOPES** LYMAN, SC

START TO FINISH: 20 MIN.
MAKES: 6 SERVINGS

- 2 **cups uncooked instant rice**
- 6 **salmon fillets (4 ounces each)**
- ⅓ **cup reduced-calorie pancake syrup**
- ⅓ **cup reduced-sodium teriyaki sauce**
- 4 **green onions, thinly sliced**
- 1 **tablespoon butter**
- 1 **package (10 ounces) frozen chopped spinach, thawed and squeezed dry**
- ½ **cup reduced-fat sesame ginger salad dressing**

1. Cook the instant rice according to package directions. Meanwhile, place salmon fillets in a 15x10x1-in. baking pan coated with cooking spray. Mix syrup and teriyaki sauce; spoon ⅓ cup mixture over fillets.
2. Bake at 400° for 10-15 minutes or until the fish flakes easily with a fork, basting frequently with the remaining syrup mixture.
3. In a large skillet, saute onions in butter until tender. Add spinach and cooked rice; saute 2 minutes longer. Stir in dressing; heat through. Serve with salmon.

MINI SALMON LOAF

Here's a classic salmon loaf with dill sauce that's the perfect size for two. I've made it many, many times with great success.
—**PATRICIA GOULD** CANAAN, NH

PREP: 15 MIN. • **BAKE:** 40 MIN.
MAKES: 2 SERVINGS

- ¾ **cup chopped celery**
- ½ **cup chopped onion**
- 2 **tablespoons canola oil**
- 1 **cup soft bread crumbs**
- 1 **large egg, lightly beaten**
- 2 **tablespoons 2% milk**
- ¼ **teaspoon salt**
- ¼ **teaspoon pepper**
- 1 **can (7½ ounces) salmon, drained, bones and skin removed**

DILL SAUCE

- ½ **cup mayonnaise**
- ¼ **cup sour cream**
- 1 **tablespoon lemon juice**
- 1 **tablespoon 2% milk**
- 2 **teaspoons snipped fresh dill**
- ½ **teaspoon sugar**
- ⅛ **teaspoon pepper**

1. In a small skillet, saute the celery and onion in oil until tender. In a large bowl, combine the bread crumbs, egg, milk, salt, pepper and celery mixture. Crumble the salmon over the mixture and mix well. Transfer to a greased 5¾x3x2-in. loaf pan.
2. Bake at 350° for 40-45 minutes or until a thermometer reads 160°. In a bowl, combine the sauce ingredients. Serve with salmon loaf.

TOP TIP

CRAB CAKE SERVING IDEAS

Dress up your crab cakes with these accompaniments and serving ideas:

- Lemon wedges, cocktail sauce or tartar sauce
- A side dish of veggie fries, mac 'n' cheese or buttered green beans
- Coleslaw or Macaroni Coleslaw (page 235) and sliced tomatoes
- Toasted dinner rolls, baby lettuce and the mustard mayo from the tuna cakes recipe on page 159 to make Crab Po' Boy Sliders

Bonus: Sides, Salads & Breads

HOMEMADE TORTILLAS

SAVORY CHEDDAR BREAD

I often serve my cheddar bread with deep bowls of steaming homemade soup. The combo helps to warm up my cattle-raiser husband and our two sons on our chilly evenings here in Canada.

—CAROL FUNK RICHARD, SK

PREP: 20 MIN. • **BAKE:** 45 MIN.
MAKES: 1 LOAF (12 SLICES)

- 2 **cups all-purpose flour**
- 4 **teaspoons baking powder**
- 1 **tablespoon sugar**
- ½ **teaspoon onion salt**
- ½ **teaspoon leaf oregano**
- ¼ **teaspoon ground mustard**
- 1¼ **cups shredded sharp cheddar cheese**
- 1 **large egg, well beaten**
- 1 **cup milk**
- 1 **tablespoon butter, melted**

1. Combine the flour, baking powder, sugar, onion salt, leaf oregano, ground mustard and shredded sharp cheddar cheese; set aside. Combine egg, milk and butter; add to the dry ingredients, stirring just until moistened.

2. Spread batter in a greased 8x4-in. loaf pan. Bake at 350° for 45 minutes or until a toothpick inserted in center comes out clean.

PER SERVING *1 slice equals 149 cal., 6 g fat (4 g sat. fat), 35 mg chol., 301 mg sodium, 18 g carb., 1 g fiber, 6 g pro. Diabetic Exchanges: 1½ starch, 1 fat.*

HOMEMADE TORTILLAS

I usually double this recipe because we go through these so quickly. The tortillas are so tender, chewy and simple, you'll never use store-bought again.

—KRISTIN VAN DYKEN KENNEWICK, WA

START TO FINISH: 30 MIN.
MAKES: 8 TORTILLAS

- 2 **cups all-purpose flour**
- ½ **teaspoon salt**
- ¾ **cup water**
- 3 **tablespoons olive oil**

1. In a large bowl, combine flour and salt. Stir in water and oil. Turn onto a floured surface; knead 10-12 times, adding a little flour or water if needed to achieve a smooth dough. Let rest for 10 minutes.

2. Divide dough into eight portions. On a lightly floured surface, roll each portion into a 7-in. circle.

3. In a large nonstick skillet coated with cooking spray, cook the tortillas over medium heat for 1 minute on each side or until lightly browned. Keep warm.

PER SERVING *1 tortilla equals 159 cal., 5 g fat (1 g sat. fat), 0 chol., 148 mg sodium, 24 g carb., 1 g fiber, 3 g pro. Diabetic Exchanges: 1½ starch, 1 fat.*

FABULOUS GREEN BEANS

SCALLOPED CARROTS

A cookbook my husband gave me as a wedding gift included this recipe—he remembers having the dish as a child at church dinners. Now I make it whenever I need a special vegetable side. It's still rich and cheesy after reheating.

—JOYCE TORNHOLM NEW MARKET, IA

PREP: 25 MIN. • **BAKE:** 35 MIN.
MAKES: 6 SERVINGS

- 12 **medium carrots, sliced ¼ inch thick (about 4 cups)**
- 1 **medium onion, finely chopped**
- ½ **cup butter, divided**
- ¼ **cup all-purpose flour**
- 1 **teaspoon salt**
- ¼ **teaspoon ground mustard**
- ¼ **teaspoon celery salt**
  Dash pepper
- 2 **cups milk**
- 2 **cups (8 ounces) shredded cheddar cheese**
- 3 **slices whole wheat bread, cut into small cubes**

1. Preheat oven to 350°. Place 1 in. of water in a large saucepan; add carrots. Bring to a boil. Reduce the heat; cover and simmer for 7-9 minutes or until crisp-tender. Drain.

2. In another saucepan, saute onion in ¼ cup butter. Stir in the flour, salt, mustard, celery salt and pepper until blended. Gradually add milk. Bring to a boil; cook and stir for 2 minutes or until thickened.

3. In a greased 11x7-in. baking dish, layer half of the carrots, cheese and white sauce. Repeat layers. Melt the remaining butter; toss with bread cubes. Sprinkle over the top. Bake, uncovered, 35-40 minutes or until hot and bubbly.

FABULOUS GREEN BEANS

My family loves this buttery sauce over green beans, whether they're garden fresh or frozen. Another great option: Try sugar snap peas.

—LORI DANIELS BEVERLY, WV

START TO FINISH: 20 MIN.
MAKES: 4 SERVINGS

- 1 **pound fresh green beans, trimmed**
- ¼ **cup butter, cubed**
- 1 **tablespoon olive oil**
- ½ **teaspoon salt**
- ½ **teaspoon Italian seasoning**
- ½ **teaspoon lemon juice**
- ¼ **teaspoon grated lemon peel**

1. Place beans in a steamer basket; place in a large saucepan over 1 in. of water. Bring to a boil; cover and steam for 8-10 minutes or until crisp-tender.

2. Meanwhile, in a small saucepan, heat remaining ingredients until the butter is melted. Transfer beans to a serving bowl; drizzle with the butter mixture and toss to coat.

HERBED-BUTTER GREEN BEANS
Saute ¼ cup chopped onion, ¼ cup chopped celery, 2 tablespoons sesame seeds, 3 minced garlic cloves, 4 teaspoons dried parsley flakes, ½ teaspoon salt, ½ teaspoon dried basil, ½ teaspoon dried oregano and ⅛ teaspoon crushed dried rosemary in 3 tablespoons butter until vegetables are tender. Toss with steamed beans.

SPICED GREEN BEANS *Toss the steamed beans with 2 tablespoons melted butter, ¼ teaspoon celery seed, ¼ teaspoon ground ginger, ¼ teaspoon ground mustard and ¼ teaspoon salt.*

DILLED GREEN BEANS *Toss the steamed beans with 2 tablespoons rice vinegar, 2 tablespoons soy sauce, 1 tablespoon snipped fresh dill and 1 tablespoon toasted sesame seeds.*

TOP TIP

WHAT'S A DASH?

When a recipe calls for a dash, it means a very small amount of seasoning added with a downward flick of the wrist.

BEST-EVER
BANANA BREAD

BEST-EVER BANANA BREAD

Whenever I pass a display of ripe bananas, I can almost smell this bread's wonderful aroma. I always stock up so I can whip up a loaf any time!

—**GERT KAISER** KENOSHA, WI

PREP: 15 MIN.
BAKE: 1¼ HOURS + COOLING
MAKES: 1 LOAF (16 SLICES)

- 1¾ cups all-purpose flour
- 1½ cups sugar
- 1 teaspoon baking soda
- ½ teaspoon salt
- 2 large eggs
- 2 medium ripe bananas, mashed (1 cup)
- ½ cup canola oil
- ¼ cup plus 1 tablespoon buttermilk
- 1 teaspoon vanilla extract
- 1 cup chopped walnuts

1. In a large bowl, stir together flour, sugar, baking soda and salt. In another bowl, combine the eggs, bananas, oil, buttermilk and vanilla; add to flour mixture, stirring just until combined. Fold in nuts.
2. Pour into a greased 9x5-in. loaf pan. Bake at 325° for 1¼-1½ hours or until a toothpick comes out clean. Cool on a wire rack.

MINTED ORZO

In just 15 minutes, I can make a warm, fresh-tasting side. Its mild flavor balances lots of entrees, especially the spicy ones.

—**DONNA CURTIS** OAKHURST, NJ

START TO FINISH: 15 MIN.
MAKES: 6 SERVINGS

- 1 cup uncooked orzo pasta
- 1 teaspoon minced garlic
- 2 tablespoons olive oil
- 2 tablespoons butter
- ½ teaspoon salt
- ¼ teaspoon pepper
- 3 tablespoons minced fresh mint

1. Cook the orzo according to the package directions. Meanwhile, in a large skillet, saute garlic in oil and butter for 2 minutes.
2. Drain orzo and add to the skillet. Sprinkle with salt and pepper; toss to coat. Sprinkle with mint.

BACON CAULIFLOWER SALAD

My Aunt Lavern's specialty side combines crispy-crunchy ingredients with a creamy dressing that's slightly sweet—and now it's a family tradition.

—**KELLY WARD-HARTMAN** CAPE CORAL, FL

PREP: 20 MIN. + CHILLING
MAKES: 4 SERVINGS

- 1 medium head cauliflower, broken into florets
- 1 pound sliced bacon, cooked and crumbled
- 1 cup cubed cheddar cheese
- 1 medium green pepper, chopped
- 1 medium onion, chopped
- 1 cup mayonnaise
- 2 to 4 teaspoons sugar

In a large salad bowl, combine the cauliflower, bacon, cheese, green pepper and onion. Combine the mayonnaise and sugar; spoon over cauliflower mixture and toss to coat. Cover and refrigerate for at least 4 hours before serving.

BACON
CAULIFLOWER SALAD

CREAMY PASTA SALAD

I love creating new and tasty foods. This salad has become popular at our house, especially in the summer. I make it often for my husband and me. Toss in cooked chicken to take it from side dish to meal.

—LORRAINE MENARD OMAHA, NE

PREP: 25 MIN. + CHILLING
MAKES: 2 SERVINGS

- 1 **cup cooked spiral pasta**
- ⅓ **cup grape tomatoes, halved**
- ¼ **cup shredded cheddar cheese**
- 3 **tablespoons chopped onion**
- 3 **tablespoons chopped cucumber**
- 3 **tablespoons chopped green pepper**
- 2 **tablespoons shredded Parmesan cheese**
- 2 **tablespoons sliced pepperoncini**
- 2 **radishes, sliced**
- ⅛ **teaspoon pepper**
- ¼ **cup ranch salad dressing**

In a small bowl, combine the first 10 ingredients. Drizzle with dressing and toss to coat. Cover and refrigerate for at least 1 hour before serving.

SUNFLOWER SEED & HONEY WHEAT BREAD

I've tried many other bread recipes, but this one is the staple in our home. I won $50 in a baking contest with a loaf that I had stored in the freezer.

—MICKEY TURNER GRANTS PASS, OR

PREP: 40 MIN. + RISING
BAKE: 35 MIN. + COOLING
MAKES: 3 LOAVES (12 SLICES EACH)

- 2 **packages (¼ ounce each) active dry yeast**
- 3¾ **cups warm water (110° to 115°)**
- ¼ **cup bread flour**
- ⅓ **cup canola oil**
- ⅓ **cup honey**
- 3 **teaspoons salt**
- 6½ to 7½ **cups whole wheat flour**
- ½ **cup sunflower kernels**
- 3 **tablespoons butter, melted**

1. In a large bowl, dissolve yeast in warm water. Add the bread flour, canola oil, honey, salt and 4 cups whole wheat flour. Beat until smooth. Stir in sunflower kernels and enough remaining flour to form a firm dough.

2. Turn dough onto a floured surface; knead until smooth and elastic, about 6-8 minutes. Place in a greased bowl, turning once to grease the top. Cover and let rise in a warm place until doubled, about 1 hour.

3. Punch dough down; divide into three portions. Shape into loaves; place in three greased 8x4-in. loaf pans. Cover and let rise until doubled, about 30 minutes.

4. Bake at 350° for 35-40 minutes or until golden brown. Brush with melted butter. Remove from pans to wire racks to cool.

FREEZE OPTION *Securely wrap and freeze cooled loaves in foil, and place in resealable plastic freezer bags. To use, thaw at room temperature.*

PER SERVING *1 slice equals 125 cal., 4 g fat (1 g sat. fat), 3 mg chol., 212 mg sodium, 19 g carb., 3 g fiber, 4 g pro.* ***Diabetic Exchanges:*** *1 starch, 1 fat.*

SUNFLOWER SEED &
HONEY WHEAT BREAD

AMBROSIA FRUIT SALAD

START TO FINISH: 10 MIN.
MAKES: 6 SERVINGS

- 1 can (8¼ ounces) fruit cocktail, drained
- 1 can (8 ounces) unsweetened pineapple chunks, drained
- 1 cup green grapes
- 1 cup seedless red grapes
- 1 cup miniature marshmallows
- 1 medium banana, sliced
- ¾ cup vanilla yogurt
- ½ cup flaked coconut

In a large bowl, combine all ingredients. Chill until serving.

PEACHY SWEET POTATOES

Microwaving a couple of sweet potatoes gets this side dish off to a fast start. Juicy slices of fresh peach and sweet cinnamon sugar help turn it into a standout.
—**JOSIE BOCHEK** STURGEON BAY, WI

START TO FINISH: 20 MIN.
MAKES: 2 SERVINGS

- 2 medium sweet potatoes
- 1 small peach, peeled and chopped
- 4½ teaspoons butter
- 1 tablespoon cinnamon sugar
  Dash salt
- 4½ teaspoons chopped pecans, toasted

1. Scrub and pierce potatoes; place on a microwave-safe plate. Microwave, uncovered, on high for 10-12 minutes or until tender, turning once.
2. Meanwhile, in a small saucepan, combine the chopped peach, butter, cinnamon sugar and salt; bring to a boil. Cook and stir for 2-3 minutes or until the peach is tender. Cut an "X" in the top of each potato; fluff the pulp with a fork. Spoon peach mixture into each potato. Sprinkle with pecans.
NOTES *This recipe was tested in a 1,100-watt microwave.*

To toast nuts, bake in a shallow pan in a 350° oven for 5-10 minutes or cook in a skillet over low heat until lightly browned, stirring occasionally.

"I start this with plenty of fruit, add the yogurt for dressing, then mix in just enough marshmallows and coconut so it tastes like the special version I grew up with. It's a well-loved recipe in my home now."
—**TRISHA KRUSE** EAGLE, ID

AMBROSIA FRUIT SALAD

APPLE CIDER SALAD

This cool, refreshing salad with crunchy nuts and apples makes me think of my mother's cooking at Thanksgiving. She would prepare it every year.
—**JEANNETTE MACK** RUSHVILLE, NY

PREP: 15 MIN. + CHILLING
MAKES: 12 SERVINGS

- 2 envelopes unflavored gelatin
- 3¾ cups apple cider, divided
- 3 tablespoons lemon juice
- 3 tablespoons sugar
- ½ teaspoon salt
- 3½ to 4 cups chopped peeled apples
- 1 cup chopped walnuts

1. In a small saucepan, sprinkle the gelatin over ¼ cup of cider; let stand for 2 minutes. Add the lemon juice, sugar, salt and remaining cider. Cook and stir over medium heat until sugar and gelatin are dissolved. Cover and refrigerate until slightly thickened, about 2½ hours.
2. Fold in the chopped apples and walnuts. Transfer to a 2-qt. serving bowl. Cover and refrigerate overnight.
PER SERVING *½ cup equals 135 cal., 6 g fat (0 sat. fat), 0 chol., 102 mg sodium, 19 g carb., 0 fiber, 4 g pro.* **Diabetic Exchanges:** *1 fruit, 1 fat, ½ starch.*

CREAMED PEAS
AND CARROTS

CREAMED PEAS AND CARROTS

A delicate cream sauce gently seasoned with salt and pepper is all it takes to turn peas and carrots into an elegant side. Try this the next time you're looking to spice up a meal!

—GAYLEEN GROTE BATTLEVIEW, ND

START TO FINISH: 25 MIN.
MAKES: 4 SERVINGS

- 4 **medium carrots, sliced**
- 2 **cups frozen peas**
- 1 **tablespoon cornstarch**
- ¼ **teaspoon salt**
- ⅛ **teaspoon pepper**
- ½ **cup heavy whipping cream**

1. Place carrots in a large saucepan; add 1 in. of water. Bring to a boil. Reduce heat; cover and simmer for 5-8 minutes or until crisp-tender.

2. Add peas; return to a boil. Reduce heat; cover and simmer 5-10 minutes longer or until vegetables are tender. Drain, reserving ½ cup cooking liquid. Return the vegetables and reserved liquid to the pan.

3. In a small bowl, combine the cornstarch, salt, pepper and cream until smooth. Stir into vegetables. Bring to a boil; cook and stir for 1-2 minutes or until thickened.

TOP TIP

CHEESY CARROTS

Have some leftover carrots? I persuade my picky eaters to eat more by melting a few slices of American cheese on top of sliced carrots.

—DOROTHY C. DECATUR, IL

CAJUN SUMMER VEGETABLES

Put your summertime veggies to good use in a colorful side dish that gets a little heat from Cajun seasoning. It pairs well with any entree, and it's quick and easy to prepare.

—**NANCY DENTLER** GREENSBORO, NC

START TO FINISH: 25 MIN.
MAKES: 6 SERVINGS

- 2 **medium yellow summer squash, sliced**
- 2 **medium zucchini, sliced**
- 1¾ **cups sliced fresh mushrooms**
- ½ **medium onion, sliced and separated into rings**
- ½ **medium red onion, sliced and separated into rings**
- 1 **cup cherry tomatoes**
- ¼ **cup sliced fresh carrots**
- 1 **teaspoon Cajun seasoning**

Place the vegetables in a grill wok or basket. Grill, uncovered, over medium heat for 8-12 minutes or until tender, stirring frequently. Transfer to a large bowl. Sprinkle with Cajun seasoning; toss to coat.

NOTE *If you do not have a grill wok or basket, use a disposable foil pan. Poke holes in the bottom of the pan with a meat fork to allow liquid to drain.*

MACARONI COLESLAW

My friend Peggy brought this coleslaw to a picnic. After one bite, we all had to have the recipe. Water chestnuts give this new summer standby a welcome crunch.

—**SANDRA MATTESON** WESTHOPE, ND

PREP: 25 MIN. + CHILLING
MAKES: 16 SERVINGS (¾ CUP EACH)

- 1 **package (7 ounces) ring macaroni or ditalini**
- 1 **package (14 ounces) coleslaw mix**
- 2 **medium onions, finely chopped**
- 2 **celery ribs, finely chopped**
- 1 **medium cucumber, finely chopped**
- 1 **medium green pepper, finely chopped**
- 1 **can (8 ounces) whole water chestnuts, drained and chopped**

DRESSING
- 1½ **cups Miracle Whip Light**
- ⅓ **cup sugar**
- ¼ **cup cider vinegar**
- ½ **teaspoon salt**
- ¼ **teaspoon pepper**

1. Cook the macaroni according to package directions; drain and rinse in cold water. Transfer to a large bowl; add the coleslaw mix, onions, celery, cucumber, green pepper and water chestnuts.

2. In a small bowl, whisk the dressing ingredients. Pour over the salad; toss to coat. Cover and refrigerate for at least 1 hour.

PER SERVING *¾ cup equals 150 cal., 5 g fat (1 g sat. fat), 6 mg chol., 286 mg sodium, 24 g carb., 2 g fiber, 3 g pro.* **Diabetic Exchanges:** *1 starch, 1 vegetable, 1 fat.*

MACARONI COLESLAW

EAT SMART
ITALIAN BROCCOLI WITH PEPPERS

START TO FINISH: 20 MIN.
MAKES: 6 SERVINGS

- 4 **cups fresh broccoli florets**
- 1 **medium sweet red pepper, julienned**
- 1 **medium sweet yellow pepper, julienned**
- 1 **tablespoon olive oil**
- 1 **garlic clove, minced**
- 1 **teaspoon dried oregano**
- ½ **teaspoon salt**
- ¼ **teaspoon pepper**
- 1 **medium ripe tomato, cut into wedges and seeded**
- 1 **tablespoon grated Parmesan cheese**

1. In a large saucepan, bring 6 cups water to a boil. Add broccoli; cook, uncovered, 3 minutes. Drain and immediately place broccoli in ice water. Drain and pat dry.

2. In a large nonstick skillet, saute peppers in oil for 3 minutes or until crisp-tender. Add the broccoli, garlic, oregano, salt and pepper; cook for 2 minutes longer. Add the tomato; heat through. Sprinkle with cheese.

PER SERVING ¾ cup equals 55 cal., 3 g fat (1 g sat. fat), 1 mg chol., 228 mg sodium, 7 g carb., 2 g fiber, 2 g pro. *Diabetic Exchanges:* 1 vegetable, ½ fat.

GARLIC-ROASTED BRUSSELS SPROUTS WITH MUSTARD SAUCE

Don't be afraid to bring out the Brussels sprouts. Mellowed by roasting and coated with mustard sauce, they may just delight even the most skeptical folks.

—BECKY WALCH ORLAND, CA

START TO FINISH: 20 MIN.
MAKES: 6 SERVINGS

- 1½ **pounds fresh Brussels sprouts, halved**
- 2 **tablespoons olive oil**
- 3 **garlic cloves, minced**
- ½ **cup heavy whipping cream**
- 3 **tablespoons Dijon mustard**
- ⅛ **teaspoon white pepper**
  Dash salt

1. Place the Brussels sprouts in an ungreased 15x10x1-in. baking pan. Combine oil and garlic; drizzle over the sprouts and toss to coat. Bake, uncovered, at 450° for 10-15 minutes or until tender, stirring occasionally.

2. Meanwhile, in a small saucepan, combine the heavy whipping cream, Dijon mustard, pepper and salt. Bring to a gentle boil; cook for 1-2 minutes or until slightly thickened. Spoon over the Brussels sprouts.

"This healthy side dish goes with just about anything. For a satisfying meal, we like it plated over pasta, grilled chicken or turkey breasts."
—MAUREEN MCCLANAHAN ST. LOUIS, MO

ITALIAN BROCCOLI WITH PEPPERS

HOW-TO
PREP BRUSSELS SPROUTS

1. Remove any yellowed or loose outer leaves. Use a knife to trim the stem end of each sprout.

2. Rinse sprouts and pat dry before adding to recipe.

**GARLIC-ROASTED
BRUSSELS SPROUTS
WITH MUSTARD SAUCE**

CORN DOG MUFFINS

Our three boys were always asking for corn dogs, so I came up with this fast way to deliver the same flavor without the fuss. Try them with a not-too-spicy chili for a fun meal the whole family will love.

—LYNITA ARTEBERRY PLANKINTON, SD

START TO FINISH: 25 MIN.
MAKES: 1½ DOZEN

- 2 packages (8½ ounces each) corn bread/muffin mix
- 2 tablespoons brown sugar
- 2 large eggs
- 1 cup milk
- 1 can (11 ounces) whole kernel corn, drained
- 5 hot dogs, chopped

1. In a large bowl, combine the corn bread mix and brown sugar. Combine eggs and milk; stir into dry ingredients until moistened. Stir in corn and hot dogs (batter will be thin).

2. Fill greased or paper-lined muffin cups three-fourths full. Bake at 400° for 14-18 minutes or until a toothpick inserted in muffin comes out clean. Serve warm. Refrigerate leftovers.

EAT SMART **FREEZE IT**
TOMATO-HERB FOCACCIA

With its medley of herbs and tomatoes, this rustic bread will liven up any occasion, whether it's a family dinner or a game-day get-together. It never lasts long!

—JANET MILLER INDIANAPOLIS, IN

PREP: 30 MIN. + RISING • **BAKE:** 20 MIN.
MAKES: 1 LOAF (12 PIECES)

- 1 package (¼ ounce) active dry yeast
- 1 cup warm water (110° to 115°)
- 2 tablespoons olive oil, divided
- 1½ teaspoons salt
- 1 teaspoon sugar
- 1 teaspoon garlic powder
- 1 teaspoon each dried oregano, thyme and rosemary, crushed
- ½ teaspoon dried basil
  Dash pepper
- 2 to 2½ cups all-purpose flour
- 2 plum tomatoes, thinly sliced
- ¼ cup shredded part-skim mozzarella cheese
- 1 tablespoon grated Parmesan cheese

TOMATO-HERB FOCACCIA

1. In a large bowl, dissolve the yeast in warm water. Add 1 tablespoon oil, salt, sugar, garlic powder, herbs, pepper and 1½ cups flour. Beat until smooth. Stir in enough remaining flour to form a soft dough (dough will be sticky).

2. Turn dough onto a floured surface; knead until smooth and elastic, about 6-8 minutes. Place in a greased bowl, turning once to grease top. Cover and let rise in a warm place until doubled, about 1 hour.

3. Punch the dough down. Cover and let rest for 10 minutes. Shape into a 13x9-in. rectangle; place on a greased baking sheet. Cover and let rise until doubled, about 30 minutes. With fingertips, make several dimples over top of dough.

4. Brush dough with remaining oil; arrange the tomatoes over the top. Sprinkle with cheeses. Bake at 400° for 20-25 minutes or until golden brown. Remove to a wire rack.

FREEZE OPTION *Freeze the cooled focaccia squares in freezer containers, separating layers with waxed paper. To use, reheat squares on a baking sheet in a preheated 400° oven until heated through.*

PER SERVING *1 piece equals 111 cal., 3 g fat (1 g sat. fat), 2 mg chol., 314 mg sodium, 17 g carb., 1 g fiber, 3 g pro.* **Diabetic Exchanges:** *1 starch, ½ fat.*

VEGETABLE AND BARLEY PILAF

My good-for-you dish stars barley, a good source of fiber, and a few of my favorite garden picks. Feel free to toss in whatever fresh veggies you have on hand.

—**JESSE KLAUSMEIER** BURBANK, CA

START TO FINISH: 30 MIN.
MAKES: 4 SERVINGS

- 1 **large zucchini, quartered and sliced**
- 1 **large carrot, chopped**
- 1 **tablespoon butter**
- 2 **cups reduced-sodium chicken broth**
- 1 **cup quick-cooking barley**
- 2 **green onions, chopped**
- ½ **teaspoon dried marjoram**
- ¼ **teaspoon salt**
- ⅛ **teaspoon pepper**

1. Saute zucchini and carrot in butter in a large saucepan until crisp-tender. Add chicken broth; bring to a boil. Stir in the barley. Reduce heat; cover and simmer 10-12 minutes or until barley is tender.

2. Stir in the onions, marjoram, salt and pepper. Remove from the heat; cover and let stand for 5 minutes.

SPINACH BARLEY PILAF *Stir in 1 cup chopped fresh spinach with the onions.*

PER SERVING *¾ cup equals 219 cal., 4 g fat (2 g sat. fat), 8 mg chol., 480 mg sodium, 39 g carb., 10 g fiber, 9 g pro.*

STUFFED GRILLED ZUCCHINI

Pair up these zucchini boats with seared pork chops, smoked fish and other grilled greats. Not warm enough for cooking alfresco? Your ol'-fashioned oven will do.

—**NANCY ZIMMERMAN**
CAPE MAY COURT HOUSE, NJ

PREP: 25 MIN. • **GRILL:** 10 MIN.
MAKES: 4 SERVINGS

- 4 **medium zucchini**
- 5 **teaspoons olive oil, divided**
- 2 **tablespoons finely chopped red onion**
- ¼ **teaspoon minced garlic**
- ½ **cup dry bread crumbs**
- ½ **cup shredded part-skim mozzarella cheese**
- 1 **tablespoon minced fresh mint**
- ½ **teaspoon salt**
- 3 **tablespoons grated Parmesan cheese**

1. Cut zucchini in half lengthwise; scoop out pulp, leaving ¼-in. shells. Brush with 2 teaspoons oil; set aside. Chop pulp.

2. In a large skillet, saute pulp and onion in remaining oil. Add garlic; cook 1 minute longer. Add bread crumbs; cook and stir for 2 minutes or until golden brown.

3. Remove from the heat. Stir in the mozzarella cheese, mint and salt. Spoon into zucchini shells. Sprinkle with Parmesan cheese.

4. Grill, covered, over medium heat for 8-10 minutes or until zucchini is tender.

STUFFED GRILLED ZUCCHINI

BONUS:
SIDES, SALADS & BREADS

"This pretty side dish's bright, citrusy flavors are a great perk-up for down-to-earth entrees—and for people who usually shy away from beets."
—**JEAN ANN PERKINS** NEWBURYPORT, MD

HARVARD
BEETS

HARVARD BEETS

START TO FINISH: 15 MIN.
MAKES: 4-6 SERVINGS

- 1 can (16 ounces) sliced beets
- ¼ cup sugar
- 1½ teaspoons cornstarch
- 2 tablespoons vinegar
- 2 tablespoons orange juice
- 1 tablespoon grated orange peel

Drain beets, reserving 2 tablespoons juice; set the beets and juice aside. In a saucepan, combine the sugar and cornstarch. Add vinegar, orange juice and beet juice; bring to a boil. Reduce the heat and simmer for 3-4 minutes or until thickened. Add the beets and orange peel; heat through.

GARBANZO BEAN SALAD

You gotta love a versatile dish—serve this one as a side, appetizer or spooned over a tossed green salad. It keeps for days in the refrigerator, but it never lasts that long in my house!

—**ELEANOR GLOFKA** MOUNTAIN TOP, PA

START TO FINISH: 15 MIN.
MAKES: 6 SERVINGS

- 2 cans (15 ounces each) garbanzo beans or chickpeas, rinsed and drained
- ½ cup chopped sweet onion
- ½ cup whole ripe olives, halved
- ¼ cup chopped sweet red pepper
- ¼ cup chopped green pepper
- 1 celery rib, chopped
- ¼ cup shredded Parmesan cheese
- ½ cup olive oil
- 3 tablespoons balsamic vinegar
- 2 tablespoons minced fresh parsley
- 1 tablespoon sugar
- ¼ teaspoon onion powder
- ⅛ teaspoon dried basil
  Dash dried oregano

In a bowl, combine the beans, onion, olives, peppers, celery and Parmesan cheese. In a jar with tight-fitting lid, combine the remaining ingredients; shake well. Pour over bean mixture and toss to coat.

PUMPKIN CHIP MUFFINS

PUMPKIN CHIP MUFFINS

My sisters, brothers and I started cooking and baking when we were young. Mom was a very good teacher—she told us we would learn our way around the kitchen. Now, I tell my kids the same thing!

—**CINDY MIDDLETON** CHAMPION, AB

PREP: 10 MIN. • **BAKE:** 15 MIN. + COOLING
MAKES: ABOUT 2 DOZEN

- 4 large eggs
- 2 cups sugar
- 1 can (15 ounces) solid-pack pumpkin
- 1½ cups canola oil
- 3 cups all-purpose flour
- 2 teaspoons baking soda
- 1 teaspoon baking powder
- 1 teaspoon ground cinnamon
- 1 teaspoon salt
- 2 cups (12 ounces) semisweet chocolate chips

1. In a large bowl, beat the eggs, sugar, pumpkin and canola oil until smooth. Combine flour, baking soda, baking powder, cinnamon and salt; gradually add to the pumpkin mixture and mix well. Fold in the chocolate chips. Fill greased or paper-lined muffin cups three-fourths full.

2. Bake at 400° for 15-18 minutes or until a toothpick inserted near the center comes out clean. Cool in the pan 10 minutes before removing to a wire rack.

ZUCCHINI & CHEESE DROP BISCUITS

These colorful little drop biscuits are ready for any meal or occasion. I serve them warm right out of the oven.

—**KEITH MESCH** MOUNT HEALTHY, OH

PREP: 25 MIN. + STANDING • **BAKE:** 25 MIN.
MAKES: 1 DOZEN

- ¾ cup shredded zucchini
- 1¼ teaspoons salt, divided
- 2½ cups all-purpose flour
- 1 tablespoon baking powder
- ½ cup cold butter, cubed
- ½ cup shredded cheddar cheese
- ¼ cup shredded part-skim mozzarella cheese
- ¼ cup shredded Parmesan cheese
- 2 tablespoons finely chopped oil-packed sun-dried tomatoes, patted dry
- 2 tablespoons minced fresh basil or 2 teaspoons dried basil
- 1 cup 2% milk

1. Preheat oven to 425°. Place the zucchini in a colander over a plate; sprinkle with ¼ teaspoon salt and toss. Let stand 10 minutes. Rinse and drain well. Squeeze the zucchini to remove excess liquid. Pat dry.

2. In a large bowl, whisk flour, baking powder and the remaining salt. Cut in butter until mixture resembles coarse crumbs. Stir in the zucchini, cheeses, tomatoes and basil. Add milk; stir just until moistened.

3. Drop batter by ⅓ cupfuls into a greased 13x9-in. baking pan. Bake 22-26 minutes or until golden brown. Serve warm.

CHINESE SPAGHETTI

Give any entree an Asian twist and a bit of heat with this tasty side dish. You can vary the vegetables as desired.

—**ANNE SMITHSON** CARY, NC

START TO FINISH: 20 MIN.
MAKES: 5 SERVINGS

- 8 ounces uncooked angel hair pasta
- 1 cup sliced fresh mushrooms
- 1 cup fresh snow peas
- ¾ cup shredded carrots
- 4 green onions, cut into 1-inch pieces
- 2 tablespoons canola oil
- 1 garlic clove, minced
- ¼ cup reduced-sodium soy sauce
- 1 teaspoon sugar
- ¼ teaspoon cayenne pepper
- 2 tablespoons sesame seeds, toasted

1. Cook pasta according to package directions. Meanwhile, in a large skillet, saute the mushrooms, snow peas, carrots and onions in oil until crisp-tender. Add the garlic; cook 1 minute longer.

2. In a small bowl, combine the soy sauce, sugar and cayenne. Drain pasta. Add pasta and soy sauce mixture to skillet and toss to coat. Heat through. Sprinkle with sesame seeds.

EAT SMART

ARUGULA SALAD WITH SHAVED PARMESAN

Fresh peppery arugula, golden raisins, crunchy almonds and shredded Parm combine in this perfect dinner salad. I first put it together for my mom, and the whole family ended up loving it!

—**NICOLE RASH** BOISE, ID

START TO FINISH: 15 MIN.
MAKES: 4 SERVINGS

- 6 cups fresh arugula
- ¼ cup golden raisins
- ¼ cup sliced almonds, toasted
- 3 tablespoons olive oil
- 1 tablespoon lemon juice
- ¼ teaspoon salt
- ¼ teaspoon freshly ground pepper
- ⅓ cup shaved or shredded Parmesan cheese

In a large bowl, combine the arugula, raisins and almonds. Drizzle with oil and lemon juice. Sprinkle with the salt and pepper; toss to coat. Divide among four plates; top with cheese.
NOTE *To toast nuts, bake in a shallow pan in a 350° oven for 5-10 minutes or cook in a skillet over low heat until lightly browned, stirring occasionally.*
PER SERVING *1 cup equals 181 cal., 15 g fat (3 g sat. fat), 4 mg chol., 242 mg sodium, 10 g carb., 2 g fiber, 4 g pro.*
Diabetic Exchanges: *3 fat, ½ starch.*

ZUCCHINI & CHEESE DROP BISCUITS

ARUGULA SALAD WITH
SHAVED PARMESAN

MINTY WATERMELON-
CUCUMBER SALAD

MINTY WATERMELON-CUCUMBER SALAD

Capturing fantastic flavors of summer, this refreshing, beautiful salad will be the talk of any picnic or potluck.

—ROBLYNN HUNNISETT GUELPH, ON

START TO FINISH: 20 MIN.
MAKES: 16 SERVINGS (¾ CUP EACH)

- 8 cups cubed seedless watermelon
- 2 English cucumbers, halved lengthwise and sliced
- 6 green onions, chopped
- ¼ cup minced fresh mint
- ¼ cup balsamic vinegar
- ¼ cup olive oil
- ½ teaspoon salt
- ½ teaspoon pepper

In a large bowl, combine watermelon, cucumbers, green onions and mint. In a small bowl, whisk remaining ingredients. Pour over the salad and toss to coat. Serve immediately or refrigerate, covered, up to 2 hours before serving.

PER SERVING ¾ *cup equals 60 cal., 3 g fat (trace sat. fat), 0 chol., 78 mg sodium, 9 g carb., 1 g fiber, 1 g pro. Diabetic Exchanges: ½ fruit, ½ fat.*

READER RAVE

"This is absolutely delicious! I will be making this again and again. I didn't have fresh mint, so I substituted fresh basil out of my garden. YUM!"

—SCHAEFERSMITH
FROM TASTEOFHOME.COM

AUTUMN BEANS

Long ago, Johnny Appleseed passed through this part of the country. Now, nearly every hill is crowned with aged apple trees. Cider is abundant in the fall, and my family looks forward to enjoying it in this bean dish!

—MARA MCAULEY HINSDALE, NY

START TO FINISH: 30 MIN.
MAKES: 6 SERVINGS

- 8 bacon strips, chopped
- ¼ cup finely chopped onion
- 1 cup apple cider
- 2 cans (16 ounces each) baked beans, undrained
- ¼ to ½ cup raisins
- ½ teaspoon ground cinnamon

1. In a skillet, lightly fry the bacon. Remove to paper towel to drain. Set aside 2 tablespoons drippings. Saute onion in the drippings until tender.
2. Stir in the remaining ingredients. Bring to a boil; reduce the heat and simmer, uncovered, 20-25 minutes, stirring occasionally.

AUTUMN BEANS

TOMATO CORN TOSS

My microwave comes in handy when preparing this dish featuring banana peppers, tomatoes and corn. If you're using fresh corn, plan on 4 to 6 ears to get the 2 cups you'll need.

—ANNETTE MARIE YOUNG
WEST LAFAYETTE, IN

START TO FINISH: 15 MIN.
MAKES: 3 SERVINGS

- 1 medium tomato, seeded and diced
- 1 to 2 banana peppers, seeded and chopped
- 2 tablespoons water
- 1 teaspoon salt-free seasoning blend
- 2 cups frozen corn, thawed
- 1 tablespoon butter

1. In a 1-qt. microwave-safe dish, combine the tomato, peppers, water and seasoning blend. Cover and microwave on high for 1 minute; stir. Cook 1 minute longer.

2. Stir in corn and butter. Cover and microwave for 2-3 minutes or until heated through and butter is melted.
NOTES *This recipe was tested in a 1,100-watt microwave. When cutting banana peppers, disposable gloves are recommended. Avoid touching your face.*
PER SERVING *¾ cup equals 147 cal., 5 g fat (3 g sat. fat), 10 mg chol., 50 mg sodium, 26 g carb., 4 g fiber, 4 g pro.* **Diabetic Exchanges:** *1½ starch, ½ fat.*

TANGY CUCUMBER SALAD

A splash of lemon juice, sweet onion and cider vinegar give a delightfully tart bite to this zesty, quick salad. Best of all, it's light on calories.

—SHARON SEVING SIDNEY, OH

PREP: 20 MIN. + CHILLING
MAKES: 6 SERVINGS

- 1 cup (8 ounces) fat-free sour cream
- 2 tablespoons cider vinegar
- 2 tablespoons lemon juice
- ¾ teaspoon salt
- ⅛ teaspoon white pepper
- 3 large cucumbers, peeled and thinly sliced
- ½ cup thinly sliced sweet onion

In a large bowl, combine sour cream, vinegar, lemon juice, salt and pepper. Add cucumbers and onion; toss to coat. Cover and refrigerate for at least 1 hour. Serve with a slotted spoon.
PER SERVING *¾ cup equals 68 cal., trace fat (trace sat. fat), 6 mg chol., 328 mg sodium, 13 g carb., 1 g fiber, 4 g pro.* **Diabetic Exchanges:** *1 vegetable, ½ starch.*

General Recipe Index

Alphabetical Recipe Index